All About Administering NIS+

Rick Ramsey

A Sun Microsystems, Inc. Business

10 9 8 7 6 5 4 3 2 1

ISBN 0-13-068800-2

SunSoft Press
A Prentice Hall Title

Preface

Not long after I began working with Solaris, I learned about a great command called name. I needed to call someone, but had forgotten his phone number. "What's Mateo's extension?" I asked my officemate. "Use name," he said without turning around. Embarrassed because I could not understand an answer that sounded so easy to understand, I sat still and stared at my computer, half-hoping it would offer to help.

```
% Pssst, what he means is, . . .
```

I wasn't about to ask my officemate what he meant; he acted as if everyone, including me own grandmother, would have understood. So I sat still and wondered whether I really need to call Mateo. But my officemate wouldn't be denied. He stood up, came over, and shouldered me away from my keyboard. Then he typed:

```
% name mateo
```

"Hit Return and watch the lights go blink-blink" he said, and walked out of the office. Cursing his entire lineage, I smacked the Return key. Lo and behold, look what appeared on my screen:

```
% name mateo
LAMBIER, MATEO (MATHEW)     elvis@graceland     B-15     ext 57612
```

I didn't know it then, but that was my first encounter with a network information service. Of course the name command is not a network information service. It is a network application that gets its information from a network information service. Nevertheless, it demonstrates how much network information services affect the working habits of not just network administrators, but workstation users.

In addition to time-saving conveniences like the name command, network information services make possible remote logins, shared filesystems, shared programs, easy access to the Internet, and a wide variety of other network services. All this in addition to their central purpose: to make the administration of medium to large networks not only manageable, but possible.

The subject of this book is not network information services in general, but a new network information service developed by SunSoft. It is part of the Open Network Computing (ONC™) suite of products, and is called NIS+, which is the acronym for Network Information Service Plus™. Because it is an ONC product, it can run on any architecture that supports ONC, whether Intel- or SPARC™-based, whether running Solaris™ or another operating system. All it requires is that the operating system support either ONC transport-specific RPC (TS-RPC™) or transport-independent RPC (TI-RPC™). At the publication date of this book, ONC was installed on over 3.1 million nodes worldwide.

Audience

This book is written primarily for system and network administrators, although MIS managers can use it to determine whether NIS+ offers what they need and exactly what is involved in setting it up and administering it.

Although this book takes some pains to introduce concepts relevant to NIS+, it makes no attempt to explain networking fundamentals or to describe the administration tools offered by the Solaris environment. If you administer networks, you already know how they work (we hope) and you have already picked out your favorite tools.

Scope and Organization

The first network information services developed for the UNIX world were DNS (Domain Naming Service™), which helped the Internet become viable as a nationwide computer network, and NIS (the Network Information Service™), which expanded the role of network information services from an "address book" to a database of network information. Because of this heritage, the book begins by comparing NIS+ to DNS and NIS. The remainder of the book deals exclusively with NIS+, except when discussing transition and compatibility issues. The book is organized into three parts:

- Understanding NIS+
- Setting Up NIS+
- Administering NIS+

Part 1 — Understanding NIS+

The first part of the book focuses on the structure of NIS+. NIS+ is a powerful and flexible system; to set it up and take advantage of all its capabilities, you must understand what it has to offer and how it is put together. Part 1 has five chapters.

Chapter 1   Understanding Network Information Services

This chapter describes the purpose of network information services, explaining the advantages they offer and why they have become popular. It also provides a high-level, comparative overview of DNS, NIS, and NIS+. In that overview, it introduces the principal features of NIS+, which are described in detail in the remainder of Part 1.

Chapter 2   Understanding the NIS+ Namespace

This chapter describes the structure of an NIS+ namespace and introduces its structural components: directories and domains. It describes NIS+ servers and clients, and how they provide and receive NIS+ service. It includes a description of the naming conventions used by NIS+.

Chapter 3   Understanding NIS+ Tables and Information

This chapter describes what NIS+ tables are, how they are structured, and what it takes to set them up and populate them. It also describes the information in each table, and how it should be formatted when loaded into NIS+ via an input file.

Chapter 4   Understanding NIS+ Security

This chapter describes the security features of NIS+. It provides an overview of the entire security process, describes the structure of NIS+ groups, credentials, and access rights, and summarizes what is involved in setting them up.

Chapter 5   Understanding the Name Service Switch

This chapter describes the Name Service Switch, a facility that allows you to specify the type of service that provides each category of information to your workstation: NIS+, NIS, DNS, or local /etc files.

Part 2 — Setting Up the NIS+ Service

This part of the book provides step-by-step instructions for setting up the components of an NIS+ namespace, from the root domain itself to individual clients. Because you can set up NIS+ in many different configurations, no one set of instructions would be adequate for everyone. Conversely, one set of instructions for every different configuration would make the book unwieldy.

Instead, the setup process has been divided into building blocks, each of which is described in its own chapter. You can "build" your namespace by putting together the building blocks that you need. For instance, to set up the root domain, follow the instructions in Chapter 7. When you need to set up a client in the root domain, go to Chapter 9. To set up a subdomain, follow the instructions in Chapter 11. Then, to set up clients for that subdomain, go back to Chapter 9. And so on.

Chapter 6   Planning for Setup

This chapter is the key chapter of Part 2. It identifies the building blocks of the setup process and maps them to the chapters that provide their instructions. It explains which decisions you need to make and what information you need to gather before you begin setting up. It also provides general guidelines for migrating from NIS to NIS+.

Chapter 7   Setting Up the Root Domain

This chapter provides step-by-step instructions for setting up the root domain, including using the NIS-compatibility mode.

Chapter 8   Setting Up NIS+ Tables

This chapter provides step-by-step instructions for populating NIS+ tables with information from input files or NIS maps.

Chapter 9   Setting Up an NIS+ Client

This chapter provides step-by-step instructions for setting up an NIS+ client and includes three different initialization methods. These instructions apply to clients in both the root domain and subdomains, whether all-NIS+ or NIS-compatible.

Chapter 10   Setting Up an NIS+ Server

This chapter provides step-by-step instructions for setting up a generic NIS+ server. These servers can be used for any role except root master.

All About Administering NIS+

Chapter 11   Setting Up a Subdomain

This chapter provides step-by-step instructions for creating and setting up a subdomain, whether normal or NIS-compatible, including designating its master and replica servers.

Chapter 12   Setting Up the Name Service Switch

This chapter provides step-by-step instructions for setting up the Name Service Switch to be used with NIS, NIS+, or DNS, as well as to provide backward compatibility with the +/– syntax.

Part 3 — Administering the NIS+ Service

The third part of this book describes the NIS+ commands. It divides them into administration categories, such as "commands used to administer credentials" and "commands used to administer groups," and places each category in its own chapter.

When first learning to use a command you may need to read through detailed instructions, but after you become familiar with a particular command, all you may need is a quick reminder of its syntax. To accommodate this usage, most command descriptions begin with a summary of the syntax.

Chapter 13   Administering NIS+ Groups

This chapter describes the syntax of group-related NIS+ commands and provides instructions for using them to administer NIS+ groups.

Chapter 14   Administering NIS+ Credentials

This chapter describes the syntax of credential-related NIS+ commands and provides instructions for using them to administer NIS+ credentials.

Chapter 15   Administering NIS+ Access Rights

This chapter describes the syntax of rights-related NIS+ commands and provides instructions for using them to administer NIS+ access rights.

Chapter 16   Administering NIS+ Directories

This chapter describes the syntax of directory-related NIS+ commands, as well as other general NIS+ commands such as `rpc.nisd`, and provides instructions for using them to administer NIS+ directories.

Chapter 17   Administering NIS+ Tables

This chapter describes the syntax of table-related NIS+ commands and provides instructions for using them to administer NIS+ tables.

Conventions Used in This Book

As with most books about Solaris, commands and filenames are written in `courier` font. *Italics* are used for emphasis and to identify variables. To give you an idea of what's inside, the first page of each chapter contains a table that lists the important sections of the chapter and the pages they begin on. In Part 1, the tables list the top-level *heads* of a chapter, like this:

The Purpose of Network Information Services	Page 3
Overview of DNS	Page 10
Overview of NIS	Page 14
Overview of NIS+	Page 17

In Part 2, the tables list the *tasks* described in a chapter, like this:

How to Populate NIS+ Tables from Files	Page 136
How to Populate NIS+ Tables from NIS Maps	Page 140

All About Administering NIS+

Not only in the table, but throughout the book, tasks are called out with an inverted triangle in the margin:

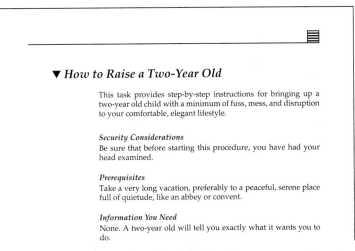

In Part 3, the tables list the commands described in the chapter, as well as the tasks described under each command, like this:

`nismkdir`	
How to Create a Directory	Page 236
How to Add a Replica to an Existing Directory	Page 237
`nisrmdir`	
How to Remove a Directory	Page 237
How to Disassociate a Replica from a Directory	Page 238

In AnswerBook, the Solaris on-line documentation tool, these cross references are hot links. If you double-click over one, AnswerBook takes you to the page on which it begins.

Acknowledgments

≡

The SunSoft NIS+ engineering team put a great deal of time and effort into the NIS+ product. Without their hard work and cooperation, there would be no book. I would like to thank, in particular:

> Helen Bradley, Director of Distributed Computing Technology, who supported the publication of this book, the first in a series on network computing, and Lou Delzompo, manager of the NIS+ team.

> Chuck McManis, who designed the heart of the product and spent countless hours explaining and re-explaining the intricacies of NIS+ to me.

> Anil Gangolli, who is responsible for my understanding of the conceptual underpinnings of NIS+, especially the information on security. He also helped set up my laboratory environment so that I could test early versions of NIS+.

> Vipin Samar, project leader of the NIS+ team, who took a personal interest in the book and provided me with details and information that I would have been unable to acquire on my own. Vipin was a great sounding board for design and presentation schemes, and did the final technical review of this book.

Joe Dere tested this manual assiduously and made part of his lab available for me to run my own tests. The results of his real-world perspective and painstaking attention to detail are evident throughout the book.

Barry Holroyd clarified the notion of an NIS+ namespace. Rosanna Lee and Vikul Khosla reviewed the introductory chapters and provided valuable suggestions. Sanjay Dani and Thomas Maslen provided the information about the Name Service Switch and corrected the mistakes in my early drafts. William Malloy reviewed and corrected my drafts of the DNS material. Bob LeFave provided guidance and information about transitioning an organization from NIS to NIS+, and gave me a thorough review of the manual from the perspective of a real-world user.

Bill Edwards, Jeff Parker, Dave Miner, Paul Sawyer, and Randy Enger of the Admintool engineering team in the SunSoft Billerica office, also helped with quick answers to my questions.

Most of the good ideas in this book come from the work done by a bicoastal team of SunSoft system and network administration writers managed by John Lazarus and led by Charla Mustard-Foote. The book's major structural elements are adapted from the design work done by Dave Damkoehler and Bruce Sesnovich, of the Sun Billerica office. The task-oriented approach came from discussions with Suzy Chapple, a SunSoft Information Products manager, and other writers in the group: Tom Amiro, Electra Coumou, and Janice Winsor. Janice was particularly helpful with design issues and with advice about what looks good on a page. Janice deserves special thanks for being a good workbuddy and putting up with my endless harangues about "good technical writing."

I would like to thank the management of SunSoft Information Products for their encouragement and support. Connie Howard, manager of DOE Documentation, for initially suggesting and encouraging my involvement with this project; Bridget Burke, SunSoft Information Products manager, for supporting this project and for providing the equipment; and, in particular, Suzy Chapple, manager of Networking Documentation, for her encouragement and appreciation. I would also like to thank Darell Sano, the illustrator at Sun Microsystems whose icons were used to create this book's beautiful cover.

Thanks are also due to Karin Ellison of SunSoft Press and Phyllis Bregman of Prentice Hall for making this book possible. Without Karin's vision of SunSoft Press and her interest in this project, this book would have never been published. Phyllis's encouragement and direction made this experience rewarding; her tolerance and wry sense of humor made it a blast.

I would also like to thank Robin Greynolds and Al Cuenco for rescuing me and my workstations on numerous occasions. Al was particularly helpful with my home workstation. Having Al nearby is as reassuring as driving through the desert with a camel in your back seat.

Finally, I owe a warm and hearty Thank You to Laura, for not only supporting this project enthusiastically, but for putting up with unmowed lawns, unwashed cars, and unkilled spiders. She also had the clever idea to put the setup charts on the inside covers of the book. I would also like to thank my 2-year old daughter, Grace, for learning so quickly that crayons do not make OpenWindows prettier, they just make the screen messy. Last of all, I would like to thank my dog, "The Chief," for sparing my hard drive that fateful Wednesday in August, when he ate his way through the rest of my office.

Contents

≡

Preface. . . . . *iii*

Acknowledgments. . . . .*xi*

Part 1 - Understanding NIS+ 1

1. Understanding Network Information Services 3

The Purpose of Network Information Services 3

Overview of DNS. 10

DNS and the Internet 11

DNS Name Resolution and Mail Delivery. 13

Overview of NIS. 14

NIS Maps 15

Overview of NIS+. 17

NIS+ Security. 19

NIS+ and the Name Service Switch 19

NIS+ and Solaris 1.x 19

NIS+ Administration Commands. 20

What Next? 22

2. Understanding the NIS+ Namespace. 23

Structure of the NIS+ Namespace 23

Directories. 25

Domains. 26

Servers 28

How Servers Propagate Changes 29

Clients 31

An NIS+ Server Is Also a Client 36

Naming Conventions (To Dot or Not) 37

NIS+ Name Expansion. 42

3. Understanding NIS+ Tables and Information 45

   NIS+ Table Structure 45

      Columns and Entries 46

      Search Paths. 47

   Ways to Set Up Tables 49

      How Tables Are Updated. 51

   Information in NIS+ Tables. 51

      Auto_Home Table. 53

      Auto_Master Table 53

      Bootparams Table 54

      Ethers Table 55

      Group Table 56

      Hosts Table. 57

      Mail Aliases Table 58

      Netgroup Table 58

      Netmasks Table 59

      Networks Table 60

      Password Table 60

      Protocols Table 61

      RPC Table. 62

      Services Table 63

      Timezone Table 63

4. Understanding NIS+ Security 65

   Overview of the Security Process. 65

      Security and Principals. 65

      Security and Servers. 66

      Security and Objects. 67

      About Setting Up NIS+ Security 69

   About NIS+ Credentials 70

      The Cred Table. 71

      How Credentials Are Created and Used 73

   About Access Rights 78

      Authorization Categories. 78

      Where Access Rights are Stored 80

      How Access Rights Are Assigned. 81

      How a Server Grants Access Rights 83

5. Understanding the Name Service Switch 89

About the Name Service Switch 89

   Format of the nsswitch.conf File 90

The nsswitch.nisplus File 93

The nsswitch.nis File 95

The nsswitch.files File 96

Part 2 - Setting Up NIS+ 97

6. Planning for Setup 99

Recommended Setup Procedure 99

Planning Guidelines 101

   Sketching a Domain Hierarchy 101

   Selecting Servers for the Namespace 104

   Determining Credential Needs of the Namespace 107

   How Many Administrative Groups? 108

   Determining Access Rights to the Namespace 109

   Where Can I Get Information About the Namespace? 112

      Table 112

Transition Guidelines 114

7. Setting Up the Root Domain 117

   ▼   How to Set Up the Root Domain 117

8. Setting Up NIS+ Tables 135

   ▼   How to Populate NIS+ Tables from Files 136

   ▼   How to Populate NIS+ Tables from NIS Maps 140

   ▼   How to Transfer Information from NIS+ to NIS 145

9. Setting Up an NIS+ Client 149

   ▼   How to Set Up an NIS+ Client 149

10. Setting Up NIS+ Servers 163

   ▼   How to Set Up an NIS+ Server 1 64

   ▼   How to Add a Replica to an Existing Domain 167

   ▼   How to Change a Server's Security Level 168

11. Setting Up a Non-Root Domain 173

▼   How to Set Up a Non-Root Domain 173

12. Setting Up the Name Service Switch 183

▼   How to Select an Alternate Configuration File 183

▼   How to Select a Configuration for using DNS 185

▼   How to Add Compatibility with +/- Syntax 186

Part 3 - Administering NIS+ 189

13. Administering NIS+ Groups 191

▼   How to Specify Group Members in all Commands 192

`niscat -o` 193

▼   How to List the Object Properties of a Group 193

`nisgrpadm` 194

▼   How to Create an NIS+ Group 194

▼   How to Delete an NIS+ Group 195

▼   How to Add Members to an NIS+ Group 196

▼   How to List the Members of an NIS+ Group 197

▼   How to Remove Members from an NIS+ Group 198

▼   How to Test for Membership in an NIS+ Group 198

14. Administering NIS+ Credentials 199

Where Credential-Related Information is Stored 200

`nisaddcred` 201

▼   How to Create the Root Master's Credentials 203

▼   How to Create Your Own Credentials 203

▼   How to Create Credentials for Others 204

▼   How to Remove Credentials 208

`chkey` 209

▼ How to Change Your DES Keys 209

    `nispasswd` 210

▼ How to Display Password Information 212

▼ How to Change Passwords 213

    `nisupdkeys` 214

▼ How to Update All Public Keys in a Directory 215

▼ How to Update the Keys of a Particular Server 215

▼ How to Clear Public Keys 215

▼ How to Update IP Addresses 216

    `keylogin` 216

▼ How to Keylogin 216

15. Administering NIS+ Access Rights 217

▼ How to Specify Access Rights in All Commands 218

    `nisdefaults` 220

▼ How to Display Default Values 221

▼ How to Change Defaults 222

▼ How to Display the Value of NIS_DEFAULTS 222

▼ How to Reset the Value of NIS_DEFAULTS. 223

▼ How to Override Defaults 223

    `nischmod` 224

▼ How to Add Rights to an Object 225

▼ How to Remove Rights to an Object 225

▼ How to Add Rights to a Table Entry 225

▼ How to Remove Rights to a Table Entry. 226

    `nistbladm -c,-u` 226

▼ How to Set Column Rights when Creating a Table. 226

▼ How to Add Rights to an Existing Table Column 227

▼ How to Remove Rights to a Table Column 228

`nischown` 228

▼ How to Change an Object's Owner 228

▼ How to Change a Table Entry's Owner 229

`nischgrp` 229

▼ How to Change an Object's Group 230

▼ How to Change a Table Entry's Group................................. 230

16. Administering NIS+ Directories... 231

`niscat -o` 232

▼ How to List the Object Properties of a Directory......................... 232

`nisls` 233

▼ How to List the Contents of a Directory — Terse 234

▼ How to List the Contents of a Directory — Verbose 235

`nismkdir` 235

▼ How to Create a Directory 236

▼ How to Add a Replica to an Existing Directory 237

`nisrmdir` 237

▼ How to Remove a Directory 237

▼ How to Disassociate a Replica from a Directory 238

`nisrm` 238

▼ How to Remove Non-Directory Objects 238

`rpc.nisd` 239

▼ How to Start the NIS+ Daemon 239

▼ How to Start an NIS-Compatible NIS+ Daemon 240

▼ How to Stop the NIS+ Daemon 240

`nisinit` 240

▼ How to Initialize a Client 241

▼ How to Initialize the Root Master Server 241

`nis_cachemgr` 242

▼ How to Start the Cache Manager 242

`nisshowcache` 242

▼ How to Display the Contents of the NIS+ Cache 243

`nisping` 243

▼ How to Display the Time of the Last Update 244

▼ How to Ping Replicas 244

▼ How to Checkpoint a Directory 245

`nislog` 245

▼ How to Display the Contents of the Transaction Log 246

`nischttl` 248

▼ How to Change the Time-to-Live of an Object 249

▼ How to Change the Time-to-Live of a Table Entry 249

17. Administering NIS+ Tables 251

`nistbladm` 252

▼ How to Create a Table 253

▼ How to Delete a Table 254

▼ How to Add an Entry to a Table 255

▼ How to Modify a Table Entry 256

▼ How to Remove a Single Entry from a Table 257

▼ How to Remove Multiple Entries from a Table 258

`niscat` 259

▼ How to Display the Contents of a Table 259

▼   How to List the Object Properties of a Table 260

   `nismatch, nisgrep` 262

▼   How to Search Through the First Column 264

▼   How to Search Through a Particular Column 264

▼   How to Search Through Multiple Columns 265

   `nisln` 265

▼   How to Create a Link 266

   `nissetup` 266

▼   How to Expand a Directory into an NIS+ Domain 267

▼   How to Expand it into an NIS-Compatible Domain 267

   `nisaddent` 268

▼   How to Load Information From a File 269

▼   How to Load Data from an NIS Map 271

▼   How to Dump the Contents of an NIS+ Table to a File 273

Appendix A.Pre-SetupWorksheets 275

Index 285

Part 1 — Understanding NIS+

Understanding Network Information Services
This chapter describes the purpose of network information services, explaining the advantages they offer and why they have become popular. It also provides an overview of DNS, NIS, and NIS+, including the NIS+ compatibility features.

Understanding the NIS+ Namespace
This chapter introduces the NIS+ namespace components: directories, groups, tables, domains, servers and clients. It explains what all these components (except groups and tables) are, how they are structured, and gives you a first look at what is involved in setting them up.

Understanding NIS+ Tables and Information
This chapter describes what NIS+ tables are, how they are structured, and what it takes to set them up and populate them. It also describes the information in each table, and how it should be formatted when loaded into NIS+ via an input file.

Understanding NIS+ Security
This chapter describes the security features of NIS+, explaining how it works and describing credentials and access rights.

Understanding the Name Service Switch
Describes the Name Service Switch, a facility that allows you to specify the type of service that provides each different category of information to your workstation: NIS+, NIS, DNS, or local `/etc` files.

Understanding
Network Information Services

You can better appreciate the features and benefits of NIS+ once you understand why network information services were developed in the first place, and how NIS+ compares to other services of its kind. This chapter describes the purpose of network information services, points out their major features and benefits, and compares three of them: DNS, NIS, and NIS+. It has four sections:

The Purpose of Network Information Services	Page	3
Overview of DNS	Page	10
Overview of NIS	Page	14
Overview of NIS+	Page	17

The Purpose of Network Information Services

Network information services store information that users, workstations, and applications must have to communicate across the network. Without a network information service, each workstation would have to maintain its own copy of this information.

For example, take a simple network of three workstations, pine, elm, and oak:

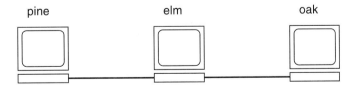

Before `pine` can send a message to either `elm` or `oak`, it must know their network addresses. For this reason, it keeps a file, `/etc/hosts`, that stores the network address of every workstation in the network, including itself.

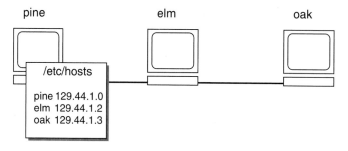

Likewise, in order for `elm` and `oak` to communicate with `pine` or with each other, they must keep similar files.

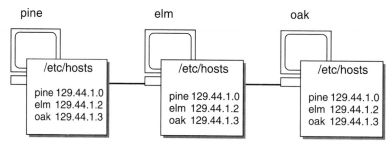

However, addresses are not the only network information that workstations need to store. They also need to store security information, mail information, information about their Ethernet interfaces, information about network services, and about groups of users allowed to

use the network, about services offered on the network, and so on. As networks offer more
services, the list grows. As a result, each workstation may need to keep an entire set of files
similar to /etc/hosts:

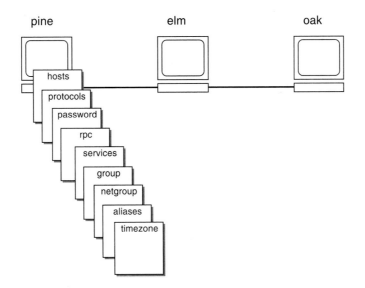

As this information changes, administrators must keep it current on every workstation in the
network. In a small network this is simply tedious, but on a medium or large network, the job
becomes not only time-consuming, but unmanageable.

A network information service solves this problem. It stores network information on a server and provides it to any workstation that asks for it:

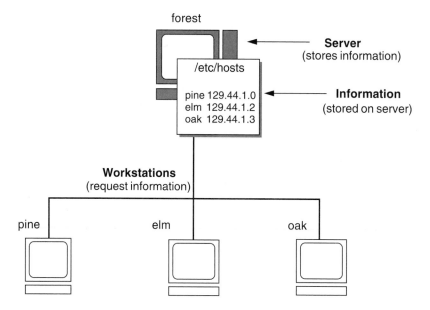

The workstations are known as *clients* of the server. Whenever information about the network changes, instead of updating each client's local file, an administrator updates only the information on the central server. This reduces errors, inconsistencies between clients, and the sheer size of the task.

This arrangement, of a server providing centralized services to clients across a network, is known as *client-server computing*.

Although the chief purpose of a network information service is to centralize information, another is to simplify network names. A network information service enables workstations to be identified by common names instead of numerical addresses. (This is why these services are sometimes called "name services.") This makes communication simpler because users don't have to remember and try to enter cumbersome numerical addresses like "129.44.1.3." Instead, they can use descriptive names like Sales, Lab1, or Arnold.

For example, assume that a fictitious company called "Wizard, Inc." has set up a network and connected it to the Internet. The Internet has assigned Wizard, Inc. the network number of

129.44.0.0 Wizard, Inc. has two divisions, "Sales" and "Eng," so its network is divided into two subnets, one for each division. Each subnet, of course, has its own address:

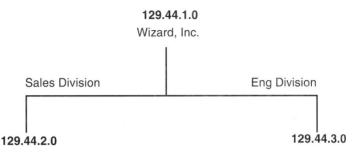

Each division could be identified by its network address, as shown above, but descriptive names made possible by network information services would clearly be preferable:

(As a convention, this book presents hardware connections with solid lines and network information service connections with less solid lines.)

So, instead of addressing mail or other network communications to 129.44.1.0, they could be addressed simply to "Wiz." Instead of addressing them to 129.44.2.0 or 129.44.3.0, they could be addressed to "Sales.Wiz." or "Eng.Wiz."

Names are also more flexible than physical addresses. While physical networks tend to remain stable, the organizations that use them tend to change. A network information service can act as a buffer between an organization and its physical network. This is because a network information service is mapped to the physical network, not hard-wired to it. This is best demonstrated with an example.

Assume that the Wiz. network is supported by three servers, S1, S2, and S3, and that two of those servers, S1 and S3, support clients:

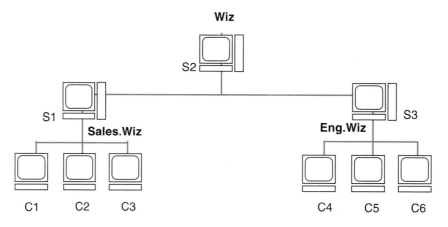

Clients C1, C2, and C3 would obtain their network information from server S1. Clients C4, C5, and C6 would obtain it from server S3. The resulting network is summarized in this table (this is a generalized representation of that network — actual network information maps do not look like this):

Network Address	Network Name	Server	Clients
129.44.1.0	Wiz.	S1	
129.44.2.0	Sales.Wiz.	S2	C1
	Sales.Wiz.	S2	C2
	Sales.Wiz.	S2	C3
129.44.3.0	Eng.Wiz.	S3	C6
	Eng.Wiz.	S3	C5
	Eng.Wiz.	S3	C6

Now assume that Wizard, Inc. created a third division, "Testing," which borrowed some resources from the other two divisions, but did not create a third subnet. Unfortunately, the physical network would no longer parallel the corporate structure:

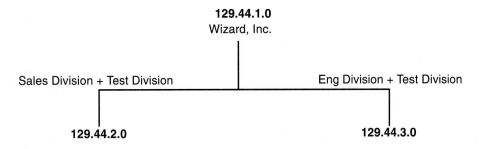

Traffic for the Test Division would not have its own subnet, but would instead be split between the 129.44.2.0 and 129.44.3.0 subnets. However, with a network information service, the Test Division traffic could have its own dedicated "network:"

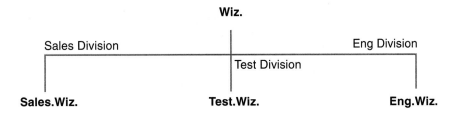

Thus, when an organization changed, its network information service would simply change its mapping:

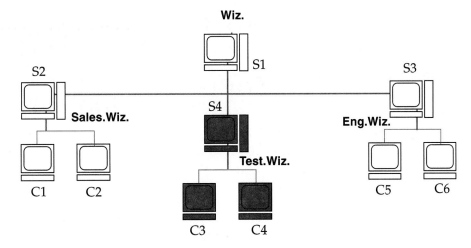

(As a convention in the illustrations used throughout this book, shading is used only to call attention to items — not to distinguish one type of item, such as a server, from another, such as a client.)

Now clients C1 and C2 would obtain their information from server S2; C3 and C4 from server S4; and C5 and C6 from server S3.

Subsequent changes in the Wizard Inc., organization would continue to be accommodated by changes to the "soft" network information structure without reorganizing the "hard" network structure.

Overview of DNS

DNS is the network information service provided by the Internet for TCP/IP networks. It was developed so that workstations on the network could be identified with common names instead of Internet addresses.

The collection of networked workstations that use DNS are referred to as the DNS *namespace*. The DNS namespace can be divided into a hierarchy of *domains*. A DNS domain is simply a group of workstations. Each domain is supported by two or more *name servers*: a principal server and one or more secondary servers:

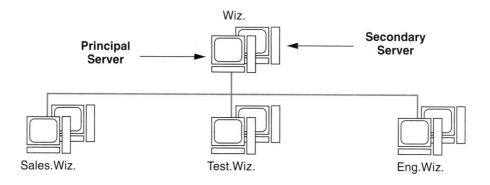

Both principal and secondary servers run the DNS software and store the names and addresses of the workstations in the domain. Principal servers store the original information and secondary servers store copies.

DNS clients request service only from the servers that support their domain. If the domain's server does not have the information the client needs, it forwards the request to its parent server, which is the server in the next-higher domain in the hierarchy. If the request reaches the top-level server, the top-level server determines whether the domain is valid. If it is *not* valid, the server returns a "Not Found" message to the client. If the domain is valid, the server routes the request down to the server that supports that domain.

DNS and the Internet

DNS is the network information service used by the Internet. The Internet is a vast network that connects many smaller networks across the World. Organizations with networks of any size can join the Internet by applying for membership. Once they are accepted, they can choose between two domain hierarchies: an organizational one and a geographical one.

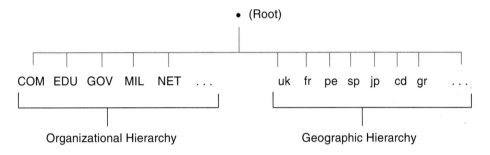

The Organizational hierarchy divides its namespace into the top-level domains listed in Table 1-1.

Table 1-1   Internet Organizational Domains

Domain	Purpose
COM	Commercial organizations
EDU	Educational institutions
GOV	Government institutions
MIL	Military groups
NET	Major network support centers
ORG	Nonprofit organizations and others
INT	International organizations

The Geographic hierarchy assigns each country in the world a two- or three-digit identifier and provides official names for the geographic regions within each country.

A site using DNS can use any top-level names it prefers, but if it wants to connect to the Internet, it cannot use any of the organizational or geographic names reserved by the Internet's top-level domains.

Networks that join the Internet append their Internet domain name to their own names. For example, if the Wiz domain from the previous example joined the Internet, it would be placed in the "COM" domain.

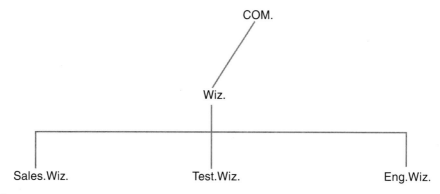

Thus the full Internet names of the Wiz domains would be:

```
Wiz.COM.
Sales.Wiz.COM.
Test.Wiz.COM.
Eng.Wiz.COM.
```

Domain names are capitalized in this book simply as a convention; the DNS service does not require them to be capitalized. Workstation names precede their DNS domain names. They are *not* capitalized in this book (also by convention), to distinguish them from domain names. Here are some examples:

```
boss.Wiz.COM.
neverhome.Sales.Wiz.COM.
quota.Sales.Wiz.COM.
lab.Test.Wiz.COM.
worknights.Eng.Wiz.COM.
```

The Internet regulates administration of its domains by granting each domain authority over the names of its workstations, and expecting each domain to delegate authority to the levels below it. Thus, the COM. domain has authority over the names of the workstations in its domain. It also authorizes the formation of the Wiz.COM. domain and delegates authority over the names in that domain. The Wiz.COM. domain, in turn, assigns names to the workstations in its domain and approves the formation of the Sales.Wiz.COM., Test.Wiz.COM., and Eng.Wiz.COM. domains.

DNS Name Resolution and Mail Delivery

DNS provides two principal services: it translates names to IP addresses (and also addresses to names) and it helps mail agents deliver mail along the Internet.

The process of translating names to addresses (and addresses to names) is called *name resolution*. To accomplish this, DNS stores the names and IP addresses of all the workstations in each domain in a set of maps, called *zone files*. One type of zone file stores IP addresses by name. When someone attempts a remote procedure such as `ftp` or `telnet`, it provides the name of the remote workstation. DNS looks up the name in the zone file and converts (or *resolves*) it into its IP address. The IP address is sent along with the remote procedure so the receiving workstation can know who sent the request. This enables the receiving workstation to reply without having to also be a DNS client.

Another type of zone file stores workstation names by IP address. It uses them to convert IP addresses to workstation names, a process called *reverse resolution*. Reverse resolution is used primarily to verify the identity of the workstation who sent a message or to authorize remote operations on a local workstation (remote operations are usually authorized per IP addresses, which are more stable than workstation names).

To deliver mail across the Internet, DNS uses *mail exchange records*. Many organizations don't allow mail that comes across the Internet to be delivered directly to workstations within the organization. Instead, they use a central mailhost (or a set of mailhosts) to intercept incoming mail messages and route them to their recipients.

The purpose of a mail exchange record is to identify the mailhost that services each workstation. Therefore, a mail exchange record lists the DNS domain names of remote organizations and either the IP address or the name of its corresponding mailhost. For example:

DNS Domain	Mailhost
International.Com.	129.44.1.1
Sales.Wiz.Com.	SalesWizMailer
Eng.Wiz.Com.	EngWizMailer
Fab.Com.	FabMailer

When the mail agent receives a request to send mail to another domain, it parses the name of the recipient backwards and looks for a match in the table. For example, if it receives a request to send mail to . . .

```
neverhome.Sales.Wiz.Com
```

. . . it first extracts the topmost label, "Com." It examines the mail exchange record to see if there is an entry for Com. Since there is none, it continues parsing. It extracts the next label and looks for an entry for "Wiz.Com." Since there is none, it continues looking. The next entry it looks for is "Sales.Wiz.Com." As you can see in the table above, the mailhost for that domain is SalesWizMailer. Because that is a workstation name, the mail agent asks DNS to resolve it. When DNS provides that mailhost's IP address, the mail agent sends the message.

If instead of the mailhost name, the mail exchange record had specified an IP address, the mail agent would have sent the message directly to that address, since it would have needed no translation from DNS.

Overview of NIS

NIS was developed independently of DNS and had a slightly different focus. Whereas DNS focused on making communication simpler by using workstation names instead of addresses, NIS focused on making network administration more manageable by providing centralized control over a variety of network information. As a result, NIS stores information not only about workstation names and addresses, but also about users, the network itself, and network services. This collection of network *information* is referred to as the NIS *namespace*.

NIS uses a client-server arrangement similar to DNS. Replicated NIS servers provide services to NIS clients. The principal servers are called *master* servers, and for reliability, they have backup, or *slave* servers. Both master and slave servers use the NIS information retrieval software and both store NIS maps.

NIS, like DNS, uses domains to arrange the workstations, users, and networks in its namespace. However, it does not use a domain hierarchy; an NIS namespace is flat. Thus, this physical network:

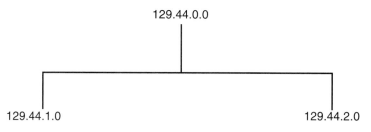

would be arranged into one NIS domain:

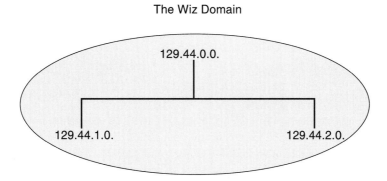

An NIS domain can't be connected directly to the Internet. However, organizations that want to use NIS and be connected to the Internet can combine NIS with DNS. They use NIS to manage all local information and DNS for name resolution. NIS provides special client routines for this purpose. When a client needs access to any type of information except IP addresses, the request goes to the client's NIS server. When a client needs name resolution, the request goes to the DNS server. From the DNS server, the client has access to the Internet in the usual way.

NIS Maps

Like DNS, NIS stores information in a set of maps. However, NIS maps were designed to replace UNIX /etc files, as well as other configuration files, so they store much more than names and addresses. As a result, the NIS namespace has a large set of maps, as shown in Table 1-2.

NIS maps are essentially bi-column tables. One column is the key and the other column is information about the key. NIS finds information for a client by searching through the keys. Thus, some information is stored in several maps because each map uses a different key. For example, the names and addresses of workstations are stored in two maps: hosts.byname and `hosts.byaddr`. When a server has a workstation's name and needs to find its address, it looks in the `hosts.byname` map. When it has the address and needs to find the name, it looks in the `hosts.byaddr` map.

Table 1-2   NIS Maps

NIS Map	Description
bootparams	Lists the names of the diskless clients and the location of the files they need during booting.
ethers.byaddr	Lists the Ethernet addresses of workstations and their corresponding names.
ethers.byname	Contains the names of workstations and their corresponding Ethernet addresses.
group.bygid	Provides membership information about groups, using the group id as the key.
group.byname	Provides membership information about groups, using the group name as the key.
hosts.byaddr	Lists the names and addresses of workstations, using the address as the key.
hosts.byname	Lists the names and addresses of workstations, using the name as the key.
mail.aliases	Lists the mail aliases in the namespace and all the workstations that belong to them.
mail.byaddr	Lists the mail aliases in the namespace, but uses the address as the key.
netgroup	Contains netgroup information, using group name as the key.
netgroup.byhost	Contains information about the netgroups in the namespace, but with workstation names as the key.
netgroup.byuser	Contains netgroup information, but with user as the key.
netid.byname	Contains the secure RPC netname of workstations and users, along with their UIDs and GIDs.
netmasks.byaddr	Contains network masks used with IP subnetting, using address as the key.
networks.byaddr	Contains the names and addresses of the networks in the namespace, and their Internet addresses.
networks.byname	Contains the names and addresses of the networks in the namespace, using the names as the key.
passwd.byname	Contains password information, with username as the key.
passwd.byuid	Contains password information, with userid as the key.
protocols.byname	Lists the network protocols used.
protocols.bynumber	Lists the network protocols used, but uses their number as the key.
publickey.byname	Contains public and secret keys for secure RPC.
rpc.bynumber	Lists the known program name and number of RPC's.
services.byname	Lists the available Internet services.
ypservers	Lists the NIS servers in the namespace, along with their IP addresses.

Overview of NIS+

NIS+ was designed to replace NIS. NIS addresses the administration requirements of client-server computing networks prevalent in the 1980's. At that time client-server networks did not usually have more than a few hundred clients and a few multipurpose servers. They were spread across only a few remote sites, and since users were sophisticated and trusted, they did not require security.

However, client-server networks have grown tremendously since the mid-1980's. They now range from 100-10,000 multi-vendor clients supported by 10-100 specialized servers located in sites throughout the world, and they are connected to several "untrusted" public networks. In addition, the information they store changes much more rapidly than it did during the time of NIS. The size and complexity of these networks required new, autonomous administration practices. NIS+ was designed to address these requirements.

The NIS namespace, being flat, centralizes administration. Because networks in the 90's require scalability and decentralized administration, the NIS+ namespace was designed with hierarchical domains, like those of DNS:

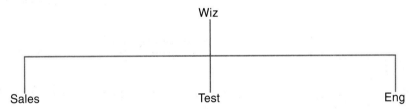

This allows NIS+ to be used in a range of networks, from small to very large. It also allows the NIS+ service to adapt to the growth of an organization. For example, if a corporation divided itself into two divisions, its NIS+ namespace could be divided into two domains, which could be administered autonomously. Just as the Internet delegates administration of domains *downward*, NIS+ domains can be administered more or less independently of each other.

Although NIS+ uses a domain hierarchy similar to that of DNS, an NIS+ domain is much more than a DNS domain. A DNS domain only stores name and address information about its clients. An NIS+ domain, on the other hand, is a collection of *information* about the workstations, users, and network services in a portion of an organization.

Although this division into domains makes administration more autonomous and growth easier to manage, it does not make information harder to access. Clients have the same access to information in other domains as they would have had under one umbrella domain. A domain can even be administered from within another domain.

The NIS+ client-server arrangement is similar those of NIS and DNS in that each domain is supported by a set of servers. The principal server is called the *master* server, and the backup servers are called *replicas*. Both master and replica servers run NIS+ server software and both maintain copies of NIS+ tables. The principal server stores the original tables, and the backup servers store copies.

However, NIS+ uses an updating model that is completely different from the one used by NIS. Since at the time NIS was developed, the type of information it would store changed infrequently, NIS was developed with an update model that focused on stability. Its updates are handled manually and, in large organizations, can take more than a day to propagate to all the replicas. Part of the reason for this is the need to remake and propagate an entire map every time any information in the map changes.

NIS+, however, accepts *incremental* changes. Changes must still be made on the master server (to avoid inconsistencies with the replicas), but once made they are automatically propagated to the replica servers and immediately made available to the entire namespace. You don't have to "make" any maps or wait for propagation.

Details about NIS+ domain structure, servers, and clients, are provided in Chapter 2, "Understanding the NIS+ Namespace."

An NIS+ domain can be connected to the Internet via its NIS+ clients, using the Name Service Switch, described below. The client, if it is also a DNS client, can set up a Switch configuration file to search for information in either DNS zone files or NIS maps — in addition to NIS+ tables.

NIS+ stores information in *tables* instead of maps or zone files. NIS+ provides 16 types of predefined, or *system*, tables:

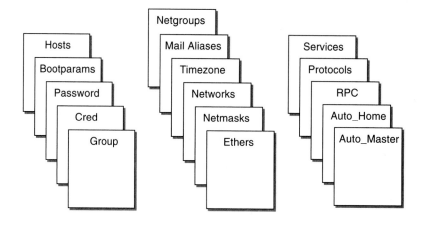

Each table stores a different type of information. For instance, the Hosts table stores information about workstation addresses, while the Password table stores information about users of the network.

NIS+ tables provide two major improvements over the maps used by NIS. First, an NIS+ table can be accessed by any column, not just the first column (sometimes referred to as the "key"). This eliminates the need for duplicate maps, such as the `hosts.byname` and `hosts.byaddr` maps used by NIS. Second, the information in NIS+ tables can be accessed and manipulated at three levels of granularity: the table level, the entry level, and the column level. NIS+ tables — and the information stored in them — are described in Chapter 3, "Understanding NIS+ Tables and Information."

NIS+ Security

NIS+ protects the structure of the namespace, and the information it stores, by the complementary processes of *authorization* and *authentication*. First, every component in the namespace specifies the type of operation it will accept and from whom. This is authorization. Second, NIS+ attempts to *authenticate* every request for access to the namespace. Once it identifies the originator of the request, it can find out whether the component has authorized that particular operation for that particular individual. Based on its authentication and the component's authorization, NIS+ carries out or denies the request for access. A full description of this process is provided in Chapter 4, "Understanding NIS+ Security."

NIS+ and the Name Service Switch

NIS+ works in conjunction with a separate facility called the *Name Service Switch*. The Name Service Switch, loosely referred to as "the Switch," enables Solaris 2.x-based workstations to obtain their information from more than one network information service; specifically, from local, or `/etc` files, from NIS maps, from DNS zone files, or from NIS+ tables. The Switch not only offers a choice of sources, but allows a workstation to specify different sources for different *types* of information. A complete description of the Switch is provided in Chapter 5, "Understanding the Name Service Switch."

NIS+ and Solaris 1.x

Although NIS+ is provided with the Solaris 2.x package, it can be used by workstations running Solaris 1.x in two different ways. First, NIS+ provides a *NIS-compatibility mode*. The NIS-compatibility mode enables an NIS+ server running Solaris 2.x to answer requests from NIS clients while continuing to answer requests from NIS+ clients. NIS+ does this by providing two service interfaces. One responds to NIS+ client requests, while the other responds to NIS client requests.

This mode does not require any additional setup or changes to NIS clients. In fact, NIS clients are not even aware that the server that is responding isn't an NIS server — except for three differences. First, the NIS+ server running in NIS-compatibility mode does not support the `ypupdate` and `ypxfr` protocols. Second, it cannot be used as a slave or master NIS server. Third, the NIS-compatibility mode does not support DNS-forwarding.

Two more differences need to be pointed out. One is that instructions for setting up a server in NIS-compatibility mode are slightly different than those used to set up a standard NIS+ server. For details, see Part II. The other is that NIS-compatibility mode has security implications for tables in the NIS+ namespace. Since the NIS client software does not have the capability to provide the credentials that NIS+ servers expect from NIS+ clients, all their requests end up classified as *unauthenticated*. Therefore, to allow NIS clients to access information in NIS+ tables, those tables must provide access rights to unauthenticated requests. This is handled automatically by the utilities used to set up a server in NIS-compatibility mode, as described in Part II. However, to understand more about the authentication process, read Chapter 4, "Understanding NIS+ Security."

Second, NIS+ provides a separate package called the *Solaris 1.x Distribution*, which enables workstations running Solaris 1.x to operate as NIS+ servers without having to upgrade to Solaris 2.x. The NIS+ Solaris 1.x Distribution consists of the NIS+ daemon, all the NIS+ commands, the NIS+ client libraries, a README file, and additional text files. It is delivered in a `tar` file, `NISPLUS.TAR`, included in the Solaris 2.x CD-ROM. To transfer the distribution from the CD-ROM to a Solaris 1.x-based workstation, first mount the CD-ROM, then transfer the `NISPLUS.TAR` file using the `tar` command. If you have network access to the Solaris 1.x Distribution, you can `ftp` or `rcp` it. Instructions for installing it are provided in the README file.

NIS+ Administration Commands

NIS+ provides a full set of commands for administering a namespace. They are described throughout this book, but mostly in Part III. Table 1-3, below, summarizes them.

Table 1-3   NIS+ Namespace Administration Commands

Command	Description	Page
nisaddcred	Creates credentials for NIS+ principals and stores them in the Cred table.	page 201
nisaddent	Adds information from /etc files or NIS maps into NIS+ tables.	page 268
nis_cachemgr	Starts the NIS+ Cache Manager on an NIS+ client.	page 242

Table 1-3   NIS+ Namespace Administration Commands (Continued)

Command	Description (Continued)	Page
niscat	Displays the contents of NIS+ tables.	page 259
nischgrp	Changes the group owner of an NIS+ object.	page 229
nischmod	Changes the access rights that an NIS+ object grants to four different categories of NIS+ principal: owner, group, world, and nobody.	page 224
nischown	Changes the owner of an NIS+ object.	page 228
nischttl	Changes an NIS+ object's time-to-live value.	page 248
nisdefaults	Lists an NIS+ object's default values: domain name, group name, workstation name, NIS+ principal name, access rights, directory search path, and time-to-live.	page 220
nisgrep	Searches for entries in an NIS+ table.	page 262
nisgrpadm	Creates or destroys an NIS+ group, or displays a list of its members. Also adds members to a group, removes them, or tests them for membership in the group.	page 194
nisinit	Initializes an NIS+ client or server.	page 240
nisln	Creates a symbolic link between two NIS+ objects.	page 265
nisls	Lists the contents of an NIS+ directory.	page 233
nismatch	Searches for entries in an NIS+ table.	page 262
nismkdir	Creates an NIS+ directory and specifies its master and replica servers.	page 235
nispasswd	Changes NIS+ password information.	page 210
nisrm	Removes NIS+ objects (except directories) from the namespace.	page 238
nisrmdir	Removes NIS+ directories from the namespace.	page 237
nissetup	Creates `org_dir` and `groups_dir` directories and a complete set of (unpopulated) NIS+ tables for an NIS+ domain.	page 266

Table 1-3   NIS+ Namespace Administration Commands (Continued)

Command	Description (Continued)	Page
nisshowcache	Lists the contents of the NIS+ shared cache maintained by the NIS+ Cache Manager.	page 242
nistbladm	Creates or deletes NIS+ tables, and modifies or deletes entries in an NIS+ table.	page 252
nisupdkeys	Updates the public keys stored in an NIS+ object.	page 214

What Next?

The remainder of this book shifts focus from network information services in general toward NIS+ in particular. DNS and NIS are no longer mentioned except when discussing how to use them with NIS+. Before attempting to set up NIS+, be sure you understand the information presented in the remaining chapters of Part I:

- Chapter 2, "Understanding the NIS+ Namespace," describes NIS+ directories, domains, servers, clients, and the NIS-compatibility mode.

- Chapter 3, "Understanding NIS+ Tables and Information," describes NIS+ tables and the information in each of the 16 system tables.

- Chapter 4, "Understanding NIS+ Security," describes the process of authentication and authorization.

- Chapter 5, "Understanding the Name Service Switch," describes the Switch.

Understanding
the NIS+ Namespace

2≡

The NIS+ service is designed to conform to the shape of the organization that installs it, wrapping itself around the bulges and corners of almost any network configuration. This is implemented through the NIS+ *namespace*. This chapter describes the structure of the NIS+ namespace, the servers that support it, and the clients that use it. It has the following sections:

Structure of the NIS+ Namespace	Page	23
Directories	Page	25
Domains	Page	26
Servers	Page	28
Clients	Page	31
Naming Conventions (To Dot or Not)	Page	37
NIS+ Name Expansion	Page	42

Structure of the NIS+ Namespace

The NIS+ namespace is the arrangement of information stored by NIS+. The namespace can be arranged in a variety of ways to suit the needs of an organization. For example, if an organization had three divisions, its NIS+ namespace would likely be divided into three parts, one for each division. Each part would store information about the users, workstations, and network services in its division, but the parts could easily communicate with each other. Such an arrangement would make information easier for the users to access and for the administrators to maintain.

Although the arrangement of an NIS+ namespace can vary from site to site, all sites use the same structural components: directories, tables, and groups. These components are called *objects*. NIS+ objects can be arranged into a hierarchy that resembles a UNIX filesystem. For example, the illustration below shows, on the left, a namespace that consists of three directory objects, three group objects, and three table objects; on the right it shows a UNIX filesystem that consists of three directories and three files:

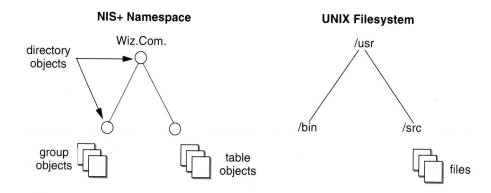

Although an NIS+ namespace resembles a UNIX filesystem, it has five important differences:

1. Although both use directories, the other objects in an NIS+ namespace are tables and groups, not files.

2. The NIS+ namespace is administered only through NIS+ administration commands (listed in Table 1-3 on page 20) or graphical user interfaces (GUI's) designed for that purpose; it cannot be administered with standard UNIX filesystem commands or GUI's.

3. The names of UNIX filesystem components are separated by slashes ("/usr/bin"), but the names of NIS+ namespace objects are separated by dots ("Wiz.Com.").

4. The "root" of a UNIX filesystem is reached by stepping through directories from right to *left* (e.g., /usr/src/file1), while the root of the NIS+ namespace is reached by stepping from left to *right* (Sales.Wiz.Com.).

5. Like UNIX files, NIS+ objects can be linked together, but NIS+ objects require the nisln command (described in Chapter 17, "Administering NIS+ Tables.") instead of the ln command.

Directories

Directory objects are the skeleton of the namespace. When arranged into a treelike structure, they divide the namespace into separate parts. You may find it helpful to visualize a directory hierarchy as an upside-down tree, with the root of the tree at the top, and the leaves toward the bottom. The topmost directory in a namespace is the *root* directory. If a namespace is flat, it has only one directory, but that directory is nevertheless the root directory. The directory objects beneath the root directory are simply called "directories:"

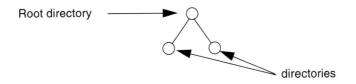

A namespace can have several levels of directories:

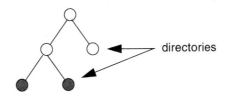

When identifying the relation of one directory to another, the directory beneath is called the *child* directory, and the directory above is called the *parent* directory.

Whereas Unix directories are designed to hold Unix files, NIS+ directories are designed to hold NIS+ objects: other directories, tables and groups. By convention, NIS+ directories that store NIS+ groups have the name "groups_dir," while directories that store NIS+ tables have been given the memorable name of "org_dir:"

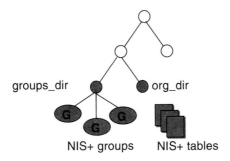

Technically, you can arrange directories, tables, and groups into any structure that you like. However, the NIS+ service is designed to work best when the directories, tables, and groups in a namespace are arranged into configurations called *domains*. Domains are designed to support separate portions of the namespace. For instance, one domain may support the Sales Division of a company, while another may support the Engineering Division.

Domains

An NIS+ domain consists of a directory object, its "org_dir" directory, its "groups_dir" directory, and a set of NIS+ tables.

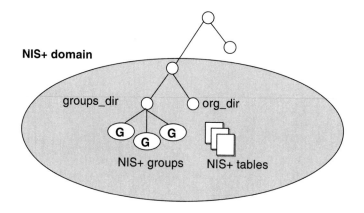

NIS+ domains are not *tangible* components of the namespace. They are simply a convenient way to *refer* to sections of the namespace that are used to support real-world organizations. Take the Wizard Corporation from Chapter 1 as an example. As you recall, at one point it had a Sales Division and an Engineering division. To support those divisions, its NIS+ namespace would most likely be arranged into three major directory groups, with a structure that looked like this:

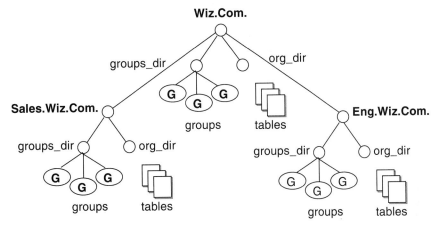

Instead of referring to such a structure as three directories, six subdirectories, and several additional objects, it is more convenient to refer to it as three domains:

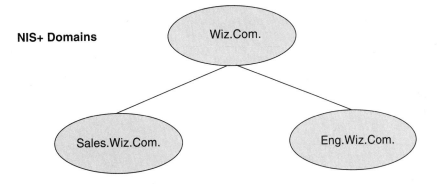

Part II of this book provides step-by-step instructions for setting up two types of domains. Chapter 7, "Setting Up the Root Domain," describes how to set up a root domain. Chapter 11, "Setting Up a Non-Root Domain," describes how to set up a non-root domain. For guidelines about which type to set up and in what order, see Chapter 6, "Planning for Setup."

Servers

Every NIS+ domain is supported by a set of NIS+ *servers*. The servers store the domain's directories, groups, and tables, and answer requests for access from users, administrators, and applications. Each domain is supported by only one set of servers. However, a single set of servers can support more than one domain:

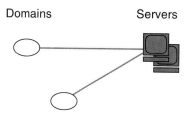

Remember that a domain is not an object, but only refers to a collection of objects. Therefore, a server that supports a domain is not actually connected to the domain, but to the domain's main *directory*:

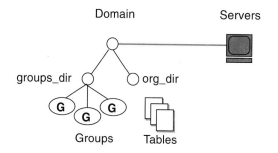

This connection between the server and the directory object is established during the process of setting up a domain. Although instructions are provided in Part II, one thing is important to mention now: when that connection is established, the directory object stores the name and IP address of its server. This information is used by clients to send requests for service, as described later in this section.

Any Solaris 2.x-based workstation can be an NIS+ server. The software for both NIS+ servers and clients is bundled together into the Solaris 2.x package. Therefore, any workstation that has Solaris 2.x installed can become a server or a client, or both. What distinguishes a client from a server is the *role it is playing*. If a workstation is providing NIS+ service, it is acting as an NIS+ server. If it is requesting NIS+ service, it is acting as an NIS+ client.

Because of the need to service many client requests, a workstation that will act as an NIS+ server might be configured with more computing power and more memory than the average client. And, because it needs to store NIS+ data, it might also have a larger disk. However, other than hardware to improve its performance, a server is not inherently different from an NIS+ client.

Two types of servers support an NIS+ domain: a master and its replicas:

Domain Servers Replica Master

The master server of the root domain is called the *root master* server. A namespace has only one root master server. The master servers of other domains are simply called master servers. Likewise, there are root replica servers and plain ol' replica servers.

Both master and replica servers store NIS+ tables and answer client requests. The master, however, stores the master copy of a domain's tables. The replicas store only duplicates. The administrator loads information into the tables in the master server, and the master server propagates it to the replica servers.

This arrangement has two benefits. First, it avoids conflicts between tables because only one set of master tables exists; the tables stored by the replicas are only copies of the masters. Second, it makes the NIS+ service much more *available*. If either the master or a slave is down, the other server can act as a backup and handle the requests for service.

How Servers Propagate Changes

An NIS+ master servers tries to "batch" updates to its objects before it propagates them to its replicas. When a master server receives an update to an object, whether a directory, group, link, or table, it waits about ten seconds for any other updates that may arrive. Once it is finished waiting, it stores the updates in three locations: memory, disk, and a *transaction log*.

The transaction log is used by master servers to store temporary changes to the namespace until they can be propagated to replicas. A transaction log has two primary components: updates and timestamps.

Transaction Log

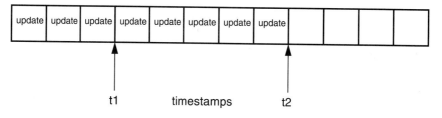

An update is an actual copy of a changed object. For instance, if a directory has been changed, the update is a complete copy of the directory object. If a table entry has been changed, the update is a copy of the actual table entry. The timestamp indicates the time at which each batch of updates was made by the master server.

After recording the change in the transaction log, the master sends a message to its replicas, telling them that it has updates to send them. Each replica replies with the timestamp of the last update it received from the master. The server then sends each server the updates it has recorded in the log since the replica's timestamp:

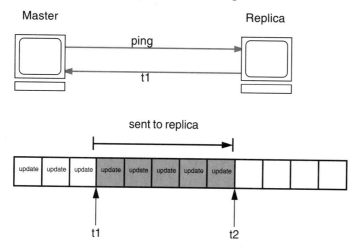

When the master server updates *all* its replicas, it clears the transaction log. In some cases, such as when a new replica is added to a domain, the master receives a timestamp from a replica that is before its earliest timestamp still recorded in the transaction log. If that happens, the master server performs a full *resynchronization*, or "resync." A resync downloads all the objects and information stored in the master down to the replica. During a resync, neither the replica nor the master can accept updates or answer requests for information. They respond with "Server Busy - Try Again" message.

Clients

An NIS+ client is a workstation that has been set up to receive NIS+ service. Setting up an NIS+ client consists of establishing security credentials, making it a member of the proper NIS+ groups, verifying its home domain, verifying its Switch configuration file and, finally, running the NIS+ initialization utility. (Complete instructions are provided in Chapter 9, "Setting Up an NIS+ Client.")

An NIS+ client can access any part of the namespace, subject to security constraints. In other words, if it has been authenticated and if it has been granted the proper permissions, it can access information or objects in any domain in the namespace.

Although a client can access the entire namespace, a client *belongs* to only one domain, which is referred to as its *home* domain. A client's home domain is usually specified during installation, but it can be changed or specified later. All the information about a client, such as its IP address and its DES credentials, is stored in the NIS+ tables of its home domain.

There is a subtle difference between being an NIS+ client and being listed in an NIS+ table. Entering information about a workstation into an NIS+ table does not automatically make that workstation an NIS+ client. It simply makes information about that workstation available to other NIS+ clients. That workstation cannot request NIS+ service unless it is actually set up as an NIS+ client.

Conversely, making a workstation an NIS+ client does not enter information about that workstation into an NIS+ table. It simply allows that workstation to receive NIS+ service. If information about that workstation is not explicitly entered into the NIS+ tables by an administrator, other NIS+ clients will not be able to get it.

Since an NIS+ client can access the entire namespace, it can receive service from any server in the namespace. The server that answers a particular request is the server that supports the domain the client is trying to access. Here is a simplified representation:

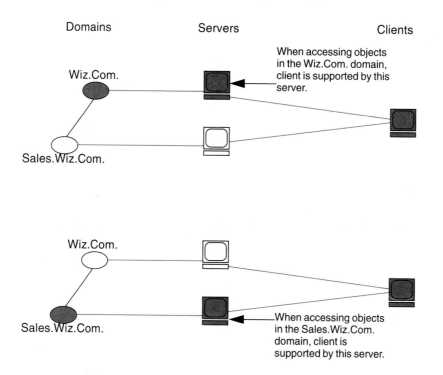

How does the client know which server that is? By a sophisticated method of trial and error. Beginning with its home server, the client tries one server, then another, until it finds the right one. When a server cannot answer the client's request, it sends the client information to help it locate the right server. Over time, the client builds up its own cache of information and becomes more efficient at locating the right server. Here are the details of the process,

When a client is initialized, it is given a *coldstart file*. The purpose of a coldstart file is to give a client a copy of a directory object that it can use as a starting point for contacting servers in the namespace. The directory object contains the address, public keys, and other information about the master and replica servers that support the directory. Normally, the coldstart file contains the directory object of the client's home domain. However, the administrator who initializes the client can place additional directory objects in its coldstart file.

A coldstart file, however, is used only to initialize a client's *directory cache*. The directory cache, managed by an NIS+ facility called the *cache manager,* stores the directory objects that enable a client to send its requests to the proper servers:

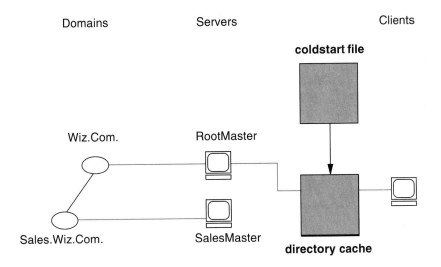

By storing a copy of the namespace's directory objects in its directory cache, a client can know which servers support which domains. Here is a simplified example[1]:

Domain	Directory Name	Supporting Server	IP Address
Wiz.Com.	Wiz.Com.	RootMaster	129.44.1.1
Sales.Wiz.Com	Sales.Wiz.Com.	SalesMaster	129.44.2.1
Eng.Wiz.Com.	Eng.Wiz.Com.	EngMaster	129.44.3.1
Intl.Sales.Wiz.Com.	Intl.Sales.Wiz.Com.	IntlSalesMaster	129.44.2.11

To keep these copies up-to-date, each directory object has a *time-to-live* value. The default is 12 hours. If a client looks in its directory cache for a directory object and finds that it has not been updated in the last 12 hours, the cache manager obtains a new copy of the object. You can change a directory object's time to live value with the `nischttl` command, as described in

---

1. To view the contents of a client's cache, use the `nisshowcache` command, described in Chapter 16, "Administering NIS+ Directories."

Chapter 16, "Administering NIS+ Directories." However, keep in mind that the longer the time to live, the higher the likelihood that the copy of the object will be out of date; and the shorter the time to live, the greater the network traffic and server load.

How does the directory cache accumulate these directory objects? As mentioned above, the coldstart file provides the first entry in the cache. Therefore, when the client sends its first request, it sends the request to the server specified by the coldstart file. If the request is for access to the domain supported by that server, the server answers the request:

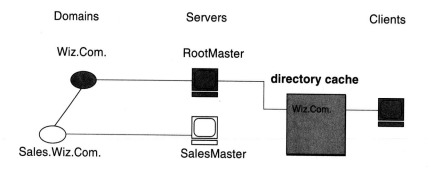

If the request is for access to another domain (e.g., "Sales.Wiz.Com.), the server tries to help the client locate the proper server. If the server has an entry for that domain in its own directory cache, it sends a copy of the domain's directory object to the client. The client loads that information into its directory cache for future reference and sends its request to that server:

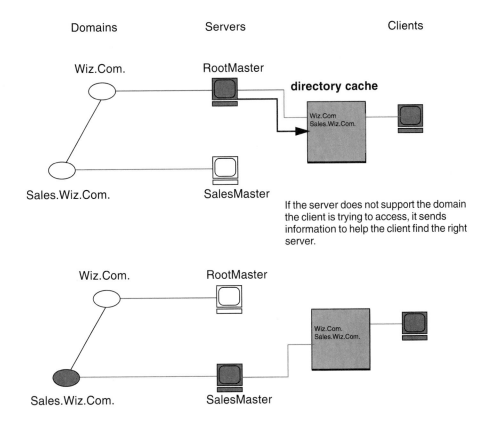

In the unlikely event that the server does not have a copy of the directory object the client is trying to access, its sends the client a copy of the directory object for its own home domain, which lists the address of the server's parent. The client repeats the process with the parent server, and keeps trying until it finds the proper server or until it has tried all the servers in the namespace. What the client does after trying all the servers in the domain is determined by the instructions in its Name Service Switch configuration file. See Chapter 5, "Understanding the Name Service Switch," for details.

Over time, the client accumulates in its cache a copy of all the directory objects in the namespace and thus, the IP addresses of the servers that support them.   When it needs to send a request for access to another domain, it can usually find the name of its server in its directory cache and send the request directly to that server.

Understanding the NIS+ Namespace   35

An NIS+ Server Is Also a Client

An NIS+ server is also an NIS+ client. In fact, before you can set up a workstation as a server (as described in Part II of this book), you must initialize it as a client. The only exception is the root master server, which is initialized as a server and client simultaneously, with its own unique setup process.

This means that in addition to *supporting* a domain, a server also *belongs* to a domain. In other words, by virtue of being a client, a server has a home domain. Its host information is stored in the Hosts table of its home domain, and its DES credentials are stored in the Cred table of its home domain. Like other clients, it sends its requests for service to the servers listed in its directory cache.

An important point to remember is that — except for the root domain — a server's home domain is the *parent* of the domain the server supports:

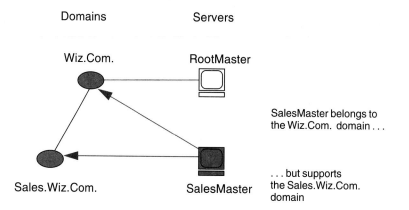

In other words, a server supports clients in one domain, but *is a client of* another domain. A server cannot be a client of a domain that it supports, with the exception of the root domain. The servers that support the root domain, because they have no parent domain, belong to the root domain itself.

All About Administering NIS+

For example, consider the following namespace:

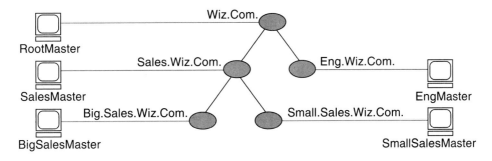

The chart below lists which domain each server supports and which domain it belongs to:

Server	Supports	Belongs to
RootMaster	Wiz.Com.	Wiz.Com.
SalesMaster	Sales.Wiz.Com.	Wiz.Com.
BigSalesMaster	Big.Sales.Wiz.Com.	Sales.Wiz.Com.
SmallSalesMaster	Small.Sales.Wiz.Com.	Sales.Wiz.Com.
EngMaster	Eng.Wiz.Com.	Wiz.Com.

Naming Conventions (To Dot or Not)

Objects in an NIS+ namespace can be identified with two types of names: *partially-qualified* and *fully-qualified*. A partially-qualified name, also called a *simple* name, is simply the name of the object or any portion of the fully-qualified name. If during any administration operation you enter the partially-qualified name of an object or principal, NIS+ will attempt to expand the name into its fully-qualified version. For details, see "*NIS+ Name Expansion*" on page 42.

A fully-qualified name is the complete name of the object, including all the information necessary to locate it in the namespace, such as its parent directory, if it has one, and its complete domain name, including a trailing dot.

This varies among different types of objects, so the conventions for each type, as well as for NIS+ principals, will be described separately. This namespace will be used as an example:

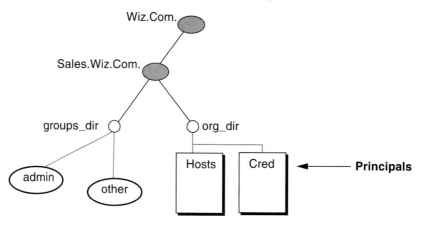

The fully-qualified names for all the objects in this namespace, including NIS+ principals, are summarized in Figure 2-1.

Figure 2-1   Fully-Qualified Names of Namespace Components

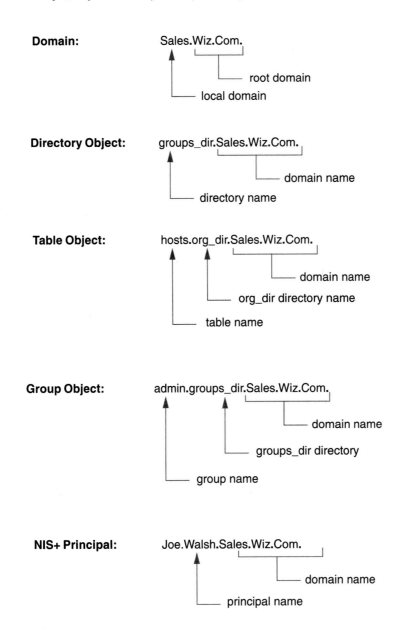

For Domains

A fully-qualified domain name is formed from left to right, starting with the local domain and ending with the root domain. For example:

> Wiz.Inc.
> Sales.Wiz.Inc.
> Intl.Sales.Wiz.Inc.

The first line above shows the name of the root domain. The root domain must always have two labels and must end in a dot. If you plan to connect the root domain to the Internet, you don't need to give it two labels; the Internet domain name that is appended to it acts as its second label:

> Wiz.   Wiz.Com.
> Sales.Wiz.   Sales.Wiz.Com.
> Intl.Sales.Wiz.   Intl.Sales.Wiz.Com.

For Directory Objects

A directory's simple name is simply the name of the directory object. It's fully-qualified name consists of its simple name plus the fully-qualified name of its domain (which always includes a trailing dot):

> groups_dir   (simple name)
> groups_dir.Eng.Wiz.Com.   (fully-qualified name)

If you set up an unusual hierarchy in which several layers of directories do not form a domain, be sure to include the names of the intermediate directories. For example:

> lowest_dir.lower_dir.low_dir.MyStrangeDomain.Com.

The simple name is normally used from within the same domain, and the fully-qualified name is normally used from a remote domain. However, by specifying search paths in a domain's NIS_PATH environment variable, you can use the simple name from remote domains (see "*NIS+ Name Expansion*" on page 42).

At this point you may wonder how to distinguish a directory name from a domain name. Well, in some cases you can't. There is no visible difference between the name of a domain and the name of its directory object. This does not confuse the NIS+ software because it knows which one it is dealing with by the type of operation it performs. For instance, when you use the `nismkdir` command, NIS+ assumes the name you provide (e.g., Wiz.Com.) is for a directory, not a domain. When you enter a domain name into the `domainname` command, the Solaris 2.x system assumes the name you provide (e.g., Wiz.Com) is for a domain.

For Tables and Groups

Fully-qualified table and group names are formed by starting with the object name and appending the directory name, followed by the fully-qualified domain name. Remember that all table objects are stored in an "org_dir" directory and all group objects are stored in a "groups_dir" directory. Here are some examples of group and table names:

admin.groups_dir.Wiz.Inc.	admin.groups_dir.Wiz.Com.
admin.groups_dir.Sales.Wiz.Inc.	admin.groups_dir.Sales.Wiz.Com.
hosts.org_dir.Wiz.Inc.	hosts.org_dir.Wiz.Com.
hosts.org_dir.Sales.Wiz.Inc.	hosts.org_dir.Sales.Wiz.Com.

For Table Entries

To identify an entry in an NIS+ table, you need to identify the table object and the entry within it. This type of name is called an *indexed* name. It has the following syntax:

[*column=value* , *column=value* , . . .] , *table-name*

Column is the name of the table column. *Value* is the actual value of that column. *Table-name* is the fully-qualified name of the table object. Here are a few examples of entries in the Hosts table:

```
[addr=129.44.2.2,name=pine],hosts.org_dir.Sales.Wiz.Com.
[addr=129.44.2.3,name=elm],hosts.org_dir.Sales.Wiz.Com.
[addr=129.44.2.4,name=oak],hosts.org_dir.Sales.Wiz.Com.
```

You can use as few column-value pairs inside the brackets as required to uniquely identify the table entry.

Some NIS+ administrative commands accept variations on this syntax. For details, see the `nistbladm`, `nismatch`, and `nisgrep` commands in Chapter 17, "Administering NIS+ Tables."

For NIS+ Principals

NIS+ principal names are sometimes confused with secure RPC netnames. Both types of names are described in Chapter 4, "Understanding NIS+ Security." However, one difference is worth pointing out now because it can cause confusion: NIS+ principal names *always* end in a dot and secure RPC netnames *never* do:

olivia.Sales.Wiz.Com.	(NIS+ principal name)
unix.olivia.@.Sales.Wiz.Com	(secure RPC netname)

Also, even though credentials for principals are stored in a Cred table, neither the name of the Cred table nor the name of the "org_dir" directory are included in the principal name.

Accepted Symbols

You can form namespace names from any printable character in the ISO Latin 1 set. However, the names cannot start with these characters:

```
@   < > +     [ ]       -
=   .   ,       :         ;
```

To use a string, enclose it in double quotes. To use a quote sign in the name, quote the sign too (for example, to use ol'yeller, type ol""yeller). To include white space (as in John Smith), use double quotes within single quotes, like this:

'"John Smith"'

NIS+ Name Expansion

Entering fully qualified names with your NIS+ commands can quickly become tedious. To ease the task, NIS+ provides a name expansion facility. When you enter a partially qualified name, NIS+ attempts to find the object by looking for it under different directories. It starts by looking in the default domain. This is the home domain of the client from which you enter the command. If it does not find the object in the default domain, NIS+ searches through each of the default domain's parent directories in ascending order until it finds the object. It stops after reaching a name with only two labels. Here are some examples (assume you are logged onto a client that belongs to the "Software.Big.Sales.Wiz.Com." domain).

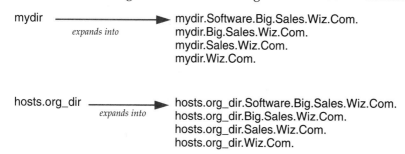

```
mydir    ─────── expands into ──────►  mydir.Software.Big.Sales.Wiz.Com.
                                       mydir.Big.Sales.Wiz.Com.
                                       mydir.Sales.Wiz.Com.
                                       mydir.Wiz.Com.

hosts.org_dir ─── expands into ──────► hosts.org_dir.Software.Big.Sales.Wiz.Com.
                                       hosts.org_dir.Big.Sales.Wiz.Com.
                                       hosts.org_dir.Sales.Wiz.Com.
                                       hosts.org_dir.Wiz.Com.
```

The NIS_PATH Environment Variable

You can change or augment the list of directories NIS+ searches through by changing the value of the environment variable NIS_PATH. NIS_PATH accepts a list of directory names separated by colons:

```
setenv NIS_PATH directory1:directory2:directory3...
```

NIS+ searches through these directories from left to right. For example:

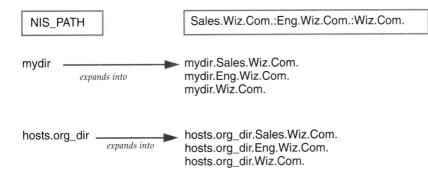

The NIS_PATH variable accepts a special symbol: $. You can append the $ symbol to a directory name or add it by itself. If you append it to a directory name, NIS+ appends the default directory to that name. For example:

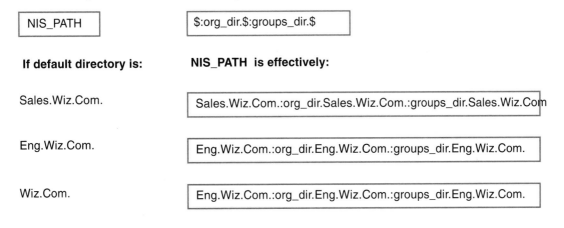

If you use it by itself (e.g., `org_dir.$:$`), NIS+ performs the standard name expansion described earlier: start looking in the default directory and proceed through the parent directories. In other words, the default value of NIS_PATH is $.

Understanding NIS+
Tables and Information

NIS+ stores a wide variety of network information in tables. This chapter describes the structure of those tables and provides brief overviews of the information in each type of table:

NIS+ Table Structure	Page	45
Ways to Set Up Tables	Page	49
Information in NIS+ Tables	Page	51

NIS+ Table Structure

NIS+ tables provide several features not found in simple text files or maps. They have a column-entry structure, they accept search paths, they can be linked together, they can be set up in several different ways, and although NIS+ provides 16 preconfigured system tables (see Table 3-1, below), you can create your own tables.

Table 3-1 System Tables

Table	Information in the Table
Hosts	Network address and hostname of every workstation in the domain
Bootparams	Location of the root, swap, and dump partition of every diskless client in the domain
Password	Password information about every user in the domain
Cred	Credentials for principals who have permission to access the NIS+ objects in the domain. (This table is described in Chapter 4, "Understanding NIS+ Security" .")
Group	Password, group id, and members of every UNIX group in the domain
Netgroup	The netgroups to which workstations and users in the domain may belong.

Table 3-1System Tables

Table	Information in the Table
Aliases	Information about the mail aliases of users in the domain.
Timezone	The timezone of every workstation in the domain
Networks	The networks in the domain and their canonical names
Netmasks	The networks in the domain and their associated netmasks
Ethers	The ethernet address of every workstation in the domain
Services	The names of IP services used in the domain and their port numbers
Protocols	The list of IP protocols used in the domain
RPC	The RPC program numbers for RPC services available in the domain.
Auto_Home	The location of all user's home directories in the domain.
Auto_Master	Automounter map information.

The information in each of these tables is described beginning on page 51.

Columns and Entries

Although NIS+ tables store different types of information, they all have the same underlying structure; they are each made up of entries and columns:

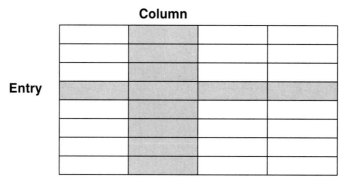

This means a client can access information not just by the table's key, but by any column. For example, to find the network address of a workstation named "baseball," a client could look through the hostname column until it found "baseball," . . .

Hostname
Column

	nose		
	grass		
	violin		
	baseball		

. . . then move along the baseball entry to find its network address:

Address   Hostname
Column   Column

	nose		
	grass		
	violin		
Baseball Row **129.44.1.2**	baseball		
←			

Because a client can access table information at the entry and column level, in addition to the object level (that is, it can access the table as a whole), NIS+ provides security mechanisms for all three levels. For instance, an administrator could assign Read rights to a table at the object level, Modify rights at the column level, but only to the owner, and Modify rights at the entry level, but to the group. Details about table security are provided in Chapter 4, "Understanding NIS+ Security" ."

Search Paths

A table contains information only about its *local* domain. For instance, tables in the "Wiz.Com." domain contain information only about the users, clients, and services of the "Wiz.Com." domain. The tables in the "Sales.Wiz.Com." domain store information only about the users, clients, and services of the "Sales.Wiz.Com." domain. And so on.

If a client in one domain tries to find information that is stored in another domain, it has to provide a fully qualified name. As described in "NIS+ Name Expansion" on page 42, if the NIS_PATH environment variable is set up properly, the NIS+ service will do this automatically.

In addition, though, every NIS+ table can specify a *search path* that a server will follow when looking for information. The search path is simply an ordered list of NIS+ tables, separated by colons:

table : *table* : *table* . . .

The table names must be fully-qualified. When a server cannot find information in its local table, it examines the table's search path. Then it proceeds to look for the information in every table named in the search path, in order, until it finds the information or runs out of names.

Here is an example that demonstrates the benefit of search paths. Assume the following domain hierarchy:

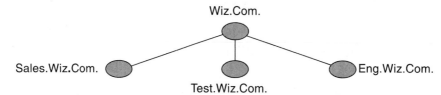

The Hosts table of the lower three domains have the following contents:

Sales.Wiz.Com.		Test.Wiz.Com.		Eng.Wiz.Com.	
127.0.0.1	localhost	127.0.0.1	localhost	127.0.0.1	localhost
129.44.2.10	vermont	129.44.4.10	nebraska	129.44.3.10	georgia
129.44.2.11	maine	129.44.4.11	oklahoma	129.44.3.11	florida
129.44.2.12	cherry	129.44.4.12	corn	129.44.3.12	orange
129.44.2.13	apple	129.44.4.13	wheat	129.44.3.13	potato
129.44.2.14	mailhost	129.44.4.14	mailhost	129.44.3.14	mailhost

Assume now that a user logged onto a client in the Sales.Wiz.Com. domain wants to login remotely to another client. If that user does not provide a fully qualified name, it can only remotely log on to five workstations: `vermont`, `maine`, `cherry`, `apple`, and the mailhost.

Now assume that the search path of the Hosts table in the Sales.Wiz.Com. domain listed the Hosts tables from the Test.Wiz.Com. and Eng.Wiz.Com. domains:

`search path`—hosts.org_dir.Test.Wiz.Com.:hosts.org_dir.Eng.Wiz.Com.

Now a user in the Sales.Wiz.Com. domain can enter something like `rlogin oklahoma`, and the NIS+ server will find it. It will first look for `oklahoma` in the local domain, but when it does not find a match, it will look in the Test.Wiz.Com. domain. How does the client know how to find the Test.Wiz.Com. domain? As described in Chapter 2, "Understanding the NIS+ Namespace" ," the information is stored in its directory cache. If it is not stored in its directory cache, the client will obtain the information by following the process described in Chapter 2.

There is a slight drawback, though, to specifying a search path. If the user were to enter an incorrect name, such as `rlogin potatoe`, the server would need to look through three tables — instead of just one — before returning an error message. If you set up search paths throughout the namespace, an operation may end up searching through the tables in 10 domains instead of just 2 or 3.

You should also be aware that since "mailhost" is often used as an alias, when trying to find information about a specific mailhost, you should use its fully-qualified name (e.g., `mailhost.Sales.Wiz.Com.`), or NIS+ will return *all* the mailhosts it finds in all the domains it searches through.

You can specify a table's search path by using the `-p` option to the `nistbladm` command, as described in Chapter 17, "Administering NIS+ Tables" ."

Ways to Set Up Tables

The second part of this book provides complete step-by-step instructions for setting up NIS+ tables, but here is an overview of the process. Setting up NIS+ tables involves three or four tasks:

1. Creating the "org_dir" directory

2. Creating the system tables

3. Creating non-system tables (optional)

4. Populating the tables with information

As described in Chapter 2, NIS+ tables are stored under an "org_dir" directory. So, before you can create any tables, you must create the "org_dir" directory that will hold them. You can do this in two ways. You can use the `nismkdir` command or you can use the `/usr/lib/nis/nissetup` utility. The `nismkdir` command, described in Chapter 16, "Administering NIS+ Directories" ," simply creates the directory. The `nissetup` utility creates the org_dir and groups_dir directories and a full set of tables.

The `nissetup` utility is the recommended way. It is described in the instructions for setting up the root domain and non-root domains. To use it, follow the instructions either in Chapter 7, "Setting Up the Root Domain" ," or Chapter 11, "Setting Up a Non-Root Domain" ."

Another benefit of the `nissetup` utility is its capability to assign the proper access rights to the tables of a domain whose servers are running in NIS-compatibility mode. When entered with the `-Y` flag, it assigns Read permissions to the "Nobody" category of the objects it creates, allowing NIS clients, who are unauthenticated, to get information from the domain's NIS+ tables.

The 16 NIS+ tables and the type of information they store are described later in this chapter. To create them, you could use the `nistbladm` command or the `nissetup` utility mentioned above. The `nistbladm` utility creates and modifies NIS+ tables. You could, conceivably, create all the tables in a namespace with the `nistbladm` command, but you would have to do a lot more typing and you would have to know the correct column names and access rights. A much, much easier way is to use the `nissetup` utility.

To create a non-system table — that is, a table that has not been preconfigured by NIS+ — use the `nistbladm` command, as described in Chapter 17, "Administering NIS+ Tables" ." Because these are not system tables, they will not be supported by an NIS+ replica server running in NIS-compatibility mode.

You can populate NIS+ tables in three ways: from NIS maps, from ASCII files (such as `/etc` files), and manually.

If you are upgrading from the NIS service, you already have most of your network information stored in NIS maps. You *don't* have to re-enter this information manually into NIS+ tables. You can transfer it automatically with the `nisaddent` utility, as described in "How to Populate NIS+ Tables from NIS Maps" on page 140.

If you are not using another network information service, but maintain network data in a set of `/etc` files, you *don't* have to re-enter this information either. You can transfer it automatically, also using the `nisaddent` utility, as described in "How to Populate NIS+ Tables from Files" on page 136.

If you are setting up a network for the first time, you may not have much network information stored anywhere. In that case, you'll need to first get the information and then enter it manually into the NIS+ tables. You can do this with the `nistbladm` command, as described in Chapter 17, "Administering NIS+ Tables" ." You can also do it by entering all the information for a particular table into an *input file* — which is essentially the same as an `/etc` file — and then transferring the contents of the file with the `nisaddent` utility, as described in "How to Populate NIS+ Tables from Files" on page 136.

How Tables Are Updated

When a domain is set up, its servers receive their first versions of the domain's NIS+ tables. These versions are stored on disk, but when a server begins operating, it loads them into memory. When a server receives an update to a table, it immediately updates its memory-based version of the table. When it receives a request for information, it uses the memory-based copy for its reply.

Of course, the server also needs to store its updates on disk. Since updating disk-based tables takes time, all NIS+ servers keep *log* files for their tables. The log files are designed to temporarily store changes made to the table, until they can be updated on disk. They use the table name as the prefix and append ".log." For example:

hosts.log
bootparams.log
password.log

You should update disk-based copies of a table on a daily basis so that the log files don't grow too large and take up too much disk space. To do this, use the `nisping -C` command, described in Chapter 17, "Administering NIS+ Tables" ."

Information in NIS+ Tables

NIS+ tables store a wide variety of information, ranging from user names to Internet services. Most of this information is generated during a setup or configuration procedure. For instance, an entry in the Password table is created when a user account is set up. An entry in the Hosts table is created when a workstation is added to the network. And an entry in the Networks table is created when a new network is set up.

Since this information is generated from such a wide field of operations, describing it thoroughly in this chapter would make this book much too large. Instead, this section defines the information contained in each column of the tables, providing details only when necessary to keep things from getting confusing, such as when distinguishing groups from NIS+ groups and netgroups. For thorough explanations of the information, consult other books about Solaris 2.x, especially those related to system and network administration. These are the tables summarized in this chapter:

Auto_Master Table	Page	53
Auto_Home Table	Page	53
Bootparams Table	Page	54

Ethers Table	Page	55
Group Table	Page	56
Hosts Table	Page	57
Mail Aliases Table	Page	58
Netmasks Table	Page	59
Netgroup Table	Page	58
Networks Table	Page	60
Password Table	Page	60
Protocols Table	Page	61
RPC Table	Page	62
Services Table	Page	63
Timezone Table	Page	63

The Cred table, because it contains only information related to NIS+ security, is described in Chapter 4, "Understanding NIS+ Security" .

As explained in Chapter 1, without a network information service, this information would be stored in /etc files. In fact, most NIS+ tables have corresponding /etc files. With the NIS service, you could combine the information in the NIS maps with the information in their corresponding /etc maps by using the +/- syntax. However, the Name Service Switch provides a better method.

The Name Service Switch allows you to specify one or more sources for different types of information. In addition to NIS+ tables, that source can be NIS maps, DNS maps, or /etc tables. The order in which you specify them determines how the information from different sources is combined. For more information, see Chapter 5, "Understanding the Name Service Switch" .

Note – If you are creating input files for any of these tables, most tables share two formatting requirements: you must use one line per entry, and you must separate columns with one or more spaces or TABs. If a particular table has different or additional format requirements, they are described under a heading called *"Input File Format."*

Auto_Home Table

The Auto_Home table is an indirect automounter map that enables an NIS+ client to mount the home directory of any user in the domain. It does this by specifying a mount point for each user's home directory, the location of each home directory, and mount options, if any. Because it is an indirect map, the first part of the mount point is specified in the Auto_Master table, and happens to be, by default, /home. The second part of the mount point (i.e., the subdirectory under /home) is specified by the entries in the Auto_Home map, and is different for each user.

The Auto_Home Table has two columns:

Column	Description
Mount Point	The login name of every user in the domain.
Options&Location	The mount options for every user, if any, and the location of the user's home directory.

For example:

```
costas          barcelona:/export/partition2/costas
```

The home directory of the user costas, which is located on the server barcelona, in the directory /export/partition2/costas, would be mounted under a client's /home/costas directory. No mount options were provided in the entry.

Auto_Master Table

The Auto_Master table lists all the automounter maps in a domain. For direct maps, the Auto_Master table simply provides a map name. For indirect maps, it provides both a map name and the top directory of its mount point. The Auto_Master table has two columns:

Column	Description
Mount Point	The top directory into which the map will be mounted. If the map is a direct map, this is a dummy directory, represented with /−.
Map Name	The name of the automounter map.

For example, assume these entries in the Auto_Master table:

```
/home          auto_home
/-             auto_man
/programs      auto_programs
```

The first entry names the Auto_Home map. It specifies the top directory of the mount point for all entries in the Auto_Home map: /home. (The Auto_Home map is an indirect map.) The second entry names the Auto_Man map. Because that map is a direct map, the entry provides only the map name. The Auto_Man map will itself provide the topmost directory, as well as the full pathname, of the mount points for each of its entries. The third entry names the Auto_Programs map and since it provides the top directory of the mount point, the Auto_Programs map is an indirect map.

All automounter maps are stored as NIS+ tables. By default, Solaris 2.x provides the Auto_Master map, which is mandatory, and the Auto_Home map, which is a great convenience. You can create more automounter maps for a domain, but be sure to store them as NIS+ tables and list them in the Auto_Master table. For more information about the automounter, consult books about the Automounter or books that describe the NFS filesystem.

Bootparams Table

The Bootparams table stores configuration information about every diskless workstation in a domain. A diskless workstation is a workstation that is connected to a network, but has no hard disk. Since it has no internal storage capacity, a diskless workstation stores its files and programs in the filesystem of a server on the network. It also stores its configuration information — or *boot parameters* — on a server.

Because of this arrangement, every diskless workstation has an initialization program that knows where this information is stored. If the network has no network information service, the program looks for this information in the server's /etc/bootparams file. If the network uses the NIS+ name service, the program looks for it in the Bootparams table, instead.

The Bootparams table can store any configuration information about diskless workstations. It has two columns: one for the configuration key, another for its value. By default, it is set up to store the location of each workstation's root, swap, and dump partitions. The default table has only two columns, but uses them to provide the following four items of information:

Column	Description
Hostname	The diskless workstation's official hostname, as specified in the Hosts table

Column	Description
Configuration	Root Partition: the location (server name and path) of the workstation's root partition
	Swap Partition: the location (server name and path) of the workstation's swap partition
	Dump Partition: the location (server name and path) of the workstation's dump partition

Input File Format

The columns are separated with a TAB character. Backslashes (\) are used to break a line within an entry. The entries for root, swap, and dump partitions have the following format:

```
client-name        root=server:path \
                   swap=server:path \
                   dump=server:path
```

Here is an example:

```
buckaroo        root=bigriver:/export/root1/buckaroo\
                swap=bigriver:/export/swap1/buckaroo\
                dump=bigriver:/export/dump/buckaroo
```

Ethers Table

The Ethers table stores information about the 48-bit Ethernet addresses of workstations on the Internet. It has two columns:

Column	Description
Ethernet-address	The 48-bit Ethernet address of the workstation.
Official-host-name	The name of the workstation, as specified in the Hosts table.

An Ethernet address has the form:

$n:n:n:n:n:n$ hostname

. . . where n is a hexadecimal number between 0 and FF, representing one byte. The address bytes are always in network order.

Group Table

The Group table stores information about workstation user groups. Solaris 2.x supports three kinds of groups: netgroups, NIS+ groups, and workstation user groups.

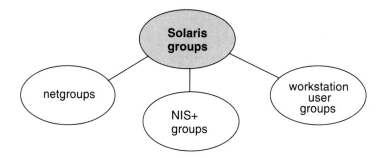

A netgroup is a group of workstations and users that have permission to perform remote operations on other workstations in the group. An NIS+ group is a set of NIS+ users that can be assigned access rights to an NIS+ object. They are described in Chapter 4, "Understanding NIS+ Security" . A workstation user group is simply a collection of users who are given additional UNIX access permissions.

Workstation user groups can be formed at two levels: the workstation and the network.

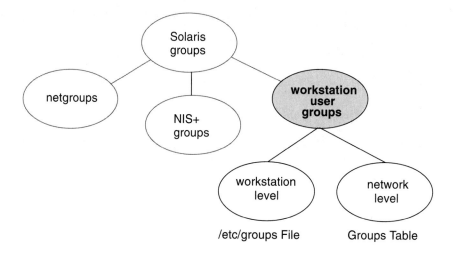

When formed at the workstation level, they are used to grant equal access to all members of a group while denying access to nonmembers. This level of workstation user group is set up and administered by the workstation owner. Thus, the files that define it (/etc/groups and /etc/passwd) are maintained locally, by the workstation owner.

When formed at the network level, workstation user groups allow a set of users on the network to access a set of files on several workstations or servers without making those files available to everyone. For example, the engineering and marketing staff working on a particular project could form a workstation user group. This type of workstation user groups is recorded in the Group Database.

The Group table has four columns:

Field	Description
Name	The group's name
Password	The group's password.
GID	The group's numerical ID.
members	The names of the group members, separated by commas.

Previous releases of SunOS used a +/- syntax in local /etc/group files to incorporate or overwrite entries in the NIS group maps. Since Solaris 2.x uses the Name Service Switch (described in Chapter 5) to specify a workstation's sources of information, this is no longer necessary. All you have to do in Solaris 2.x systems is edit a client's /etc/nsswitch.conf file to specify "files," followed by "nisplus" as the sources for the group information. This effectively adds the contents of the Group table to the contents of the client's /etc/group file.

Hosts Table

The Hosts table associates the names of all the workstations in a domain with their IP addresses. The workstations are usually also NIS+ clients, but they don't have to be. Other tables, such as Bootparams, Group, and Netgroup, rely on the network names stored in this table. They use them to assign other attributes, such as home directories and group memberships, to individual workstations. The Hosts table has four columns:

Column	Description
IP Address	The workstation's IP address (network number plus workstation ID number)
Hostname	The workstation's official name
Nickname	An optional name used in place of the hostname to identify the workstation
Comment	An optional comment about the record

Mail Aliases Table

The Mail Aliases table lists the domain's mail aliases recognized by `sendmail`. It has two columns:

Column	Description
Alias Name	The name of the alias
Members	A list containing the members that receive mail sent to this alias. Members can be users, workstations, or other aliases.

Input File Format

Each entry has the following format:

alias-name : *member* [, *member*] . . .

To extend an entry over several lines, use a backslash.

Netgroup Table

The Netgroup table defines network-wide groups used to check permissions for remote mounts, logins, and shells. The members of netgroups used for remote mounts are workstations; for remote logins and shells, they are users. The Netgroup table has two columns:

Column	Description
Group Name	The name of the network group.
List of Members	A list of the members in the group.

Input File Format

The input file consists of a groupname and any number of members:

groupname member-specification . . .

A member specification can be the name of another netgroup or an ordered list with three fields:

member-spec : : = *group-name* |
         (*hostname*, *username*, *domainname*)

The first field specifies the name of a workstation. The second field specifies the name of a user. The third field specifies the domain in which the member specification is valid.

A missing field indicates a wildcard. So, this netgroup . . .

```
everybody (,,)
```

. . . includes all workstations and users in all domains.

A dash in a field is the opposite of a wildcard; it indicates that no workstations or users belong to the group. Here are two examples:

```
(host1, -,Wiz.Com.)
(-,joe,Wiz.Com.)
```

The first specification includes one workstation, host1, in the Wiz.Com. domain, but excludes all users. The second specification includes one user in the Wiz.Com. domain, but excludes all workstations.

Netmasks Table

The Netmasks table contains the network masks used to implement standard Internet subnetting. The table has two columns:

Column	Description
Network Number	The IP number of the network.
Subnet Mask	The network mask to use on the network.

For network numbers, you can use the conventional IP dot notation used by workstation addresses, but leave zeroes in place of the workstation addresses. For example, this entry:

128.32.0.0   255.255.255.0

. . . means that class B network 128.32.0.0 should have 16 bits in its network field, eight bits in its subnet field, and eight bits in its host field.

Networks Table

The Networks table lists the networks of the Internet. This table is normally created from the official network table maintained at the Network Information Control Center (NIC), though you may need to add your local networks to it. It has three columns:

Column	Description
Network Name	The official name of the network, supplied by the Internet
Network Number	The official IP number of the network
Aliases	An unofficial name for the network

Password Table

The Password table contains information about the accounts of users in a domain. These users generally are, but do not have to be, NIS+ principals. Remember though, that if they are NIS+ principals, their credentials are not stored here, but in the domain's Cred table. The Password table usually grants Read permission to the World (or to Nobody).

The information in the password table is added when users' accounts are created. The Password table contains the following columns:

Column	Description
User Name	The user's login name, which is assigned when the user's account is created. The name can contain no uppercase characters and can have a maximum of eight characters.
Password	The user's encrypted password.
UID	The user's numerical ID, assigned when the user's account is created.
Group ID	The numerical ID of the user's group.
GCOS	The user's real name plus information that the user wishes to include in the "From:" field of a mail-message heading. An & in this column simply uses the user's login name.
Home Directory	The pathname of the user's home directory; that is, the directory the user is placed in after logging in.
Login Shell	The user's initial shell program. The default is the c-shell: /usr/bin/csh.

The Password table has an additional column: the Shadow column. It stores restricted information about user accounts. It includes the following information:

Item	Description
Lastchg	The number of days between January 1, 1970, and the date the password was last modified.
Min	The minimum number of days recommended between password changes.
Max	The maximum number of days that the password is valid.
Warn	The number of days' warning a user receives before being notified that his or her password has expired.
Inactive	The number of days of inactivity allowed for the user.
Expire	An absolute date past which the user's account is no longer valid.
Flag	Reserved for future use. Currently set to 0.

Previous releases of SunOS used a +/- syntax in local /etc/passwd files to incorporate or overwrite entries in the NIS password maps. Since Solaris 2.x uses the Name Service Switch (described in Chapter 5) to specify a workstation's sources of information, this is no longer necessary. All you have to do in Solaris 2.x systems is edit a client's /etc/nsswitch.conf file to specify "files," followed by "nisplus" as the sources for the passwd information. This effectively adds the contents of the Password table to the contents of the /etc/passwd file.

However, if you still want to use the +/- method, edit the client's nsswitch.conf file to specify "compat" for the passwd source.

Protocols Table

The Protocols table lists the protocols used by the Internet. It has four columns:

Column	Description
Protocol Number	The name of the protocol
Protocol Name	The protocol number
Aliases	An unofficial alias used to identify the protocol
Comments	Comments about the protocol

Here is an example of an input file for the Protocols table:

```
#
#  Internet (IP) Protocols
#
ip          0        IP        # internet protocol, pseudo protocol number
icmp        1        ICMP      # internet control message protocol
ggp         3        GGP       # gateway-gateway protocol
tcp         6        TCP       # transmission control protocol
pup         12       PUP       # PARC universal packet
udp         17       UDP       # user datagram protocol
#
```

RPC Table

The RPC table lists the names of RPC programs. It has four columns:

Column	Description
RPC program name	The name of the program
RPC program number	The program number
Aliases	Other names that can be used to invoke the program
Comments	Comments about the RPC program

Here is an example of an input file for the RPC table:

```
#
#  rpc file
#
rpcbind      100000    portmap   sunrpcportmapper
rusersd      100002    rusers
nfs          100003    nfsprog
mountd       100005    mount     showmount
walld        100008    rwall     shutdown
sprayd       100012    spray
llockmgr     100020
nlockmgr     100021
status       100024
bootparam    100026
keyserv      100029    keyserver
#
```

Services Table

The Services table stores information about the Internet services available on the Internet. It has four columns:

Column	Description
Service Name	The official Internet name of the service.
Port/Protocol	The port number and protocol through which the service is provided (for instance, 512/tcp)
Aliases	The list of alternate names by which the service can be requested.
Comments	Comments about the service

Timezone Table

The Timezone table lists the default timezone of every workstation in the domain. The default timezone is used during installation, but can be overridden by the installer. The table has three columns:

Field	Description
Timezone name	The name of the timezone (e.g., US/Pacific)
Workstation or Domain Name	The name of the workstation or, if using only one line in the entire table, the name of the domain
Comments	Comments about the timezone

Understanding NIS+ Security

NIS+ offers security features to protect the information in the namespace, as well as the structure of the namespace itself, from unauthorized access. Without security, any NIS+ client could not only obtain and change information stored in the namespace, but could also change or destroy objects in the namespace. This chapter has the following sections:

Overview of the Security Process	Page	65
About NIS+ Credentials	Page	70
About Access Rights	Page	78

Overview of the Security Process

Access to the namespace is granted primarily to NIS+ *principals*, enforced by NIS+ servers, and spelled out by each object in the namespace.

Security and Principals

An NIS+ principal is a client user or a client workstation whose *credentials* have been stored in the namespace. The namespace maintains credentials for individuals who may log onto NIS+ clients, and for the root identity of client workstations themselves (credentials are described later in this chapter). Thus, a user can log into an NIS+ client as himself or herself and request access to the namespace based on his or her credentials. Or, a user can log into an NIS+ client as root and request access to the namespace based on the credentials of the client workstation.

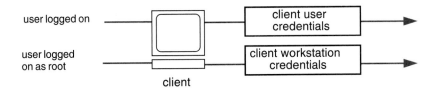

Security and Servers

When a client sends a request to a server, it automatically includes the credentials of the NIS+ principal making the request, whether that is the client user or the client workstation. The NIS+ server that checks those credentials places the request in one of two categories: *authenticated* or *unauthenticated*.

The authenticated category is for requests whose principal the server has been able to identify. This identification is used later to determine the authorization category — Owner, Group, or World — into which that principal has been placed.

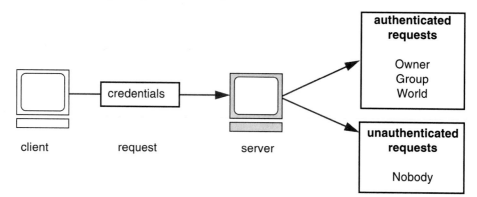

The unauthenticated category is for requests whose sender the server has been *unable* to identify. The server could have failed to identify the sender for several different reasons. Perhaps the credentials were not valid, or they were placed in a different domain, or the request did not come from an NIS+ principal to begin with. This does not mean the request is denied. As explained in "*About Access Rights,*" later in this chapter, NIS+ has set aside a special category for unauthorized requests. That category has been named, in what suggests bemused acquiescence, the "Nobody" category. If the Nobody category has the appropriate rights, the request is granted even though the sender is not identified.

Which of these categories the request is placed in depends first on the security level of the server that receives the request, and second on the validity of the credentials. Table 4-1, below, describes the three server security levels.

Table 4-1   NIS+ Security Levels

Security Level	Description
0	Security level 0 does not examine the credentials sent along with a request. It simply considers all requests unauthenticated and places them all in the Nobody category.
	This level is designed for testing and setting up the initial NIS+ namespace.
1	Security level 1 examines the credentials supplied by the request and accepts either LOCAL or DES credentials. As described later in this chapter, LOCAL credentials are one of two types of credentials accepted by NIS+; the other type is DES. When a server is running at security level 1, requests that supply valid LOCAL credentials are authenticated. Requests that supply invalid LOCAL credentials or don't supply any at all, are considered unauthenticated and relegated to the Nobody category.
	Because LOCAL credentials are easily forged, use security level 1 only for testing. Do not use it on networks to which untrusted servers may have access.
2	Security level 2 looks for DES credentials. A request with valid DES credentials is authenticated. Requests that supply LOCAL credentials or none at all are considered unauthenticated and placed in the Nobody category. Requests that supply invalid DES credentials are denied.
	This is the highest level of security currently provided by the NIS+ service. It is also the default level assigned to the server.

Security and Objects

Every communication from an NIS+ client to an NIS+ server requests access to some kind of NIS+ *object*. For example, if a client requests the IP address of another workstation, it is effectively requesting access to the Hosts table object, which stores that type of information. An administrator who asks the server to add a directory to the NIS+ namespace is actually requesting access to the directory's parent object.

Not only is every request directed at a particular object, it also specifies a type of operation. The operations vary among different types of objects, but they fall into four categories: read, modify, create, and destroy.

Every object, as part of its definition, specifies the *access rights* that it grants to authenticated NIS+ principals and unauthenticated requests. These access rights correspond to the types of operations just described; they are Read, Modify, Create, and Destroy. So, if the operation that a principal tries to perform on an object is *authorized* by the object's definition (i.e., the access rights match the type of operation), the server performs it. If not, the request is denied.

There is one more wrinkle in this process. An object does not directly grant access rights to a particular principal. Instead, it grants access rights to four *authorization categories*: Owner, Group, World, and Nobody. The principal who happens to be the object's owner gets the rights granted to the Owner category. The principals who belong to the object's Group category get the rights granted to the Group[1]. And so on. In this way, if the object changes owners or groups, its rights don't have to be updated. These categories are described later in this chapter, on page 78.

Figure 4-1, on the following page, summarizes the entire process. When a principal sends a request to a server, the server examines the principal's credentials and authenticates the request. The server determines the type of operation the principal has requested and the object it applies to. Then it examines the object's definition.

The server first determines which of the object's authorization categories the principal fits into: Owner, Group, World, or Nobody. Then it determines the access rights that the object has granted that category. If the access rights match the operation, the server performs it. Otherwise, it denies the request.

---

1. This is an NIS+ group, by the way, not a UNIX group. NIS+ groups are described on page 78.

All About Administering NIS+

Figure 4-1   Summary of NIS+ Security Process

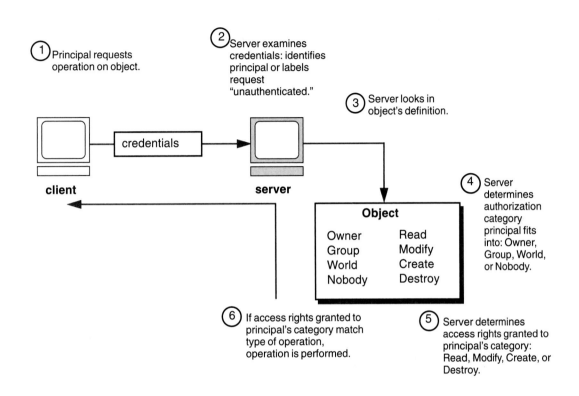

The details of this process are described in the remainder of this chapter.

About Setting Up NIS+ Security

Security is not a layer of features that you can simply add to an existing namespace; you can't set up security and the namespace independently. For this reason, instructions for setting up security are woven through the steps for setting up different components of the namespace, and are described in Part II of this book.

About NIS+ Credentials

An NIS+ credential is the authentication information about an NIS+ principal that the client software sends along with each request to an NIS+ server. The credential identifies the principal who sent the request. An NIS+ server uses that information to identify the principal and thus determine its access rights to the object it is trying to access.

NIS+ accepts two types of credentials: LOCAL and DES. A LOCAL credential is simply the UID of an NIS+ principal. Since the UID of every workstation is zero, a LOCAL credential doesn't make sense for a client *workstation*; thus, it is allowed only for a client *user*. An NIS+ server uses a LOCAL credential's UID to look up the identity of the principal who sent the request so it can determine its rights to the object.

A DES credential is more complex than a LOCAL credential, not only because of the information it requires, but because of the process involved in creating and using it. To understand how DES authentication works, you need to distinguish between the credential itself and the information that is used to generate and verify it. To keep our terminology straight, we'll reserve the term *credential* for the former and use the term *credential information* for the latter. Thus, the credential is the magic bundle of numbers that is sent by the client to the server, and the credential information is the data that is stored in a Cred table (described below), and used by the client to generate the credential and by the server to verify the credential.

The DES credential itself consists of a principal's *secure RPC netname* plus a *verification* field:

DES Credential:

Secure RPC Netname	Verification Field

The secure RPC netname portion of the credential can be formed for both client users and client workstations, and has the following syntax:

> Secure RPC netname:
>
> unix.*userid@domainname*
> unix.*hostname@domainname*

Every secure RPC netname begins with the prefix "unix." If the principal is a client user, the second field in the netname is the user's UID. If the principal is a client workstation, the second field in the netname is the workstation's hostname. The last field is the principal's home domain:

If the Principal Is	The Domain Must Be
A client user	The domain that contains the user's password entry and DES credentials.
A client workstation	The domain name returned by executing the `domainname` command on that workstation.

A brief reminder about naming conventions: an NIS+ principal name *always* has a trailing dot, while a secure RPC netname *never* does.

An NIS+ server uses the secure RPC netname to identify the principal so it can determine its access rights to the object. However, when examining DES credentials, the server also checks the verification field to make sure the credential is not forged.

The verification field is complex data that is encrypted using information stored in the Cred table. The field is decrypted by the server, also using information stored in the Cred table. First we'll describe the Cred table, then the encryption and decryption process.

The Cred Table

The Cred table stores LOCAL credentials and the information used to encrypt and decrypt DES credentials. There is one Cred table in the org_dir directory of every NIS+ domain. DES credential information, whether for a principal that is a client user or a client workstation, can only be stored in the principal's home domain. Both the client and the server use the DES credential information to encrypt and decrypt the verification field of the DES credential.

A client user can have LOCAL credentials in both its home domain and in other domains. In fact, in order to access objects in a remote domain that do not provide access rights to the Nobody category, a client user *must* have LOCAL credentials stored in the Cred table of the remote domain. If the server supporting the remote domain is running at security level 2, it can obtain the client user's DES credentials from its local domain by examining its LOCAL credentials stored in the remote domain.

Because a client workstation cannot have LOCAL credentials, and because it can store DES credentials only in its home domain, it has no way to access objects in remote domains — unless those objects have granted access rights to the Nobody category.

The Cred table has five columns:

NIS+ Principal Name	Authentication Type	Authentication Name	Public Data	Private Data
NIS+ principal name of a client user	LOCAL	UID	GID list	none
NIS+ principal name of a client user or client workstation	DES	Secure RPC netname	Public key	Encrypted Private key

The first column, NIS+ Principal Name, contains the fully-qualified name of an NIS+ principal. When the authentication type (second column) is LOCAL, the first column can only contain the principal name of a client user, since client workstations cannot have LOCAL credentials. When the authentication type is DES, the principal name can be that of a client user or a client workstation.

The second column, Authentication Type, specifies whether the three columns to the right store a LOCAL credential or DES credential information. For a LOCAL credential, the client user's UID is placed in the Authentication Name column. In addition, the client user's group ID (GID) is placed in the Public Data field, even though it is not part of the credential. The last column is not used for a LOCAL credential.

For DES credential information, the principal's secure RPC netname is placed in the Authentication Name column and two parts of the information used to encrypt and decrypt the verification field are placed in the last two columns: the principal's public key is placed in the Public Data column, and its encrypted private key is placed in the Private Data column. These keys, as well as the other components used to encrypt and decrypt a DES credentials are described in the following section. Here is a comparison of a DES credential and the DES credential information stored in the Cred table:

DES Credential:

Secure RPC Netname	Verification Field

DES Credential Information:

Secure RPC Netname	Public Key	Encrypted Private Key

How Credentials Are Created and Used

Even though step-by-step instructions for creating credentials are provided in Parts II and III, understanding the process by which credentials are created and used will prove helpful.

As described in Part II, one of the critical steps in setting up a domain is to create credentials for the domain's administrators. Once the administrators have credentials, they can continue to set up the namespace and create credentials for other principals. Or they can ask the other principals to create their own credentials. In both instances, nisaddcred is the command used to create the credentials.

The nisaddcred command creates either LOCAL credentials or DES credential information. When used to create LOCAL credentials, it simply extracts the client user's UID (and GID) from the client's login record and places it in the domain's Cred table.

When used to create DES credential information, it goes through a two-step process. To create the first part of the information, the secure RPC netname, it obtains the principal's userid from the password record and places it in the domain's Cred table. However, to generate the second part of the information, the public key and the encrypted private key, it must go to a little more trouble.

To generate the private key, it needs the principal's network password. So, when the nisaddcred command is invoked with the des argument, the first thing it does is ask the principal to enter a network password. Normally, this password *is the same as the principal's login password*[1]. From this password the nisaddcred command generates a pair of random, but mathematically-related, 192-bit authentication keys. (Neither of these is the "DES key" that forms the basis of the credential's verification field. They are used to encrypt and decrypt the DES key, but they are not *the* DES key.)

---

1. If it is different, additional steps are required, as described on page 76.

One of these is the private key, the other is the public key. The public key is placed in the "Public Data" field of the Cred table. The private key is placed in the "Private Data" field, but encrypted with the principal's network password:

nisaddcred:

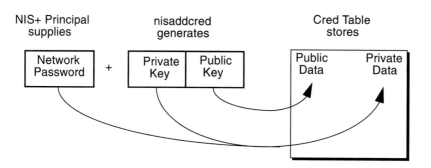

The principal's private key is encrypted as a security precaution because the Cred table, by default, is readable by all NIS+ principals, even unauthenticated ones.

The process for creating credentials is different from the process for using them. When an NIS+ client needs to send a request to an NIS+ server, it does not know the security level at which the server is running, so it sends along a DES credential first. If that doesn't work, it tries a LOCAL credential.

To generate a DES credential, the client depends on a previous procedure called *keylogin*. When an NIS+ principal logs on to an NIS+ client, the client does an automatic keylogin. The purpose of the keylogin is for the client to obtain all the authentication information it requires to operate in the namespace. The keylogin fetches the principal's public and private keys from the

Cred table, decrypts the secret key with the principal's login password (remember that the secret key was originally encrypted with the principal's network password), and stores them locally for future NIS+ requests:

keylogin:

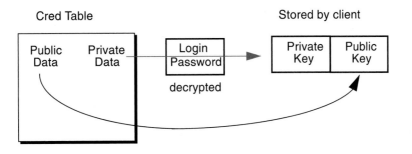

To complete this process, the client must use the public key of the server to which it will send the request. This information is stored in the client's directory cache. Once the client has this information, it can form the verification field of the credential. That is a complex process, but here is a simplified explanation. First, the client uses its own secret key and the server's public key to generate the DES key (a random number). It also generates a time stamp. It then encrypts the timestamp with the DES key, and combines it with other credential-related information into the verification field:

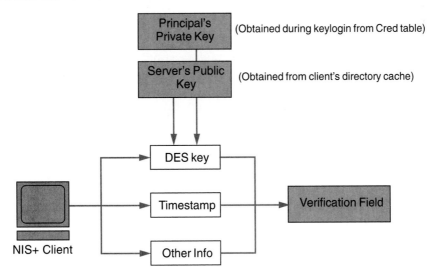

To decrypt the DES credential, the server essentially reverses the encryption process performed by the client. First, the server uses the secure RPC netname portion of the credential to look up the principal's public key in the Cred table. Then, using its own private key (keep in mind that servers also have credentials) and the principal's public key, it decrypts the DES key. Then it uses the DES key to decrypt the timestamp. If the timestamp is within a predetermined tolerance of the time the server received the message, the server authenticates the request.

This process satisfies the server. However, to let the client know that the information it receives indeed comes from a trusted server, the server encrypts the timestamp with the DES key and sends it back to the client.

To verify a LOCAL credential, the server simply looks up the principal's UID the third column of the Cred table. If it matches the UID supplied by the client, the credential is verified.

If the Network Password Is Different from the Login Password

A principal's network password is usually the same as its login password, as mentioned earlier. They can, however, be different. If so, the following happens.

When the principal logs on to the client, the client does an automatic keylogin, as usual. In other words, the client fetches the principal's keys from the Cred table, decrypting the secret key with the principal's login password. However, the secret key was *encrypted* with the principal's *network* password. As a result, the private key cannot be decrypted by the client and cannot be used for authentication:

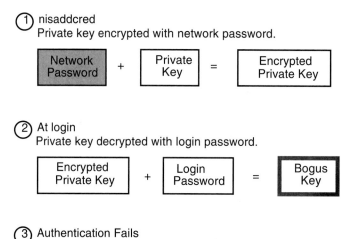

① nisaddcred
Private key encrypted with network password.

② At login
Private key decrypted with login password.

③ Authentication Fails

All About Administering NIS+

To solve this problem, the NIS+ principal must give the NIS+ client a network password after he or she logs on. This requires an explicit *keylogin*. In general, a principal must keylogin any time he or she changes credentials. In this particular case, it should be after giving the nisaddcred command a network password that is different from the login password:

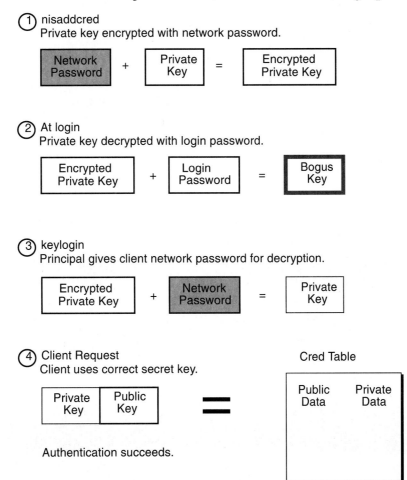

① nisaddcred
Private key encrypted with network password.

| Network Password | + | Private Key | = | Encrypted Private Key |

② At login
Private key decrypted with login password.

| Encrypted Private Key | + | Login Password | = | Bogus Key |

③ keylogin
Principal gives client network password for decryption.

| Encrypted Private Key | + | Network Password | = | Private Key |

④ Client Request
Client uses correct secret key.

Cred Table

| Private Key | Public Key | = | Public Data | Private Data |

Authentication succeeds.

Instructions for performing a keylogin are provided on page 216.

About Access Rights

Access rights specify the type of operation that NIS+ principals, both authenticated and unauthenticated, can perform on an NIS+ object. NIS+ offers four types of access rights:

Access Right	Description
Read	Principal can read the contents of the object.
Modify	Principal can modify the contents of the object.
Destroy	Principal can destroy objects in a table or directory.
Create	Principal can create new objects in a table or directory.

These rights are granted by each object, not to a particular NIS+ principal, but to four different categories of NIS+ principal. These are called *authorization categories*.

Authorization Categories

To assign access rights, every NIS+ object uses four authorization categories: Owner, Group, World, and Nobody. An object can grant one to four access rights to each of these categories. For instance, an object could grant Read access to the World category, but Modify access only to the Group and Owner. Thus, any NIS+ principal that belonged to the World category could read the object, but only the NIS+ principals that belong to the Group and Owner category could modify the object. Each category is described below.

The Object's Owner

The Owner is a single NIS+ principal. By default, an object's owner is the principal that created the object. However, an object's owner can cede ownership to another principal — in two ways. One way is for the principal to specify a different owner at the time it creates the object (see "*How to Override Defaults*" on page 223). Another way is for the principal to change the ownership of the object after the object is created (see "*nischown*" on page 228).

Once a principal gives up ownership, it gives up all owner's access rights to the object and keeps only the rights the object assigns to either the Group, the World, or Nobody.

The Object's Group

The object's group is a single NIS+ group. An NIS+ group is simply a collection of NIS+ principals, grouped together as a convenience for providing access to the namespace. The access rights granted to an NIS+ group apply to all the principals that are members of that group. By default, when an object is created, it is assigned the NIS+ principal's default group. (An object's Owner, however, does not need to belong to the object's Group.)

Information about NIS+ groups is *not* stored in the NIS+ Group table. That table stores information about UNIX groups. Information about NIS+ groups is stored in NIS+ group *objects*, under the `groups_dir` subdirectory of every NIS+ domain:

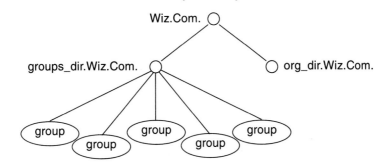

Instructions for administering NIS+ groups are provided in Chapter 13.

The World

The World is the category of all NIS+ principals that are authenticated by NIS+. Access rights granted to the World apply to all authenticated principals.

Nobody

Nobody is a category reserved for unauthenticated requests. Any request that cannot be authenticated by an NIS+ server receives the rights specified for the Nobody category. Note that requests that are not authenticated because they sent along invalid credentials are simply denied, and not given any access rights, not even those of the Nobody category.

Where Access Rights are Stored

An object's access rights are specified in its definition. (Note that this information is part of the object's *definition*; it is *not* an NIS+ table.)

Object's Owner	Object's Group Owner	Access Rights: Owner	Access Rights: Group	Access Rights: World	Access Rights: Nobody
The NIS+ principal that created the object was assigned ownership by the nischown command. The object owner is the only principal allowed to modify the access rights in the right four columns.	The NIS+ group to which the object's owner belongs.	The access rights granted to the object owner	The access rights granted to the principals in the object's group.	The access rights granted to any authenticated NIS+ principal.	The access rights granted to everyone, whether authenticated or not.

Access rights are displayed as a list of 16 characters, like this:

```
r---rmcdr---r---
```

Each character represents a type of access right. Thus, "r" represents Read, "m" represents Modify, "d" represents Destroy, "c" represents Create, and "-" represents no access rights. The first four characters represent the access rights granted to Nobody, the next four to the Owner, the next four to the Group, and the last four to the World:

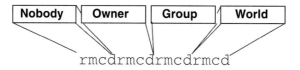

Note that unlike UNIX filesystems, the first set of rights is for Nobody, not for the Owner.

How Access Rights Are Assigned

When you create an object, NIS+ assigns the object a default owner, group, and set of access rights. The default owner is the NIS+ principal who creates the object. The default group is the group named in the NIS_GROUP environment variable. The default set of access rights is:

Nobody	Owner	Group	World
-	Read	Read	Read
-	Modify	-	-
-	Create	-	-
-	Destroy	-	-

NIS+ provides several different ways to change these default rights. The first is the NIS_DEFAULTS environment variable. That variable stores a set of security related default values, one of which is access rights. The defaults stored in the NIS_DEFAULTS variable are assigned to every object that is created while they are in effect. If the value of this variable is changed on a particular client, any object created from that client will be assigned the new values. However, previously created objects will not be affected. Instructions for changing the NIS_DEFAULTS variable are provided in the section titled "*How to Change Defaults*" on page 222.

A second way to affect access rights is with the -D option that is available with several NIS+ commands. The -D option specifies the default values that will be applied to all the objects acted upon by the command. In other words, it overrides the default values stored by the NIS_DEFAULTS variable, but only for the object affected by that particular instance of the command. For instructions, see "*How to Override Defaults*" on page 223.

The third way is to explicitly change an object's access rights (or other security defaults) using one of the NIS+ commands designed for that purpose, such as nischmod. Instructions are provided in Chapter 15, "Administering NIS+ Access Rights."

NIS+ tables provide additional levels of security not provided by other types of NIS+ objects. As described in Chapter 3, information in an NIS+ table can be accessed by column or entry:

Column

Entry

In addition to the rights that can be assigned to the table as a whole, NIS+ allows you to assign access rights to the columns and entries of a table. Those rights can provide *additional* access, but they cannot restrict the access provided by the table as a whole. For instance, if the table provided Read rights to the World category, a column could give the World category Modify rights, but it could not restrict Read access to only the Owner or the Group[1].

A column or entry can provide additional access in two ways: by extending the rights to additional principals or by providing additional rights to the same principals. Of course both ways can be combined. Here are a couple of examples.

Assume a table object granted Read rights to the table's Owner:

	Nobody	Owner	Group	World
TABLE	-	read	-	-

This means that only the table's owner can read the contents of the entire table. However, an entry in the table can grant Read rights to the Group:

	Nobody	Owner	Group	World
TABLE		read		
ENTRY1			read	

---

1. Actually, it could assign Read rights to the Owner or Group, but since the table already provides them to the World, the rights assigned by the column would have no effect on those assigned by the table object.

This means that although only the owner can read all the contents of the table, any member of the table's group can read the contents of that particular entry. In addition, however, a particular column can grant Read rights to the World:

	Nobody	Owner	Group	World
TABLE		read		
ENTRY1			read	
COLUMN1				read

As a result, only the owner can read the entire table, any member of the table's group can read ENTRY1, and any member of the World category (i.e., any authenticated NIS+ principal) can read COLUMN1.

Here is another example. Assume a table assigns Read rights to the Group:

	Nobody	Owner	Group	World
TABLE			read	

This means that any member of the group may read the contents of the entire table. A particular entry, however, can assign the group Modify rights:

	Nobody	Owner	Group	World
TABLE			read	
ENTRY1			modify	

As a result, members of the object's group can read the contents of the table, but they can also modify the contents of that particular entry (ENTRY1).

How a Server Grants Access Rights

This process has already been described for access rights at the object level (see "*Overview of the Security Process,*" starting on page 65). However, because of the overlapping rights of table objects, columns, and entries, it is worthwhile to go over how a server grants access to tables objects, entries, and columns during each type of operation: read, modify, destroy, and create.

As described earlier, after authenticating a request, an NIS+ server determines the type of operation and the object of the request. If that object is a directory or group, the server simply examines the object's definition and grants the request, providing the object has assigned the proper rights to the principal. However, if the object is a table, the server follows a more involved process. The process varies somewhat depending on the operation, but it follows this general rule of thumb:

First, check rights at the object level

Then at the entry level

Then at the column level.

Following are detailed examples of the process involved in each type of operation. While going through them, keep in mind the four factors that a server must consider when deciding whether to grant access:

1. The type of operation requested by the principal

2. The table, entry, or column the principal is trying to access

3. The authorization category the principal belongs to for that particular object

4. The access rights that the table, entry, or column has assigned to the principal's authorization category.

Granting Access to Read or Modify a Table

When a principal requests to read or modify the contents of a table (for example, by issuing the `niscat` or `nistbladm` command), an NIS+ server employs the following logic to grant access to the principal. For this example, assume that the principal is a member of the *group* named in the table's group authorization category, and is trying to *read* the entire table. The same logic applies whether the operation is to read or to modify the table.

The server first checks the table object's rights. If the table grants Read access to the group, the principal is allowed to read all the contents of the table, and the server does not proceed to check rights of columns or entries. (The shaded boxes represent the columns and entries that the principal is allowed to read.)

Rights to Entire Table Granted to Group: READ				
	Col 1	Col 2	Col 3	Col 4
Entry 1				
Entry 2				
Entry 3				
Entry 4				
Entry 5				
Entry 6				
Entry 7				

If the table object does not grant Read access to the group, the server checks the access rights granted by each individual table entry.

If an entry grants its group Read rights, and if the principal belongs to that group (which may be different from the table's group), the server allows the principal to read that entry's contents. Then it checks the rights granted by the next entry. (The shaded rows below represent the entries that have given the group Read rights.)

	Rights	Col 1	Col 2	Col 3	Col 4
Entry 1	READ				
Entry 2					
Entry 3	READ				
Entry 4					
Entry 5	READ				
Entry 6	READ				
Entry 7					

The server proceeds to check column rights only if no entry has granted the group Read rights. If any entry grants the group Read rights, the server does not check column rights.

If a server finds that no columns in the table grant their group Read rights, it returns an error message, stating that the principal does not have permission to access the object. However, if any column grants its group Read rights, and if the principal belongs to that group (which may also be different from the table or even the entries' group), the server displays the body of the table, but censors the columns that do not grant their group Read rights. Censored columns display the string *NP* (for "no permission").

	Col 1	Col 2	Col 3	Col 4
Rights	READ		READ	
Entry 1		*NP*		*NP*
Entry 2		*NP*		*NP*
Entry 3		*NP*		*NP*
Entry 4		*NP*		*NP*
Entry 5		*NP*		*NP*
Entry 6		*NP*		*NP*
Entry 7		*NP*		*NP*

Granting Access to Destroy Table Entries

When a principal requests to delete a table, the server checks the access rights granted to the principal *by the table's org_dir* directory. However, when a principal requests to delete a table entry, the server employs the following logic. Assume that the principal is a member of the group named in the table's group authorization category, and that the principal is trying to delete entries 1 and 5.

If the table object grants its group Destroy rights, the principal is allowed to remove any entry from the table (columns cannot be removed). The server checks no further. If the table object does not grant the group Destroy rights, the server checks access rights at the entry level.

At the entry level, the server only checks the rights of the entries that the principal is trying to destroy; i.e., 1, and 5. If one of those entries grants its group Destroy rights, and if the principal belongs to that group, the principal is allowed to delete that entry. If one of those entries does not grant the group Destroy rights, or if the principal does not belong to the entry's group authorization category, the principal is not allowed to delete the entry.

If no entries grant their group Destroy rights, an error message is returned, stating that the principal does not have permission to access the object.

Since no columns can be deleted from a table, the server does not check column access rights during a Destroy operation.

Granting Access to Create Table Entries

When a principal tries to create a table, the server checks the access rights granted to the principal by the *org_dir directory* under which the table will be created. However, when a principal tries to add new table entries to an existing table, the server employs the following logic. For this example, assume that the principal is a member of the group named in the table's group authorization category, and that the principal is trying to add entries 8 and 9.

If the table object grants its group Create rights, the principal is allowed to add entries to the table (columns cannot be added). The server checks no further. However, if the object does not grant its group Create rights, the server checks whether the entry that the principal is trying to create already exists.

If the entry indeed exists, the server checks whether the table object has granted its group Modify rights. If it has, the server replaces the existing entry with the new one and checks no further. If the table has not granted its group Modify rights, the server checks rights at the entry level.

At the entry level, the server checks not whether the entry has granted the group Create rights, but whether it has granted the group *Modify* rights. If the entry has granted Modify rights to its group, and if the principal is a member of that group (which may not be the same as the table object's group), the server replaces the existing entry with the new one and no further checking is done.

If the entry has not granted Modify rights to its group, or if the principal is not a member of that group, an error message is returned, stating that the principal does not have permission to modify the object.

Since no columns can be added to a table, the server does not check column access rights during a Create operation.

Understanding the
Name Service Switch $5\equiv$

The Name Service Switch, referred to as the "Switch," is not really part of NIS+, but it allows NIS+ clients (actually, clients of getXXbyYY() routines) to obtain their network information from one or more of these *sources*: NIS+ tables, NIS maps, a DNS hosts table, and local /etc files. This chapter describes the Switch and what it can do. It has five sections:

About the Name Service Switch	Page	89
The nsswitch.nisplus File	Page	93
The nsswitch.nis File	Page	95
The nsswitch.files File	Page	96

About the Name Service Switch

An NIS+ client can obtain its information from one or more of the Switch's sources in place of, or in addition, to NIS+ tables. For example, an NIS+ client could obtain its hosts information from an NIS+ table, its group information from NIS maps, and its password information from a local /etc file. Plus, it could specify the conditions under which the Switch must use each source (see "*Search Criteria*" on page 92).

These choices are called out in a special configuration file called nsswitch.conf. This file is automatically loaded into every workstation's /etc directory by Solaris 2.x, along with three alternate versions:

- /etc/nsswitch.nisplus
- /etc/nsswitch.nis
- /etc/nsswitch.files

These alternate files contain the default Switch configurations used by the NIS+ service, NIS, and local files. (They are described later in this section.) No default file is provided for DNS, but you can edit any of these files to use DNS, as described in Chapter 12, "Setting Up the Name Service Switch."

When Solaris 2.x is first installed on a workstation, the installer must select the workstation's default naming service: NIS+, NIS, or local files. During the installation itself, the corresponding configuration file is copied into the /etc/nsswitch.conf file.

You can change the sources of information used by an NIS+ client by creating your own customized configuration file and copying it over /etc/nsswitch.conf. Its syntax is described below, and instructions are provided in Chapter 12.

Format of the nsswitch.conf File

The nsswitch.conf file is essentially a list of 14 types of information and their sources, not necessarily in this order:

```
aliases:                    source(s)
bootparams:                 source(s)
ethers:                     source(s)
group:                      source(s)
hosts:                      source(s)
netgroup:                   source(s)
netmasks:                   source(s)
networks:                   source(s)
passwd: (includes shadow)   source(s)
protocols:                  source(s)
publickey:                  source
rpc:                        source(s)
services:                   source(s)

automount:                  source(s)
```

The information for the Auto_Home and Auto_Master tables is combined into one category, called "automount." The timezone table does not use the Switch, so it is not included in the list. A source can be any of the following:

Source	Description
files	A local file stored in the client's /etc directory (e.g., /etc/passwd
nisplus	An NIS+ table

All About Administering NIS+

Source	Description
nis	An NIS map
compat	Only for the Password and Group entries, supports the old-style "+" or "-" syntax in the /etc/passwd, /etc/shadow, and /etc/group files.
dns	DNS, but only for the hosts entry.

If an information type has only one source, the switch searches for the information in that source only. (If it does not find the information, it stops searching and returns a status message[1].)

If a table has more than one source, the Switch starts by searching for the information in the first source. If it does not find the information there, it tries the next source. It continues searching through the sources until it has tried them all:

```
passwd:     files nis
group:      files nis
aliases     files nis

-----searches sources in order-------->
```

If it still does not find the information, it stops searching and returns a status message. However, the Switch allows you to specify a different course of action, such as continuing to search for the information. This is done with *search criteria*.

---

1. That message is passed to the library routine that requested the information. What the routine does with the status message varies from routine to routine.

Search Criteria

The Switch searches through the sources one at a time. If it finds the information it is looking for in the first source, it returns a successful status message and passes the information to the library routine that asked for it. If it does *not* find the information, it returns one of three unsuccessful status messages, depending on the reason for not finding the information, and moves to the next source. The four possible status messages are:

Status	Meaning
SUCCESS	The requested entry was found in the source.
UNAVAIL	The source is not responding or is corrupted.
NOTFOUND	The source responded with "No such entry."
TRYAGAIN	The source is busy; it might respond next time.

You can instruct the Switch to respond to status messages with either of these two *actions*:

Action	Meaning
return	Stop looking for the information.
continue	Try the next source, if there is one.

Default Search Criteria

The Switch's default search criteria are the same for every source. Described in terms of the status messages listed above, they are:

> *The default search criteria are:*
>
> SUCCESS=return
> UNAVAIL=continue
> NOTFOUND=continue
> TRYAGAIN=continue

You can change the default search criteria for any source, using the STATUS=action syntax shown above. Here is an example:

```
hosts:     nis
networks:  nis [NOTFOUND=return] files
protocols: nis [NOTFOUND=return] files
```

In the second line of the example above, when the switch searches for information in NIS maps and gets a NOTFOUND status message, instead of searching through the second source, it stops looking. It would search through files only if the NIS service was unavailable.

What if the Syntax is Wrong?

Client library routines contain compiled-in default entries that are used if an entry in the nsswitch.conf file is either missing or syntactically incorrect. These entries are the same as the default nsswitch.conf file.

The name service switch assumes that the spelling of table and source names is correct. If you misspell a table or source name, the switch looks for it and, when it does not find it, returns an UNAVAIL status.

The Default nsswitch.conf File

The default nsswitch.conf file shipped with Solaris 2.x is actually a copy of the nsswitch.nis file, described below. You can change it to the NIS+ version by copying the nsswitch.nisplus file over the /etc/nswitch.conf file, as described in Chapter 12.

The Switch provides three alternate configuration files in addition to the default /etc/nsswitch.conf file. Each is described below.

The nsswitch.nisplus File

This configuration file specifies NIS+ as the primary source for all information except passwd, group, automount, and aliases. For those files, the primary source is local /etc files and the secondary source is an NIS+ table. The [NOTFOUND=return] search criterion instructs the

Switch to stop searching the NIS+ tables if it receives a "No such entry" message from them. It searches through local files only if the NIS+ server is unavailable. Here is a copy of the file with all the comments stripped out:

```
passwd:      files nisplus
group:       files nisplus

hosts:       nisplus [NOTFOUND=return] files
services:    nisplus [NOTFOUND=return] files
networks:    nisplus [NOTFOUND=return] files
protocols:   nisplus [NOTFOUND=return] files
rpc:         nisplus [NOTFOUND=return] files
ethers:      nisplus [NOTFOUND=return] files
netmasks:    nisplus [NOTFOUND=return] files
bootparams:  nisplus [NOTFOUND=return] files

publickey:   nisplus

netgroup:    nisplus

automount:   files nisplus
aliases:     files nisplus
```

The nsswitch.nis File

This configuration file is almost identical to the NIS+ configuration file, except that it specifies NIS maps in place of NIS+ tables.

```
passwd:      files nis
group:       files nis

hosts:       nis [NOTFOUND=return] files
services:    nis [NOTFOUND=return] files
networks:    nis [NOTFOUND=return] files
protocols:   nis [NOTFOUND=return] files
rpc:         nis [NOTFOUND=return] files
ethers:      nis [NOTFOUND=return] files
netmasks:    nis [NOTFOUND=return] files
bootparams:  nis [NOTFOUND=return] files
publickey:   nis [NOTFOUND=return] files

netgroup:    nis

automount:   files nis
aliases:     files nis
```

Because the search order for passwd and group is "files nis," you don't need to place the "+" entry in the /etc/passwd and /etc/group files.

The nsswitch.files File

This configuration file simply specifies local /etc files as the only source of information for the workstation.

```
passwd:        files
group:         files
hosts:         files
networks:      files
protocols:     files
rpc:           files
ethers:        files
netmasks:      files
bootparams:    files
publickey:     files

netgroup:      files¹

automount:     files
aliases:       files
services:      files
```

1.There is no "files" source for netgroup, so the client simply won't use it.

Part 2—Setting Up NIS+

6   *Planning for Setup*
This chapter identifies the building blocks of the setup process and maps them to the chapters that provide their instructions. Explains the decisions you must make and the information you need to gather before you begin setting up.

7   *Setting Up the Root Domain*
This chapter provides step-by-step instructions for setting up the root domain, whether NIS-compatible or standard NIS+.

8   *Setting Up NIS+ Tables*
This chapter provides step-by-step instructions for populating NIS+ tables, whether in the root domain or a subdomain, with information from input files or NIS maps.

9   *Setting Up an NIS+ Client*
This chapter provides step-by-step instructions for setting up an NIS+ client. The instructions apply to clients in the root domain and in non-root domains.

10   *Setting Up a Root Replica Server*
This chapter provides step-by-step instructions for setting up a server that will become a replica in the root domain.

11   *Setting Up a Non-Root Server*
This chapter provides step-by-step instructions for setting up a server that will become either a master or a replica in any domain except the root.

12   *Setting Up a Non-Root Domain*
This chapter provides step-by-step instructions for creating and setting up a non-root domain, including designating its master and replica servers.

13   *Setting Up the Name Service Switch*
This chapter provides step-by-step instructions for setting up the Name Service Switch for use with NIS+, NIS, and DNS, as well as to provide backward compatibility with the +/- syntax.

Planning for Setup 6≣

This chapter provides information to help you plan the setup and administration of your NIS+ service. It begins by recommending a setup procedure that works for most namespaces. Based on the steps of that procedure, it points out the decisions you need to make and the information you need to gather *before* you begin to set up NIS+.

Because many sites already use NIS, this chapter also provides guidelines for managing the transition from the NIS service to NIS+. The chapter has the following sections:

Recommended Setup Procedure	Page	99
Planning Guidelines	Page	101
Transition Guidelines	Page	114

Recommended Setup Procedure

Figure 6-1, on the following page, summarizes the recommended setup procedure. The blocks on the left represent the major setup activities, such as setting up the root domain or setting up a client. The text in the middle describes the blocks. The chapter numbers and tasks on the right point to the instructions that describe how to carry out each block.

Figure 6-1   Recommended NIS+ Setup Procedure

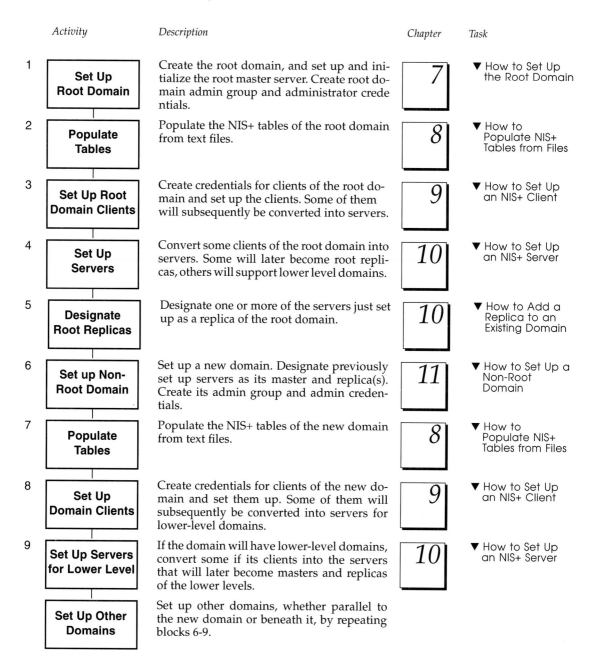

Activity	Description	Chapter	Task
1. **Set Up Root Domain**	Create the root domain, and set up and initialize the root master server. Create root domain admin group and administrator credentials.	7	▼ How to Set Up the Root Domain
2. **Populate Tables**	Populate the NIS+ tables of the root domain from text files.	8	▼ How to Populate NIS+ Tables from Files
3. **Set Up Root Domain Clients**	Create credentials for clients of the root domain and set up the clients. Some of them will subsequently be converted into servers.	9	▼ How to Set Up an NIS+ Client
4. **Set Up Servers**	Convert some clients of the root domain into servers. Some will later become root replicas, others will support lower level domains.	10	▼ How to Set Up an NIS+ Server
5. **Designate Root Replicas**	Designate one or more of the servers just set up as a replica of the root domain.	10	▼ How to Add a Replica to an Existing Domain
6. **Set up Non-Root Domain**	Set up a new domain. Designate previously set up servers as its master and replica(s). Create its admin group and admin credentials.	11	▼ How to Set Up a Non-Root Domain
7. **Populate Tables**	Populate the NIS+ tables of the new domain from text files.	8	▼ How to Populate NIS+ Tables from Files
8. **Set Up Domain Clients**	Create credentials for clients of the new domain and set them up. Some of them will subsequently be converted into servers for lower-level domains.	9	▼ How to Set Up an NIS+ Client
9. **Set Up Servers for Lower Level**	If the domain will have lower-level domains, convert some if its clients into the servers that will later become masters and replicas of the lower levels.	10	▼ How to Set Up an NIS+ Server
Set Up Other Domains	Set up other domains, whether parallel to the new domain or beneath it, by repeating blocks 6-9.		

Planning Guidelines

The order of activities shown in Figure 6-1 is not mandatory. You could set up your namespace differently. For instance, you could set up all your servers first, then create their domains. However, to keep this planning discussion clear, we will discuss only the scenario in Figure 6-1. Based on that scenario, we recommend that before you begin to set up your namespace, you go through the following planning phases:

- Sketching a Domain Hierarchy
- Selecting Servers for the Namespace
- Determining Credential Needs of the Namespace
- How Many Administrative Groups?
- Determining Access Rights to the Namespace

Each phase is described in its own section, below. In addition, each section includes a summary of the information you should have gathered for that phase.

A Summary Planning Sheet is provided at the end of this section, on page 112. If you fill it out, you will have much of the information you need to begin setting up your namespace. Additional copies are provided in Appendix A.

Sketching a Domain Hierarchy

The first planning step we recommend is to sketch a domain hierarchy. Make a map of how you expect the hierarchy to look when you are finished. This will be a useful reference when you are in the midst of the setup procedure. As a minimum, you will need to consider the following questions:

- What Kind of Hierarchy?
- Should the Root Domain Support Clients?
- Which Domain Names?
- What Security Levels?
- Which Directories Will Support the Domains?

What Kind of Hierarchy?

As described in Part I, one of the major benefits of NIS+ is its capability to divide the namespace into smaller, manageable parts. You could create a hierarchy of organizations, such as those of the imaginary Wizard, Inc.:

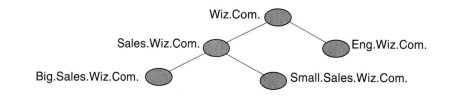

You could also organize the hierarchy by buildings instead of organizations:

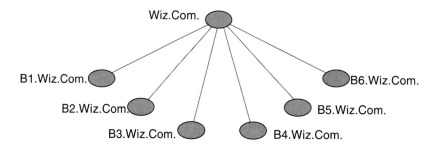

The scheme you select depends primarily on how you prefer to administer the namespace and how clients will tend to use the namespace. For example, if clients of "Eng.Wiz.Com." will be distributed throughout the buildings of the Wizard Corporation, you shouldn't organize the namespace by building. Since the clients would need to constantly access other domains, you would need to add their credentials to the other domains and you would increase traffic flow through the root master server. A better scheme would be to arrange them by organization. On the other hand, building-sized domains are immune to the reorganizations that require organization-based domains to be restructured.

Don't be limited by the physical layout of the network, since an NIS+ namespace does not have to be congruent with the physical network.

The number of domains your namespace needs depends on the kind of hierarchy you select, but keep in mind that smaller domains process NIS+ requests faster than large domains.

Should the Root Domain Support Clients?

In the two domain hierarchies illustrated above, are all the clients placed in domains beneath the root domain? Or do some belong to the root domain? Is the purpose of the root domain only to act as the root for its subdomains or will it support its own group of clients? You could place all clients in the lowest layer of domains, and only those used for administration in the intermediate domains. For example, in the first illustration, all clients would belong to the "Big.Sales.Wiz.Com.," "Small.Sales.Wiz.Com.," and "Eng.Wiz.Com." domains, and only clients used for administration would belong to the "Wiz.Com." and "Sales.Wiz.Com." domains.

Or, you could place the clients of general-purpose departments in higher level domains. For example, in the second illustration, you could put the clients of the Facilities Department in the Wiz.Com. domain.

Which Domain Names?

See "*Naming Conventions (To Dot or Not)*" on page 37 for details about domain naming conventions. Within the constraints described in that section, you can choose any names you like, but here are two suggestions. First, pick names that are descriptive. "Sales" is considerably more descriptive than "BW23A." Second, pick short names. You want to avoid appending something as odious as "EmployeeAdministrationServices.WizardCorporation" to object names when you administer the namespace.

Remember that all root domains must have at least two labels. One of those can be the name of an Internet domain.

What Security Levels?

In most cases, you'll run the namespace at Security Level 2. However, if you plan to use different security levels for different domains, you should identify them now. Chapter 4, "Understanding NIS+ Security," describes all three security levels offered by NIS+.

Which Directories Will Support the Domains?

Remember, a domain is simply a particular grouping of directories. You may create additional directories between domains for administrative purposes, although you don't have to. If you do, sketch a map of your namespace directories, complete with "org_dir" and "groups_dir" directories, so you don't get confused during setup.

Summary

As a result of these steps, you should have:

> **For the Domain Hierarchy**
> - A map of the namespace with the names of all the domains
> - A brief description of the purpose of each domain (e.g., whether for clients or administrators, or to support which part of the organization, etc.)
> - The security level of each domain
> - Optionally, a map of the directories that form the framework of your namespace.

Selecting Servers for the Namespace

Once you know the domain structure of the namespace, you can select the servers that will support them. When selecting servers, you need to differentiate between the requirements imposed by the NIS+ service and those imposed by the traffic load of your namespace.

The NIS+ service requires you to assign at least one server, the master, to each NIS+ domain. You can assign as many replicas as required[1]. How many servers a domain requires is determined by the traffic load and the configuration of its servers.

The traffic loads you anticipate will determine the total number of servers used to support the namespace, how much storage and processing speed each will require, and whether a domain needs replicas to ensure its availability. How can you determine how many servers you need? Here's a recommended sequence of steps:

---

1. An NIS+ server is capable of supporting more than one domain, but we don't advise this except in small namespaces or testing situations.

All About Administering NIS+

1. A good way to begin is by assigning one master server to each domain in the hierarchy:

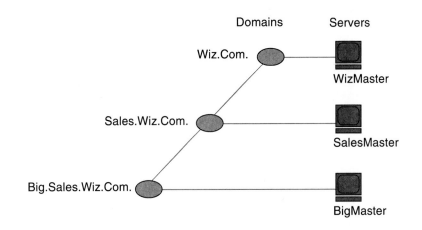

2. If certain domains must always be available, add replicas to them; one or more. We recommend always adding a replica to a domain.

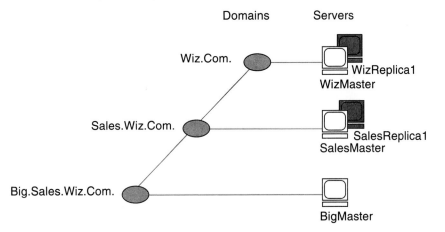

3. Determine the disk space requirements of each server (see *"Disk Space and Memory Recommendations,","* below). Based on the required disk space, estimate whether one server will be enough for each domain.

Disk Space and Memory Recommendations

How much disk space you need depends on four factors:

- Disk Space Consumed by Solaris 2.x
- Disk Space for /var/nis (and /var/yp)
- Amount of Memory
- Swap Space Required for NIS+ processes.

Solaris 2.x can consume between 90 Mbytes and 130 Mbytes of disk space, including OpenWindows, depending on how much of it you install. (This is an estimate; for exact numbers, see the Solaris 2.x installation manual.) You should also count the disk space consumed by other software the server may use. NIS+ is part of the Solaris 2.0 distribution, so it does not consume additional disk space.

NIS+ directory objects, groups, tables, and client information are stored in /var/nis. As a rule of thumb, /var/nis uses about 1K of disk space per client. So if a namespace has 10,000 clients, /var/nis requires about 10 megabytes of disk space. However, because transaction logs (also kept in /var/nis) can grow large, you may want additional space per client —we recommend an additional 60 - 70 percent. In other words, for 10,000 clients, allocate 16 to 17 megabytes for /var/nis. You can reduce this if you update transaction logs regularly. If you will use NIS+ concurrently with NIS, allocate an equal amount of space for /var/yp to hold NIS maps that you may transfer from NIS. By the way, if you can, keep /var/nis on a separate partition.

Although 32 megabytes is the minimum memory requirement for servers, we recommend that you equip servers of medium to large domains with at least 64 megabytes.

You also need swap space equal to three times the server's memory— in addition to the server's normal swap space requirements. Most of this space is used when directories are checkpointed (with nisping -C), since during a checkpoint, an entire NIS+ server process is forked.

Summary

As a result of these steps, you should have:

> *For Servers*
>
> - A list of all the servers required by the namespace, their disk, swap space, and memory requirements, and the domain(s) each server will support. For example, for a namespace with 10,000 clients:
>   - 130 Mbytes for Solaris 2.x.
>   - 17 Mbytes for `/var/nis` (plus 17 Mbytes more for `/var/yp`)
>   - 32 to 64 Mbytes memory
>   - swap space equal to triple the memory (in addition to normal swap space)
> - A map of all the domains in the namespace with the names of the servers that will support them.

Determining Credential Needs of the Namespace

Once you know the domain hierarchy of the namespace and your server specifications, you should determine what kind of credentials will be required in the namespace. When doing so, you should consider the factors discussed below.

For the Client User or for the Client Workstation?

As described in Chapter 4, "Understanding NIS+ Security," NIS+ principals can be client users or the root identity on the client workstation. When you determine the credentials you need to create, make sure you know which type of principal the credential is for.

For instance, when you set up an NIS+ client according to the instructions in Chapter 9, you will create credentials for the client workstation, not for the client user. Unless credentials for the client user are created, the client user would only have the access rights granted to the Nobody category. This can work perfectly well if that's how you choose to set up your namespace. But if you don't give any access rights to the Nobody category, the namespace won't be available to the client users.

Which Type of Credential?

The type of credentials required in a namespace is determined primarily by the security level at which each domain is running. If a domain is going to be operated in NIS-compatibility mode (security level 0), no one needs credentials of any kind. If the domain is going to operate at security level 1, any NIS+ principal that will have access rights, in addition to those granted to the Nobody category, needs LOCAL credentials. At security level 2, they need DES credentials.

For Which Domains?

For security level 2, all NIS+ principals must have DES credentials in their home domain. A client workstation cannot have credentials in any other domain. However, a client user can have LOCAL credentials in other domains, in addition to the DES credentials in its home domain. So, if you anticipate that users will request information from other domains in the namespace, you can give them the proper access in one of two ways. You can create LOCAL credentials for them in additional domains, or you can assign those domains Read rights to the World category, which includes all authenticated NIS+ principals. Which you select depends on how secure you want to make your namespace.

Summary

As a result of these steps, you should have:

For Credentials
- The security level of each domain
- A list of the type of credential required for servers, clients, administrators, and users, per domain.

How Many Administrative Groups?

After identifying the type of credentials you'll need, you would normally try to select the access rights that are required in the namespace. To make that task easier, you should first figure out how many administrative groups you'll need. Will you create one group for the entire namespace or one group per domain? Using separate groups is useful if you want to assign them different rights.

To determine the number of groups you need, determine the classes of principals you will have in your namespace. Then create a group for each class. You can also create groups of groups. For example, principals who are simple users of the namespace form one class of principal. They only need Read access to the tables in the namespace. On the other hand, principals who administer the namespace need much greater access rights. Some of them may only perform basic administration tasks, like adding user accounts, so they simply require Read and Modify rights to the namespace tables. Others, however, may actually set up or modify the namespace, so they will need Read, Modify, Create, and Delete rights to the entire namespace — or perhaps only to a single domain in the namespace. The instructions in the remainder of Part II include steps for setting up each domain's main administrative group. You can set up additional groups after setting up the namespace.

Here's an example of groups for the namespace of the Wizard Corporation:

Group Name	Description
clients.Wiz.	All clients in the Wiz.Com domain
clients.Sales.Wiz.	All clients in the Sales.Wiz.Com domain
clients.Eng.Wiz.	All clients in the Eng.Wiz.Com domain
admin.Wiz.	All administrators in the Wiz.Com domain only
admin.Sales.Wiz.	All administrators in the Sales.Wiz. domain
admin.Eng.Wiz.	All administrators in the Eng.Wiz. domain
adminall.Wiz	All administrators in the Wizzard Inc. namespace

You don't need a group for all the principals in the namespace, something like "all.Wiz.," because the "World" category already accomplishes that.

Summary

As a result of these steps, you should have:

> **For Groups**
> - A list of the groups in the namespace, with a description of their membership.

Determining Access Rights to the Namespace

After arranging your principals into groups, you should determine the kind of access rights granted by the objects in the namespace to those groups, as well as to the other categories of principal (Owner, World, and Nobody). Planning these assignments ahead of time will help you establish a coherent security policy.

NIS+ provides preset defaults that apply to every object created in the namespace. They are:

Nobody	Owner	Group	World
	Read	Read	Read
	Modify		
	Create		
	Destroy		

You can use these defaults for all your objects or assign different rights to different types of objects. You'll need to consider two main factors:

- The type of object
- The domain.

Here's a useful way to proceed:

1. Read the discussion about *"Types of Principals,"* below. Use it to help you determine the kinds of access rights different types of principals will require.

2. Read the discussion about *"Types of Objects,"* below. It divides the objects normally found in a namespace into several classes. This is an informal division; you can divide the objects in your namespace into any classes you prefer.

3. For each domain, determine the access rights each class of object should assign to each category of principal: Owner, Group, World, and Nobody. For the Group category, don't just specify the access rights, also specify one of the groups you already selected for the namespace.

4. During setup, as you create an object, classify it by type and assign it the rights specified in your table.

Types of Principals

NIS+ divides principals into four categories: Owner, Group, World, and Nobody. You can determine most of the access rights you'll need by using these categories. For instance, if you don't want any unauthenticated requests to be granted, don't assign any rights to the Nobody category. On the other hand, if you expect to have some clients make unauthenticated requests, you can assign Read rights to the Nobody category.

Depending on the type of table information, you should assign the World category at least Read rights, since it comprises all authenticated principals in the namespace. That allows a Read request from an authenticated client anywhere in the namespace to be granted.

For each type of object (see *"Types of Objects,"* below), you can pick an "owning" group. Depending on how you plan to administer the namespace, you can assign all the available administrative rights to the group, or only some of them. For instance, if only one administrator will create and modify the root domain, you should not assign the owning group Create and Destroy rights to the objects in the root domain. Instead, assign those rights only to the objects' Owner. However, if several administrators may be involved in the setup process, put them all in a group and assign full rights to it. That is easier than switching ownership back and forth.

Finally, the owner should have full rights, although this is not as important if the group does. A namespace is more secure if you give only the owner full rights, but easier to administer if you give the administrative group full rights.

Types of Objects

Objects in an NIS+ namespace can be informally classified into two categories: administrative and informative. Directories and groups are strictly administrative. There is no need to give the World category, for instance, Modify rights to a directory or group. It would compromise security and the structure of the namespace.

Tables and their entries are informative. The World category, and perhaps the Nobody category, should have Read rights to tables and entries. Depending on how secure you want the namespace, you may be willing to grant Modify rights for certain table entries to the groups that comprise all clients in a domain.

Summary

As a result of these steps, you should have:

> **For Access Rights**
> - A chart that specifies the types of objects in each domain and, for each category of NIS+ principal, the access rights granted by each type of object.

Where Can I Get Information About the Namespace?

NIS+ provides several commands that provide information about the data and objects in the namespace. Here is a list:

Command	Lists	See
niscat -o	Object properties	Chapter 16
niscat	Table contents	Chapter 17
nisls	The contents and other particulars of a directory	Chapter 16
nislog	The contents of a transaction log	Chapter 17
nisshowcache	The contents of the directory cache	Chapter 16

By the way, to exit from an NIS+ command, simply use Control-c.

Table

When you have designed the namespace and selected its servers, types of credentials, groups, and access rights, you have gathered most of the information you'll need to set up the namespace. You might want to summarize all this information in a worksheet that you can keep handy while you set up the namespace. Table 6-1, below, provides a sample worksheet that uses fictitious information for the Wizard, Inc. namespace. Appendix A provides additional blank worksheets in case you would like to use them.

Table 6-1   Sample Pre-Setup Worksheet

Domain: Wiz.Com.

Servers	Type	Name	Specifications
	Master	rootmaster	
	First Replica	rootreplica	
	Second Replica	rootreplica2	
Credentials	**Type of Principal**	**Type of Credential**	
	Servers	DES	
	Clients	DES	
	Administrators	LOCAL and DES	
	Users	LOCAL and DES	

Table 6-1   Sample Pre-Setup Worksheet

Domain: | Wiz.Com.

Servers	Type	Name				Specifications
Rights	**Types of Objects**	**Category & Rights**				
	Directories	**N**	**O**	**G**	**W**	**Use Defaults?**
	Wiz.Com.	r	rmcd	rmcd	r	no
	org_dir.Wiz.Com.	r	rmcd	rmcd	r	no
	groups_dir.Wiz.Com.	r	rmcd	rmcd	r	no
	Sales.Wiz.Com.	r	rmcd	rmcd	r	no
	Groups	**N**	**O**	**G**	**W**	**Description**
	admin.Wiz.Com.	r	rmcd	r	r	Admins who manage structure and security
	admin2.Wiz.Com.	r	rmcd	r	r	Admins who manage information

Table 6-1   Sample Pre-Setup Worksheet (Continued)

Domain: | Wiz.Com.

Rights	**Types of Objects**	**Category & Rights**				
	Tables	**N**	**O**	**G**	**W**	**Notes**
	hosts	-	rmcd	rmcd	r	
	bootparams	-	rmcd	rmcd	r	
	passwd	-	rmcd	rmcd	r	
	cred	-	rmcd	rmcd	r	
	group	-	rmcd	rmcd	r	
	netgroup	-	rmcd	rmcd	r	
	aliases	-	rmcd	rmcd	r	
	timezone	-	rmcd	rmcd	r	

Table 6-1   Sample Pre-Setup Worksheet (Continued)

Domain: | Wiz.Com.

networks	-	rmcd	rmcd	r	
netmasks	-	rmcd	rmcd	r	
ethers	-	rmcd	rmcd	r	
services	-	rmcd	rmcd	r	
protocols	-	rmcd	rmcd	r	
rpc	-	rmcd	rmcd	r	
auto_home	-	rmcd	rmcd	r	
auto_master	-	rmcd	rmcd	r	

Transition Guidelines

This section provides information and guidelines about the transition from NIS to NIS+. The transition from NIS to NIS+ can be handled in several different ways. Following are some guidelines.

1. Have the administrators who will convert your site from NIS to NIS+ build a small NIS+ namespace so they can become familiar with NIS+ before they have to deal with the added complications of a transition from NIS. When you set up the test domain, make small, manageable domains. Set up the namespace first as a pure NIS+ domain, then convert it to NIS-compatibility mode. Then import real NIS information to test.

   You may also want to consider how to train the rest of your administration staff, as well as how to communicate the changeover to your NIS clients.

2. Design the final NIS+ namespace, following the guidelines in the first part of this chapter. Consider whether you need to maintain existing email addresses of clients as well as existing login and hostnames.

3. Consider how NIS+ will interact with DNS. If the DNS domains are repositioned, you'll need to redefine new DNS zone files; otherwise, no changes are required in the DNS environment. Clients, however, do require some adjustments. See Task 7, below.

4. Determine whether you'll need to change your email environment.

    Because NIS+ offers a domain hierarchy but NIS has a flat domainspace, changing to NIS+ can have effects on your mail environment. With NIS, only one mailhost is required. If you use a domain hierarchy for NIS+, you may need one mailhost for each domain in the namespace.

    In addition, the clients who are not in the root domain will have their email addresses changed. You'll have to find a way to compensate, such as using aliases files or correcting the "From:" fields.

5. Select the domains that will operate in NIS-compatibility mode. These domains will be less secure than NIS+ domains. In addition, changing passwords in NIS requires the `yppasswd` command. To make this change take effect in the NIS+ domain, you must repeat it with the `nispasswd` command.

    You'll need to figure out a way to keep the NIS+ domains in sync with the NIS domains. At first, you may want to update the NIS+ tables nightly with the latest NIS information. Be sure to also update the NIS maps from the NIS+ tables. Instructions for both types of transfers are provided in Chapter 8, "Setting Up NIS+ Tables."

    At first, NIS will no doubt be the primary service. As you become familiar with the intricacies of sharing information, you'll be able to plan a transition into making NIS+ the primary service.

    Some NIS+ clients may want the capability to switch back and forth between the main NIS domain and the new NIS+ domain. Consider whether you can provide a script that helps them do this easily.

6. Take stock of your NIS servers, keeping in mind the requirements for your NIS+ servers. If you plan to eventually use them for the NIS+ service, upgrade them to the NIS+ recommendations. Identify which NIS servers will eventually be used to support which NIS+ domains, and in what capacity (master or replica).

    Since NIS+ is provided in a Solaris 1.x distribution, determine whether the servers will need to be upgraded to Solaris 2.x or whether they will use the Solaris 1.x distribution.

    If possible, plan to use your NIS+ servers ony for NIS+. This may require you to transfer other network services, such as DNS name services, home directories, NFS, etc., to servers not scheduled for NIS+ use.

7. Make a list of your NIS clients and map them to their eventual NIS+ domains. Determine whether they will need to be upgraded to Solaris 2.x or whether they will use the Solaris 1.x distribution of NIS+.

    NIS servers handle DNS request made from Solaris 1.x clients. However, NIS+ servers don't provide this service. As a result, all NIS clients must have an `/etc/resolv.conf` file and the DNS resolver libraries installed locally before they are disconnected from their NIS servers.

8. Resolve conflicts between login names and hostnames. Although it gives login names precedence, NIS+ does not distinguish hostnames from login names, so if the same name is used for both, you'll run into problems with permissions and the automounter tables. You may need to alias the duplicate hostnames.

9. Change the dots in your automounter files to underscores. NIS+ uses dots to separate directories, so the dots in the automounter files will confuse it. Replace them with underscores. This involves several steps.

    First, change the file names. Verify that the automounter still works in your NIS environment. Then add the new automounter targets in each NIS domain master's `/var/yp/Makefile`, and build the maps. Also doublecheck the contents of all the automounter files and change any automounter references that appear in them. Finally, install the new, just built maps into each NIS server in each domain, using `ypxfr`.

    Getting the automounter maps working properly before the transition will eliminate them as a possible cause of post-transition problems, if any occur.

Setting Up the Root Domain 7≡

This chapter provides step-by-step instructions for one task:

▼ How to Set Up the Root Domain	Page 117

This task sets up the root domain with DES authentication. It walks through the setup process at a leisurely pace, pointing out the effects of each step and related information that might be of interest. Once you are familiar with the setup process and prefer a quicker-paced approach, you can use the summary that is provided at the end of the chapter.

Differences Between Standard and NIS-Compatible Setup Procedures

The steps in this section apply to both a standard NIS+ root domain and an NIS-compatible root domain. There are, however, some important differences. The NIS+ daemon for an NIS-compatible domain must be started with the -Y option, which allows the root master server to answer requests from NIS clients. This is described in Step 7. The equivalent step for standard NIS+ domains is Step 8.

An NIS compatible domain also requires its tables to provide Read rights for the Nobody category, which allows NIS clients to access the information stored in them. This is accomplished with the -Y option to the nissetup command, in Step 9. The standard NIS+ domain version uses the same command but without the -Y option, so it is described in the same step.

▼ How to Set Up the Root Domain

This task describes how to set up the root domain for DES operation; that is, with the root master server running at security level 2. Setting up the root domain involves three major tasks:

- Preparing the root master server

- Creating the root domain

- Creating credentials for the root domain

117

However, setting up the root domain is not as simple as performing these three tasks in order; they are intertwined with each other. For instance, you must specify some security parameters before you create the root directory; the rest, after. To make the root domain easier to set up, this section separates these tasks into individual steps and arranges them into their most efficient order.

Here is a summary of the entire setup process:

Step 1 Log on — as root — to the root master server.

Step 2 Check the root master server's domain name.

Step 3 Check the root master server's Switch configuration file.

Step 4 Clean out leftover NIS+ material and processes.

Step 5 Name the root domain's admin group.

Step 6 Create the root directory and initialize the root master server.

Step 7 —NIS-Compatibility Only— Start the NIS+ daemon with -Y.

Step 8 —Standard NIS+ Only— Start the NIS+ daemon.

Step 9 Create the root domain's subdirectories and tables.

Step 10 Create DES credentials for the root master server.

Step 11 Create the root domain's admin group.

Step 12 Assign the new group to the root directory object.

Step 13 Assign full group access rights to the root directory object.

Step 14 Add the root master to the root domain's admin group.

Step 15 Update the root domain's public keys.

Step 16 Restart the NIS+ daemon with security level 2.

Step 17 Add your LOCAL credentials to the root domain.

Step 18 Add your DES credentials to the root domain.

Step 19 Add credentials for other administrators.

Step 20 Add self and other administrators to root domain's admin group.

Security Considerations

NIS+ provides preset security defaults for the root domain. These are stored in the NIS_DEFAULTS environment variable, and apply to every object that is created in the root domain. As described on page 81 (Chapter 4), you can override or change these security defaults. To do this while setting up the root domain, read the instructions in Chapter 15, "Administering NIS+ Access Rights."

Prerequisites

The /etc/passwd file on the root master server must contain an entry for you and every other administrator whose credentials will be added to the root domain in this setup process.

Information You Need

- The root password of the workstation that will become the root master server (for Step 1)

- The name of the root domain (for Step 2)

- The name of the root domain's admin group (for Step 5)

- Your UID and password

- The UID of any administrator whose credentials you will add to the root domain.

Instructions

1. **Log on — as root — to the root master server.**
   Log on as *root* to the workstation that will become the root master server. The examples in these steps use "rootmaster" as the root master server and "Wiz.Com." as the root domain.

   ```
   rootmaster% su
   Password: <enter-password>
   rootmaster#
   ```

2. **Check the root master server's domain name.**
   Make sure the root master server is using the correct domain name. Use the domainname command, as shown below:

   ```
   rootmaster# domainname
   domainname
   ```

The `domainname` command returns a workstation's current domain name. If the name is not correct, change it. Complete instructions are provided in Chapter 9, "Setting Up an NIS+ Client," but here is an example. It changes the domain name of the root master server from StrangeDomain to Wiz.Com (do not include a trailing dot in this instance):

```
rootmaster# domainname
Strange.Domain
rootmaster# domainname Wiz.Com
rootmaster# domainname
Wiz.Com
rootmaster# domainname > /etc/defaultdomain
```

3. **Check the root master server's Switch configuration file.**
   Make sure the root master server is using the NIS+ version of the `nsswitch.conf` file, even if it will run in NIS-compatibility mode. This step ensures that the primary source of information for the root master will be NIS+ tables. Figure 7-1 shows the NIS+ version of the file.

```
rootmaster# more /etc/nsswitch.conf
```

Figure 7-1   NIS+ Version of nsswitch.conf *File*

```
rootmaster# more /etc/nsswitch.conf
#
# /etc/nsswitch.nisplus:
#
# An example file that could be copied over to /etc/nsswitch.conf; it
# uses NIS+ (NIS Version 3) in conjunction with files.
#
# "hosts:" and "services:" in this file are used only if the
/etc/netconfig
# file contains "switch.so" as a nametoaddr library for "inet" transports.

# the following two lines obviate the "+" entry in /etc/passwd and
# /etc/group.
passwd:      files nisplus
group:       files nisplus

# consult /etc "files" only if nisplus is down.
hosts:       nisplus [NOTFOUND=return] files
#Uncomment  the following line, and  comment  out  the  above,
#to  use  both  DNS  and  NIS+
#hosts:       nisplus dns [NOTFOUND=return] files

services:   nisplus [NOTFOUND=return] files
networks:   nisplus [NOTFOUND=return] files
protocols:  nisplus [NOTFOUND=return] files
rpc:        nisplus [NOTFOUND=return] files
ethers:     nisplus [NOTFOUND=return] files
netmasks:   nisplus [NOTFOUND=return] files
bootparams: nisplus [NOTFOUND=return] files

publickey:  nisplus

netgroup:   nisplus

automount:  files nisplus
aliases:    files nisplus
```

If the root master server's configuration file is different from the one in Figure 7-1, change it to the NIS+ version. Complete instructions are provided in Chapter 12, "Setting Up the Name Service Switch," but here is an example:

```
rootmaster# cp /etc/nsswitch.nisplus /etc/nsswitch.conf
rootmaster# ps -e | grep keyserv
    root   145    1  67  16:34:44   ?   keyserv
        .
        .
        .
rootmaster# kill 145
rootmaster# rm -f /etc/.rootkey
rootmaster# keyserv
```

4. **Clean out leftover NIS+ material and processes.**

   If the workstation you are working on was previously used as an NIS+ server or client, remove any files that might exist in /var/nis and kill the cache manager, if it is still running. In this example, a coldstart file and a directory cache file still exist in /var/nis:

```
rootmaster# ls /var/nis
NIS_COLD_START      NIS_SHARED_CACHE
rootmaster# rm -rf /var/nis/*
rootmaster# ps -ef | grep nis_cachemgr
    root   295   260 10 15:26:58 pts/0  0:00 grep nis_cachemgr
    root   286     1 57 15:21:55 ?       0:01 /usr/sbin/nis_cachemgr
rootmaster# kill -9 286
```

   This step makes sure files left in /var/nis or directory objects stored by the cache manager are completely erased so they do not conflict with the new information generated during this setup process. If you have stored any admin scripts in /var/nis, you may want to consider storing them elsewhere temporarily, until you finish setting up the root domain.

5. **Name the root domain's admin group.**

   Although you won't actually create the admin group until Step 11, you need to identify it now. This ensures that the root domain's org_dir directory object, groups_dir directory object, and all its table objects are assigned the proper default group when the are created in Step 9. However, this does not affect the root directory object, which is created in Step 6. For that reason, you'll have to explicitly assign the root directory object's group, as instructed in Step 12.

Set the value of the environment variable NIS_GROUP to the name of the root domain's admin group. Here are two examples, one for `csh` users, and one for `sh`/`ksh` users. They both set NIS_GROUP to "admin.Wiz.Com."

```
rootmaster# setenv NIS_GROUP admin.Wiz.Com.      # for csh

rootmaster# NIS_GROUP=admin.Wiz.Com.             # for sh/ksh
rootmaster# export NIS_GROUP                     # for sh/ksh
```

6. **Create the root directory and initialize the root master server.**

Namespace   Servers

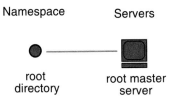

root
directory

root master
server

This step creates the first object in the namespace — the root directory — and converts the workstation you have been working on into the root master server. Use the `nisinit -r` command, as shown below[1]

```
rootmaster# nisinit -r

This machine is in the Wiz.Com. NIS+ domain
Setting up root server ...
All done.
```

---

1. This is the only instance in which you will create a domain's directory object and initialize its master server in one step. In fact, `nisinit -r` performs an automatic `nismkdir` for the root directory. In any case except the root master, these two processes are performed as separate tasks.

7. —NIS-Compatibility Only— Start the NIS+ daemon with -Y.

Namespace   Servers

root
directory   root master server
running NIS+ in NIS-
compatibility mode

Perform this step only if you are setting up the root domain in NIS-compatibility mode; if setting up a standard NIS+ domain, perform Step 8 instead.

This step consists of two sub-steps, a and b. Step a starts the NIS+ daemon in NIS-compatibility mode and Step b makes sure that when the server is rebooted, the NIS+ daemon restarts in NIS-compatibility mode. After Step b, skip to Step 5.

a. Use `rpc.nisd` **with the** `-r`, `-Y`, **and** `-S 0` **options:**

```
rootmaster# rpc.nisd -r -Y -S 0
```

The `-r` option runs the root domain's version of a master server, which is slightly different from a non-root domain's version. The `-Y` option invokes an interface that answers NIS requests in addition to NIS+ requests. The `-S 0` flag sets the server's security level to 0, which is required at this point for bootstrapping. Since no Cred table exists yet, no NIS+ principals can have credentials; if you used a higher security level, you would be locked out of the server.

b. Edit the `/etc/init.d/rpc` **file.**
Search for the string `EMULYP="Y"` in the `/etc/init.d/rpc` file and uncomment the whole line (remove the # character from the beginning of the line). Be sure to save the file.

```
rootmaster# vi /etc/init.d/rpc

    ---uncomment the line that contains EMULYP="Y"---
```

As a result of these steps, you now have a root directory and, serving it, a root master server running the NIS+ daemon. This step also creates the master server's NIS_COLD_START file, which is placed in /var/nis. You can now examine the root directory object, using niscat -o:

```
rootmaster# niscat -o Wiz.Com.
Object Name    : Wiz
Owner          : rootmaster.Wiz.Com.
Group          :
Domain         : Com.
Access Rights  : r---rmcdr---r---
   .
   .
   .
```

Of special interest are the facts that the root directory object has no group and that it assigns only Read rights to whichever group it is eventually assigned.

8. **—Standard NIS+ Only— Start the NIS+ daemon.**

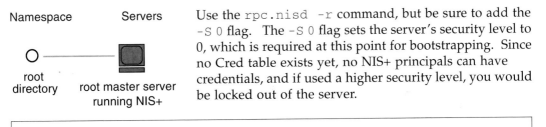

Namespace   Servers

root
directory   root master server
                running NIS+

Use the rpc.nisd -r command, but be sure to add the -S 0 flag. The -S 0 flag sets the server's security level to 0, which is required at this point for bootstrapping. Since no Cred table exists yet, no NIS+ principals can have credentials, and if used a higher security level, you would be locked out of the server.

```
rootmaster# rpc.nisd -r -S 0
```

To verify that the NIS+ daemon is indeed running, use the ps command, as shown below:

```
rootmaster# ps -ef | grep rpc.nisd
root 1081     1  61  16:43:33  ?       0:01  rpc.nisd -r -S 0
root 1087  1004  11  16:44:09  pts/1   0:00  grep rpc.nisd
```

As a result of this, you now have a root directory and, serving it, a root master server running the NIS+ daemon. This step also creates the master server's NIS_COLD_START file, which is placed in /var/nis. You can now examine the root directory object, using niscat -o:

```
rootmaster# niscat -o Wiz.Com.
Object Name    : Wiz
Owner          : rootmaster.Wiz.Com.
Group          :
Domain         : Com.
Access Rights  : r---rmcdr---r---
    .
    .
    .
```

Of special interest are the facts that the root directory object has no group and that it assigns only Read rights to whichever group it is eventually assigned.

9. **Create the root domain's subdirectories and tables.**

Namespace   Servers

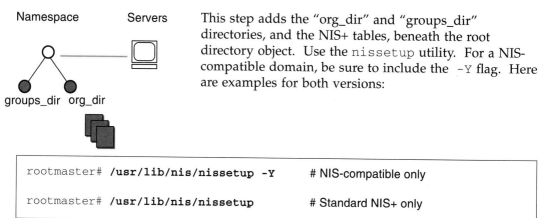

groups_dir org_dir

This step adds the "org_dir" and "groups_dir" directories, and the NIS+ tables, beneath the root directory object. Use the nissetup utility. For a NIS-compatible domain, be sure to include the -Y flag. Here are examples for both versions:

```
rootmaster# /usr/lib/nis/nissetup -Y      # NIS-compatible only

rootmaster# /usr/lib/nis/nissetup         # Standard NIS+ only
```

Each object added by the utility is listed in the output:

```
rootmaster# /usr/lib/nis/nissetup
org_dir.Wiz.Com. created
groups_dir.Wiz.Com. created
auto_master.org_dir.Wiz.Com. created
auto_home.org_dir.Wiz.Com. created
bootparams.org_dir.Wiz.Com. created
cred.org_dir.Wiz.Com. created
ethers.org_dir.Wiz.Com. created
group.org_dir.Wiz.Com. created
hosts.org_dir.Wiz.Com. created
mail_aliases.org_dir.Wiz.Com. created
sendmailvars.org_dir.Wiz.Com. created
netmasks.org_dir.Wiz.Com. created
netgroup.org_dir.Wiz.Com. created
networks.org_dir.Wiz.Com. created
passwd.org_dir.Wiz.Com. created
protocols.org_dir.Wiz.Com. created
rpc.org_dir.Wiz.Com. created
services.org_dir.Wiz.Com. created
timezone.org_dir.Wiz.Com. created
```

The -Y option creates the same tables and subdirectories as for a standard NIS+ domain, but assigns Read rights to the Nobody category so that requests from NIS clients, which are unauthenticated, can access information in the NIS+ tables.

You can examine the object properties of the subdirectories and tables by using the niscat -o command. If you do, note that even though the root directory object was not assigned a group, both the subdirectories and all the tables were. You can also use the niscat option without a flag to examine the information in the tables, although at this point they are empty.

10. **Create DES credentials for the root master server.**

The root master server requires DES credentials so that its own requests can be authenticated. To create those credentials, use the nisaddcred command as shown below. When prompted, enter the server's root password:

```
rootmaster# nisaddcred des
DES principal name : unix.rootmaster@Wiz.Com
Adding key pair for unix.rootmaster@Wiz.Com (rootmaster.Wiz.Com.).
Enter login password: <enter-login-password>
Wrote secret key into /etc/.rootkey
```

If you enter a password that is different from the server's root password, you'll get a warning message and a prompt to repeat the password:

```
Enter login password: <if-you-enter-different-password>
nisaddcred: WARNING: password differs from login password.
Retype password:
```

You can persist and retype the same password, and NIS+ will still create the credential. The new password will be stored in /etc/.rootkey and used by the keyserver when it starts up. To give the keyserver the new password right away, do a keylogin -r, as described in Chapter 14, "Administering *NIS+ Credentials.*"

If you desist and decide to use your login password after all, press Control-C and start the sequence over. If you were to simply retype your login password as encouraged by the server, you would get an error message designed for another purpose, but which in this instance, given the server's instructions, could be irritating:

```
nisaddcred: WARNING: password differs from login password.
Retype password: <enter-login-password>
nisaddcred: password incorrect.
nisaddcred: unable to create credential.
```

If for any reason you need to change the root master's DES credential, you can remove the old credential with the nisaddcred -r command, as described in Chapter 14.

As a result of this step, the root server's private and public keys are stored in the root domain's Cred table ("cred.org_dir.Wiz.Com.") and its secret key is stored in /etc/.rootkey. You can verify the existence of its credentials in the Cred table by using the niscat command. Since the default domain name is Wiz.Com., you don't have to enter the Cred table's fully-qualified name; the "org_dir" suffix is enough:

```
rootmaster# niscat cred.org_dir
rootmaster.Wiz.Com.:DES:unix.rootmaster@Wiz.Com.<public key> <encrypted field>
```

You can locate the root master's credential by looking for its secure RPC netname, as shown above. The niscat command is described in Chapter 14.

11. Create the root domain's admin group.

This step creates the admin group named in Step 5. Use the `nisgrpadm` with the `-c` option. The example below creates the "admin.Wiz.Com." group:

```
rootmaster# nisgrpadm -c admin.Wiz.Com.
Group "admin.Wiz.Com." created.
```

This step only creates the group — it does not identify its members. That is done in Step 14.

12. Assign the new group to the root directory object.

As mentioned in Step 5, the root directory object has no group. This step assigns it the group you created in the previous step. Use the `nischgrp` command, which has the following syntax:

nischgrp *group-name object*

Here is an example:

```
rootmaster# nischgrp admin.Wiz.Com. Wiz.Com.
```

Now if you examine the root directory object with `niscat -o`, it finally has the proper group:

```
rootmaster# niscat -o Wiz.Com.
Object Name   : Wiz
Owner         : rootmaster.Wiz.Com.
Group         : admin.Wiz.Com.
Domain        : Com.
Access Rights : r---rmcdr---r---
    .
    .
    .
```

13. Assign full group access rights to the root directory object.

By default, the root directory object only grants its group Read access, which makes the group no more useful than the World category. To make the setup of clients and subdomains easier, change the access rights that the root directory object grants its group from Read to Read, Modify, Create, and Destroy. Use the `nischmod` command, as shown below:

```
rootmaster# nischmod g+rmcd Wiz.Com.
```

14. Add the root master to the root domain's admin group.

Since at this point, the root master server is the only NIS+ principal that has DES credentials, it is the only member you should add to the admin group. Use the `nisgrpadm` command again, but with the `-a` option. The first argument is the group name, the second is the name of the root master server. This example adds "rootmaster.Wiz.Com." to the "admin.Wiz.Com." group:

```
rootmaster# nisgrpadm -a admin.Wiz.Com.  rootmaster.Wiz.Com.
Added "rootmaster.Wiz.Com." to group "admin.Wiz.Com."
```

To verify that the root master is indeed a member of the group, use the `nisgrpadm` command with the `-l` option (see Chapter 13, "Administering NIS+ Groups"):

```
rootmaster# nisgrpadm -l admin.Wiz.Com.
Group entry for "admin.Wiz.Com." group:
    Explicit members:
        rootmaster.Wiz.Com.
    No implicit members
    No recursive members
    No explicit nonmembers
    No implicit nonmembers
    No recursive nonmembers
```

15. Update the root domain's public keys.

Normally, directory objects are created by an NIS+ principal who already has DES credentials. In this case, however, the root master server could not acquire DES credentials until *after* it created the Cred table (since there was no parent domain in which to store its credentials). As a result, three directory objects — root, "org_dir," and "groups_dir" — do not have a copy of the root master server's public key. (You can verify this by using the `niscat -o` command with any of the directory objects. Look for the "Public Key:" field. Instructions are provided in Chapter 16, "Administering NIS+ Directories.")

To propagate the root master server's public key from the root domain's Cred table to those three directory objects, use the `/usr/lib/nis/nisupdkeys` utility for each directory object, as shown below:

```
rootmaster# /usr/lib/nis/nisupdkeys Wiz.Com.
rootmaster# /usr/lib/nis/nisupdkeys org_dir.Wiz.Com.
rootmaster# /usr/lib/nis/nisupdkeys groups_dir.Wiz.Com.
```

After each instance, you'll get a confirmation message such as this one:

```
Fetch Public key for server rootmaster.Wiz.Com.
    netname = 'unix.rootmaster@Wiz.Com.'
Updating rootmaster.Wiz.Com.'s public key.
    Public key : public-key
```

Now, if you look in any of those directories (use `niscat -o`), you'll see this entry under the "Public Key:" field:

```
Public Key : Diffie-Hellman (196 bits)
```

16. Restart the NIS+ daemon with security level 2.

Now that the root master server has DES credentials and the root directory object has a copy of the root master's public key, you can restart the root master with security level 2. First kill the existing daemon, then restart one with security level 2. Be sure to use the `-r` flag and, for a NIS-compatible root domain, the `-Y` flag. Here is an example:

```
rootmaster# ps -e | grep rpc.nisd
root 1081     1  61  16:43:33   ?       0:01  rpc.nisd -r -S 0
root 1087  1004  11  16:44:09   pts/1   0:00  grep rpc.nisd
rootmaster# kill 1081
rootmaster# rpc.nisd -r -Y            # NIS-compatible NIS+ domain
rootmaster# rpc.nisd -r               # Standard NIS+ domain
```

Since security level 2 is the default, you don't need to use the `-S 2` flag.

17. Add your LOCAL credentials to the root domain.

Since you don't have access rights to the root domain's Cred table, you must perform this operation as root. In addition, as mentioned in "*Prerequisites,*" the root master's `/etc/passwd` file must contain an entry for you. Use the `nisaddcred` command with the `-p` and `-P` flags. Here is the syntax, followed by an example:

        nisaddcred -p *uid* -P *principal-name* local

The *principal-name* consists of the administrator's login name and domain name. This example adds a LOCAL credential for an administrator with a UID of 11177 and an NIS+ principal name of "topadmin.Wiz.Com.:

```
rootmaster# nisaddcred -p 11177 -P topadmin.Wiz.Com. local
```

For more information about the `nisaddcred` command, see Chapter 14.

18. Add your DES credentials to the root domain.

Use the `nisaddcred` command again, but with the following syntax:

        nisaddcred -p *secure-RPC-netname* -P *principal-name* des

The secure RPC netname consists of the prefix "unix." followed by your UID, the symbol "@" and your domain name, but *without* a trailing dot. The principal name is the same as for LOCAL credentials: your login name followed by your domain name, *with* a trailing dot.

```
rootmaster# nisaddcred -p unix.11177@Wiz.Com -P topadmin.Wiz.Com. des
Adding key pair for unix.11177@Wiz.Com (topadmin.Wiz.Com.).
Enter login password: <enter-login-password>
```

Early versions of Solaris 2.x have a minor bug that can become evident at this point. If after entering your login password you get a warning such as this one . . .

```
nisaddcred: WARNING: password differs from login password.
Retype password:
```

. . . and yet the password you entered is your correct login password, press Control-c to interrupt the command. Then go to the `/etc/passwd` table and remove the "x" from the second field in your password entry. The `nisaddcred` code did not take this field into account. Now you can repeat the `nisaddcred` command as described above.

19. Add credentials for other administrators.

Add the credentials, both LOCAL and DES, of the other administrators who will work in the root domain. You can do this in two different ways. One way is to ask them to add their own credentials. However, they will have to do this as root. Here is an example that adds credentials for an administrator with a UID of 33355 and a principal name of "bobee.Wiz.Com."

```
rootmaster# nisaddcred -p 33355 -P bobee.Wiz.Com. local
rootmaster# nisaddcred -p unix.33355@Wiz.Com -P bobee.Wiz.Com. des
Adding key pair for unix.33355@Wiz.Com (bobee.Wiz.Com.).
Enter login password: <enter-bobee's-login-password>
```

The other way is for you to create temporary credentials for the other administrators, using dummy passwords (note that each administrator must have an entry in the NIS+ Passwd table):

```
rootmaster# /usr/lib/nis/nisaddent -a -f /etc/passwd.xfr  passwd
rootmaster# nisaddcred -p 33355 -P bobee.Wiz.Com. local
rootmaster# nisaddcred -p unix.33355@Wiz.Com -P bobee.Wiz.Com. des
Adding key pair for unix.33355@Wiz.Com (bobee.Wiz.Com.).
Enter bobee's login password: <enter-dummy-password>
nisaddcred: WARNING: password differs from login passwd.
Retype password: <re-enter-dummy-password>
```

Each administrator can later change his or her network password using the chkey command. Chapter 14, "Administering NIS+ Credentials," describes how to do this.

20. Add self and other administrators to root domain's admin group.

You don't have to wait for the other administrators to change their dummy passwords to perform this step. Use the nisgrpadm command with the -a option. The first argument is the group name, the remaining arguments are the names of the administrators. This example adds two administrators, topadmin and bobee, to the "admin.Wiz.Com." group:

```
rootmaster# nisgrpadm -a admin.Wiz.Com.  topadmin.Wiz.Com. bobee.Wiz.Com.
Added "topadmin.Wiz.Com." to group "admin.Wiz.Com.".
Added "bobee.Wiz.Com." to group "admin.Wiz.Com.".
```

This step completes this task. A summary of the entire task is provided below.

Summary

Below is a summary of the steps required to set up the root domain. It assumes the simplest case, so be sure you are familiar with the more thorough task descriptions before you use this summary as a reference. Also, this summary does not show the server's responses to each command.

```rootmaster% su```	1. Log on, as root, to root master.
```Password: <enter-root-password>```	
```# domainname```	2. Check domain name
```# more /etc/nsswitch.conf```	3. Check Switch file.
```# rm -rf /var/nis*```	4. Remove leftover NIS+ material.
```# NIS_GROUP=admin.Wiz.Com.;```	5. Name the admin group.
``` export NIS_GROUP```	
```# nisinit -r```	6. Initialize the root master.
	7. NIS-compat only:
```# rpc.nisd -r -Y -S 0```	a. Start daemon with -Y, S 0.
```# vi /etc/inet.d/rpc```	b. Uncomment EMULYP="Y" line.
```# rpc.nisd -r -S 0```	8. NIS+-Only: Start daemon with S 0.
```# /usr/lib/nis/nissetup```	9. Create org_dir, groups_dir, tables.
```# nisaddcred des```	10. Create DES credentials for root master.
```Enter login password:```	
``` <enter-login-password>```	
```# nisgrpadm -c admin.Wiz.Com.```	11. Create admin group.
```# nischgrp admin.Wiz.Com. Wiz.Com.```	12. Assign admin group to root directory.
```# nischmod g+rmcd Wiz.Com.```	13. Assign full group rights to root directory.
```# nisgrpadm -a admin.Wiz.Com.```	14. Add root master to admin group.
``` rootmaster.Wiz.Com.```	
```# /usr/lib/nis/nisupdkeys Wiz.Com.```	15. Update root directory's keys.
```# /usr/lib/nis/nisupdkeys```	Also update org_dir's keys.
``` org_dir.Wiz.Com.```	
```# /usr/lib/nis/nisupdkeys```	Also update groups_dir's keys.
``` groups_dir.Wiz.Com.```	
``# ps -ef	grep rpc.nisd```	16. Restart the NIS+ daemon w/ sec 2.
```# kill -9 <process-id>```	First kill existing daemon.
```# rpc.nisd -r [-Y]```	Use -Y for NIS compat.
```# nisaddcred -p 11177 -P```	17. Add your LOCAL credentials.
```topadmin.Wiz.Com. local```	
```# nisaddcred -p unix.11177@Wiz.Com \```	18. Add your DES credentials.
``` -P topadmin.Wiz.Com. des```	
```Enter login password:```	
``` <enter-login-password>```	
```# nisaddcred . . .```	19. Add credentials for other admins.
```# nisgrpadm -a admin.Wiz.Com. member ...```	20. Add admins to admin group.

Setting Up NIS+ Tables 8

This chapter provides step-by-step instructions for populating NIS+ tables. The tables should have already been created with the `nissetup` utility in the process of setting up a domain, either root or non-root. Although you can populate a domain's tables at any time after they are created, the Planning chapter recommends you do so immediately after completing the setup of the domain. This enables you to add clients more easily, since the required information about the clients would already be available in the domain's tables. If you waited till later, you would have to add the clients' information into the master's `/etc` files.

You can populate NIS+ tables in two ways: from files or from NIS maps. This chapter provides a task for each. It also describes how to transfer information back from NIS+ tables to NIS maps, a procedure that may be required during a transition from NIS to NIS+.

▼ How to Populate NIS+ Tables from Files	Page 136
▼ How to Populate NIS+ Tables from NIS Maps	Page 140
▼ How to Transfer Information from NIS+ to NIS	Page 145

Although these tasks are not as involved as the task for setting up a root domain, a task summary is provided at the end of this chapter —just in case you got used to it.

Replace vs Append vs Merge

When you populate a table — whether from a file or an NIS map —, you can use any of three options: replace, append, or merge. The append option simply adds the source entries to the NIS+ table.

With the replace option, NIS+ first deletes all existing entries in the table and then adds the entries from the source. In a large table, this adds a large set of entries into the table's `.log` file (one set for removing the existing entries, another for adding the new ones), taking up space in `/var/nis` and making propagation to replicas time-consuming.

The merge option produces the same result as the replace option, but uses a different process, one that can greatly reduce the number of operations that must be sent to the replicas. With the merge option, NIS+ handles three types of entries differently:

- Entries that exist only in the source are added to the table.
- Entries that exist in both the source and the table are updated in the table.
- Entries that exist only in the NIS+ table are deleted from the table.

When updating a large table with a file or map whose contents are not vastly different from those of the table, the merge option can spare the server a great many operations. Because it only deletes the entries that are not duplicated in the source (the replace option deletes *all* entries, indiscriminately), it saves one delete and one add operation for every duplicate entry.

▼ How to Populate NIS+ Tables from Files

This task transfers the contents of an ASCII file, such as /etc/hosts, into an NIS+ table. Here is a list of the steps:

Step	1	Log on to an NIS+ client.
Step	2	Add /usr/lib/nis to the search path for this shell.
Step	3	Use nisaddent to transfer any of these files, one at a time:
Step	4	Transfer the publickey file.
Step	5	Transfer the automounter information.
Step	6	Checkpoint the table directory.

Security Considerations

You can perform this task from any NIS+ client, including the root master server, as long as you have the proper credentials and access rights. If you are going to replace or merge the entries in the table with the entries from the text file, you must have Create and Destroy rights to the table. If you are going to append the new entries, you only need Create rights.

After you complete this operation, the table entries will be owned by the NIS+ principal that performed the operation and the group specified by the NIS_GROUP environment variable.

Prerequisites

- The domain must have already been set up and its master server must be running.

- The domain's servers must have enough swap space to accommodate the new table information. See "*Swap Space Requirements*" on page 114.

- The information in the file must be formatted appropriately for the table into which it will be loaded. Chapter 3, "Understanding NIS+ Tables and Information" describes the format a text file must have to be transferred into its corresponding NIS+ table. Local /etc files are usually formatted properly, but may have several comments that you would need to remove.

Information You Need

You need the name and location of the text files that will be transferred.

Instructions

1. **Log on to an NIS+ client.**
   You can perform this task from any NIS+ client— just be sure that the client belongs to the same domain as the tables into which you want to transfer the information. The examples in this task use the root master server. Since the administrator in these examples is logged on as root, the NIS+ principal actually performing this operation (and thus needing the proper credentials and access rights) is the root master server.

2. **Add** /usr/lib/nis **to the search path for this shell.**
   Since you will be using the /usr/lib/nis/nisaddent command once per table, adding its prefix to the search path will save you the trouble of typing it each time. Here are two examples, one for csh users, one for sh/ksh users:

```
rootmaster# setenv PATH $PATH:/usr/lib/nis      # csh users

rootmaster# PATH=$PATH:/usr/lib/nis             # sh/ksh users
rootmaster# export PATH
```

3. Use `nisaddent` **to transfer any of these files, one at a time:**

aliases	netmasks
bootparams	networks
ethers	passwd
group	protocols
hosts	rpc
netgroup	services

The publickey and automounter files require slightly different procedures; for the publickey file, go to Step 4, and for the automounter files, go to Step 5.

By default, `nisaddent` *appends* the file information to the table information. To replace or merge instead, use the `-m` or `-r` options.

```
rootmaster# nisaddent -r -f filename table [domain]    # to replace
rootmaster# nisaddent -a -f filename table [domain]    # to append
rootmaster# nisaddent -m -f filename table [domain]    # to merge
```

Filename is the name of the file. *Table* is the name of the NIS+ table. The *domain* argument is optional; use it only to populate tables in a different domain. Here are some examples, entered from the root domain's master server. The source files are simply edited versions of the /etc files:

```
rootmaster# nisaddent -m -f /etc/hosts.xfr hosts
rootmaster# nisaddent -m -f /etc/passwd.xfr passwd
rootmaster# nisaddent -m -f /etc/groups.xfr groups
```

If you perform this operation from a non-root server, keep in mind that a non-root server belongs to the domain above the one it supports. Therefore, it is a client of another domain. For example, the Sales.Wiz.Com. master server belongs to the Wiz.Com. domain. To populate tables in the Sales.Wiz.Com. domain from that master server, you would have to append the Sales.Wiz.Com. domain name to the `nisaddent` statement. For example:

```
salesmaster# nisaddent -r -f /etc/hosts.xfr hosts Sales.Wiz.Com.
```

For more information about `nisaddent`, see Chapter 17, "Administering NIS+ Tables."

To verify that the entries were transferred into the NIS+ table, use the `niscat` command (described in Chapter 17, "Administering NIS+ Tables"). Here is an example:

```
rootmaster# niscat group.org_dir
root::0:root
other::1::
bin::2:root,bin,daemon
  .
  .
  .
```

4. **Transfer the publickey file.**
   Since the domain's Cred table already stores some credentials, you need to make sure they are not overwritten by the contents of the publickey text file that you transfer into the Cred table. You can avoid this by removing those credentials from the publickey text file. For rootmaster, that line would be:

   > `unix.rootmaster@Wiz.Com.` *public-key : private-key*

   Then you can transfer the contents of the publickey file into the Cred table. Use `nisaddent`, but with the `-a` option.

```
rootmaster# nisaddent -a -f /etc/publickey.xfr cred [domain]
```

5. **Transfer the automounter information.**
   Although the `nissetup` utility creates auto_master and auto_home tables, they are not considered standard NIS+ tables. Therefore, transferring information into them requires a slightly different syntax; in particular, you must use the `-t` flag and specify that the table is of type "key-value":

```
rootmaster# nisaddent -m -f auto.master.xfr \
                -t auto_master.org_dir   key-value
rootmaster# nisaddent -m -f auto.home.xfr \
                -t auto_home.org_dir   key-value
```

6. Checkpoint the table directory.

This step ensures that all the servers supporting the domain transfer the new information from their `.log` files to the disk-based copies of the tables. If you have just setup the root domain, this step affects only the root master server, since the root domain does not yet have replicas. Use the `nisping` command with the `-C` (upper case) option:

```
rootmaster# nisping -C org_dir
Checkpointing replicas serving directory org_dir.Wiz.Com.:
Master server is rootmaster.Wiz.Com.
    Last update occurred at <date>

Master server is rootmaster.Wiz.Com.
checkpoint succeeded.
```

If you don't have enough swap space, the server will be unable to checkpoint properly, but it won't notify you. One way to make sure all went well is to list the contents of a table with the `niscat` command. If you don't have enough swap space, you'll get this error message:

```
can't list table: Server busy, Try Again.
```

Even though it doesn't *seem* to, this message indicates that you don't have enough swap space. Increase the swap space and checkpoint the domain again.

This step completes this task.

▼ How to Populate NIS+ Tables from NIS Maps

This task transfers the contents of an NIS map into an NIS+ table.   Here is a list of the steps:

Step	1	Log on to an NIS+ client.
Step	2	Add /usr/lib/nis to the search path for this shell.
Step	3	Use nisaddent to transfer any of these maps, one at a time:

Step   4   Transfer the publickey map.

Step   5   Transfer the automounter information.

Step   6   Checkpoint the table directory.

Security Considerations

You can perform this task from any NIS+ client as long as you (or root on the client) have the proper credentials and access rights. If you are going to replace or merge the entries in the table with the entries from the NIS map, you must have Create and Destroy rights to the table. If you are going to append the new entries, you only need Create rights.

After you complete this operation, the table entries will be owned by the NIS+ principal that performed the operation (either you or, if logged on as root, the client) and the group specified by the NIS_GROUP environment variable.

Prerequisites

- The domain must have already been set up and its master server must be running.

- The dbm files (.pag and .dir files) for the NIS maps you are going to load into the NIS+ tables must already be in a subdirectory of /var/yp. If they are not, you can use /usr/lib/netsvc/yp/ypxfr to get the maps from an NIS server.

Information You Need

You need the name and location of the NIS maps.

Instructions

1. **Log on to an NIS+ client.**
    You can perform this task from any NIS+ client— just be sure that the client belongs to the same domain as the tables into which you want to transfer the information. The examples in this task use the root master server. Since the administrator in these examples is logged on as root, the NIS+ principal actually performing this operation (and thus needing the proper credentials and access rights) is the root master server.

2. **Add** /usr/lib/nis **to the search path for this shell.**
Since you will be using the /usr/lib/nis/nisaddent command once per table, adding its prefix to the search path will save you the trouble of typing it each time. Here are two examples, one for csh users, one for sh/ksh users:

```
rootmaster# setenv PATH to $PATH:/usr/lib/nis      # csh users

rootmaster# PATH=$PATH:/usr/lib/nis                # sh/ksh users
rootmaster# export PATH
```

If you are using the Solaris 1.x distribution of NIS+, the path may be different; check the README file.

3. **Use** nisaddent **to transfer any of these maps, one at a time:**

aliases	netmasks
bootparams	networks
ethers	passwd
group	protocols
hosts	rpc
netgroup	services

The publickey and automounter maps require slightly different procedures; for the publickey file, go to Step 4, and for the automounter files, go to Step 5.

By default, nisaddent *appends* the file information to the table information. To replace or merge instead, use the -m or -r options:

```
rootmaster# nisaddent -r -y nisdomain table        # to replace
rootmaster# nisaddent -a -y nisdomain table        # to append
rootmaster# nisaddent -m -y nisdomain table        # to merge
```

The -y (lower case) option indicates a NIS domain instead of a text file. The *nisdomain* argument is the name of the NIS domain whose map you are going transfer into the NIS+ table. You don't have to name the actual map; the `nisaddent` utility automatically selects the NIS map that correspond to the *table* argument. Here are some examples:

```
rootmaster# nisaddent -m -y OldWiz hosts
rootmaster# nisaddent -m -y OldWiz passwd
rootmaster# nisaddent -m -y OldWiz groups
```

The first example transfers the contents of the hosts.byname and hosts.byaddr maps in the OldWiz (NIS) domain to the NIS+ Hosts table in the root domain (NIS+). The second transfers the NIS maps that store password-related information into the NIS+ Passwd table. The third does the same with group-related information. For more information about the `nisaddent` command, see Chapter 17, "Administering NIS+ Tables."

4. **Transfer the publickey map.**
   Since the domain's Cred table already stores some credentials, you need to make sure they are not overwritten by the contents of the publickey map that you transfer into the Cred table. First, dump the publickey map to a file:

```
rootmaster# makedbm -u /var/yp/OldWiz/publickey.byname > \
                    /etc/publickey.xfr
rootmaster# vi /tmp/publickey
```

Open the file and remove the credentials of the workstation you are logged onto from the publickey map. For rootmaster, that line would be:

```
unix.rootmaster@Wiz.Com.        public-key:private-key
```

Now you can transfer the contents of the *file* — not the map — into the Cred table. Use `nisaddent`, but with the -a option.

```
rootmaster# nisaddent -a -f /etc/publickey.xfr cred
```

5. **Transfer the automounter information.**

Although the `nissetup` utility creates auto_master and auto_home tables, they are not considered standard NIS+ tables. Therefore, transferring information into them requires a slightly different syntax:

```
rootmaster# nisaddent -m -y OldWiz -Y auto.master  \
                   -t auto_master.org_dir key-value Wiz.Com.
rootmaster# nisaddent -m -y OldWiz -Y auto.home \
                   -t auto_home.org_dir key-value Wiz.Com.
```

The -r and -y options are still required, as is the NIS domain name (in this instance, OldWiz). However, you must precede the name of the NIS map (e.g., auto.master) with a -Y (upper case). Then, as is required when transferring automounter *text files*, you must use the -t option, which indicates that this is a non-standard NIS+ table. Its arguments are first, the name of the NIS+ table (auto_master.org_dir) and second, the type of table (key-value). Also be sure to append the "org_dir" suffixes to the NIS+ table names and, as a last argument, include the NIS+ domain name.

6. **Checkpoint the table directory.**

This step ensures that all the servers supporting the domain transfer the new information from their .log files to the disk-based copies of the tables. If you just finished setting up the root domain, this step affects only the root master server, since the root domain does not yet have replicas. Use the nisping command with the -C (upper case) option:

```
rootmaster# nisping -C org_dir
Checkpointing replicas serving directory org_dir.Wiz.Com.:
Master server is rootmaster.Wiz.Com.
     Last update occurred at <date>

Master server is rootmaster.Wiz.Com.
checkpoint succeeded.
```

If you don't have enough swap space, the server will be unable to checkpoint properly, but it won't notify you. One way to make sure all went well is to use list the contents of a table with the niscat command. If you don't have enough swap space, you'll get this error message:

```
can't list table: Server busy, Try Again.
```

Even though it doesn't *seem* to, this message indicates that you don't have enough swap space. Increase the swap space and checkpoint the domain again.

This step completes this task.

▼ How to Transfer Information from NIS+ to NIS

This task transfers the contents of NIS+ tables into the NIS maps on a Solaris 1.x NIS master server. Here is a list of the steps:

Step	1	Log on to the Solaris 1.x NIS+ server.
Step	2	Transfer the NIS+ tables into output files.
Step	3	Transfer the contents of the output files into the NIS maps.

Security Considerations

To perform this task, you must have Read access to each table whose contents you transfer.

Prerequisites

* The maps must have already been built on the NIS server.

* The Solaris 1.x server must have been set up as an NIS+ server.

Instructions

1. **Log on to the Solaris 1.x NIS+ server.**

   This example uses the server named "dualserver."

2. **Transfer the NIS+ tables into output files.**

   Use the nisaddent command with the -d option, as shown below, once for each table.

   ```
   dualserver% /usr/lib/nis/nisaddent -d -t table > filename
   ```

   The -d option dumps the contents of *table* to *filename*, converting the contents back to standard /etc file format.

3. Transfer the contents of the output files into the NIS maps.

The NIS+ output files are ASCII files that you can use as input files for the NIS maps. Use `makedbm` as usual:

```
dualserver#  makedbm flags output-file NIS-dbm-file
```

Summary

This is a summary of the steps required to populate NIS+ tables. It assumes the simplest case, so be sure you are familiar with the more thorough task descriptions before you use this summary as a reference. For brevity, this summary does not show the server's responses to each command.

To Transfer Files Into NIS+ Tables:

`rootmaster%`	1. Log on to an NIS+ client.
`% PATH=$PATH:/usr/lib/nis`	2. Add /usr/lib/nis to search path.
`% export PATH`	
`% nisaddent -m -f /etc/hosts.xfr hosts`	3. Transfer each file, one at a time.
`%.`	
`%.`	
`%.`	
`% vi /etc/publickey.xfr`	4. Transfer publickey file. First remove new credentials from the file. Then transfer it.
`% nisaddent -a -f /etc/publickey.xfr \` `   cred`	

`% nisaddent -r -f auto.master.xfer \`
`   -t auto_master.org_dir \`
`   key-value`
	5. Transfer the automounter files.

`% nisaddent -r -f auto.home.xfr \` `   -t auto_home.org_dir key-value`	
`% nisping -C org_dir`	6. Checkpoint the table directory.

To Transfer Maps into NIS+ Tables:

| ```
rootmaster%
% PATH=$PATH:/usr/lib/nis; \
       export PATH
% nisaddent -m -y OldWIz hosts
%.
%.
%.
% makedbm -u
  /var/yp/OldWiz/publickey.byname > \
  /etc/publickey.xfr
% vi /etc/publickey.xfer
% nisaddent -a -f /etc/publickey.xfr \
  cred
% nisaddent -m -y OldWiz \
  -Y auto.master \
  -t auto_master.org_dir \
  key-value Wiz.Com.
% nisaddent -m -y OldWiz \
  -Y auto.home \
  -t auto_home.org_dir \
  key-value Wiz.Com.
% nisping -C org_dir
``` | 1. Log on to an NIS+ client.<br>2. Add /usr/lib/nis to search path.<br><br>3. Transfer each map, one at a time.<br><br><br><br>4. Transfer publickey file.<br>  First dump the publickey map to a file.<br><br>  Then remove new credentials.<br>  Then transfer the file.<br><br>5. Transfer the automounter maps.<br><br><br><br><br><br><br><br><br>6. Checkpoint the table directory. |

To Transfer NIS+ Tables into NIS Maps:

| ```
dualserver%
% /usr/lib/nis/nisaddent -d -t \
  table > filename
%.
%.
%.
% makedbm flags output-file NIS-dbm-file
``` | 1. Log on to Solaris 1.x NIS+ server.<br>2. Transfer NIS+ tables to files.<br><br><br><br>3. Transfer files to NIS maps. |

Setting Up an NIS+ Client 9

This chapter provides step-by-step instructions for the following tasks:

▼ How to Set Up an NIS+ Client	Page	149
▼ How to Change a Workstation's Domain Name	Page	156
▼ How to Initialize an NIS+ Client by Broadcast	Page	158
▼ How to Initialize an NIS+ Client by Hostname	Page	159
▼ How to Initialize an NIS+ Client by Coldstart File	Page	160

The central task in this chapter is, of course, how to set up an NIS+ client. It applies to clients in a standard NIS+ domain and in a NIS-compatible domain. In that task, Step 7 instructs you to initialize the client by one of three methods: broadcast, hostname, or coldstart file. Since each method is implemented differently, each has its own task description. After initializing a client by one of these methods, you can continue setting up the client by returning to Step 8.

The last task in the chapter describes how to change a workstation's domain name. This task is referenced by several different setup procedures in Part II and is closely related to setting up a client, so it seems fitting to include it here.

This chapter walks through the client setup process at the same leisurely pace as the task for setting up the root domain. For a quicker pace, see the summary at the end of the chapter.

▼ How to Set Up an NIS+ Client

This task describes how to set up a typical NIS+ client, whether in the root domain or in a non-root domain. It applies to regular NIS+ clients and to those clients that will later become NIS+ servers. It applies, as well, to clients in a standard NIS+ domain and those in an NIS-compatible domain. Setting up an NIS+ client involves the following tasks:

- Creating credentials for the client
- Preparing the workstation
- Initializing the workstation as an NIS+ client.

However, as with setting up the root domain, setting up a client is not as simple as carrying out these three tasks in order. To make the set up process easier to execute, these tasks have been broken down into individual steps, and the steps have been arranged into the most efficient order. They are:

Step	1	Log on to the domain's master server.
Step	2	Create DES credentials for the new client workstation.
Step	3	Log on —as root— to the client.
Step	4	Assign the client its new domain name.
Step	5	Check the client's Switch configuration file.
Step	6	Clean out leftover NIS+ material and processes.
Step	7	Initialize the client.
Step	8	Kill and restart the keyserv daemon.
Step	9	Run keylogin.
Step	10	Reboot the client.

Security Considerations

Setting up a client has two main security requirements: both the administrator and the client must have the proper credentials and access rights. If you are setting up the client according to the sequence recommended in the Planning chapter, you already have the proper credentials and access rights.

Otherwise, the only way for a client to obtain credentials in a domain running at security level 2 is for them to be created by an administrator who has valid DES credentials and Modify rights to the Cred table in the client's home domain. The administrator can either have DES credentials in the client's home domain, or a combination of DES credentials in his or her home domain and LOCAL credentials in the client's domain.

Once an administrator creates the client's credentials, the client can complete the setup process. However, the client still needs Read access to the directory object of its home domain. If you set up the client's home domain according to the instructions in either Chapter 7 or Chapter 11, Read access was provided to the World category by the NIS+ commands used to create the directory objects (`nisinit` and `nismkdir`, respectively).

You can check the directory object's access rights by using the `niscat -o` command. It displays the properties of the directory, including its access rights. Here is an example:

```
rootmaster# niscat -o Wiz.Com.
ObjectName    : Wiz
Owner         : rootmaster.Wiz.Com.
Group         : admin.Wiz.Com.
Domain        : Com.
Access Rights : r---rmcdr---r---
       .
       .
       .
```

You can change the directory object's access rights, provided you have Modify rights to it yourself, by using the `nischmod` command, described in Chapter 15, "Administering NIS+ Access Rights."

Prerequisites

- The administrator setting up the client's credentials must have valid DES credentials and Modify rights to the Cred table in the client's home domain.

- The client must have Read rights to the directory object of its home domain.

- The client's home domain must already be set up and running NIS+.

- The client's name and IP address must be recognized by the domain's master server. In other words, the client must have an entry either in the master server's `/etc/hosts` file or in its domain's Hosts table.

Information You Need

- The name of the client's home domain

- The root password of the workstation that will become the client

- The IP address of an NIS+ server in the client's home domain.

Instructions

1. **Log on to the domain's master server.**

2. **Create DES credentials for the new client workstation.**
   Use the `nisaddcred` command with the `-p` and `-P` arguments. Here is the syntax, followed by an example:

```
nisaddcred -p secure-RPC-netname -P principal-name des [ domain ]
```

The secure RPC netname consists of the prefix "unix." followed by the client's hostname, the symbol "@" and the client's domain name, but without a trailing dot. The principal name consists of the client's hostname and domain name, with a trailing dot. If the client belongs to a different domain than the server from which you enter the command, append the client's domain name after the second argument.

This example adds a DES credential for a client workstation named "client1" in the Wiz.Com. domain:

```
rootmaster% nisaddcred -p unix.client1@Wiz.Com  -P client1.Wiz.Com. des
Adding key pair for unix.client1@Wiz.Com (client1.Wiz.Com.).
Enter client1.Wiz.Com.'s root login passwd: <enter-password>
Retype password: <enter-password>
```

For more information about the `nisaddcred` command, see Chapter 14, "Administering NIS+ Credentials."

3. **Log on —as root— to the client.**
   Now that the client workstation has credentials, you can log out of the master server and begin working from the client itself. You can do this locally or remotely.

4. **Assign the client its new domain name.**
   Assign the client its new domain name, using the task titled *"How to Change a Workstation's Domain Name"* on page 156. Then return to Step 5.

5. **Check the client's Switch configuration file.**
   Make sure the client is using the NIS+ version of the `nsswitch.conf` file. This ensures that the primary source of information for the client will be NIS+ tables. Figure 9-1 shows the correct version of the file.

```
client1# more /etc/nsswitch.conf
```

Figure 9-1   NIS+ Version of `nsswitch.conf` *File*

```
rootmaster# more /etc/nsswitch.conf
#
# /etc/nsswitch.nisplus:
#
# An example file that could be copied over to /etc/nsswitch.conf; it
# uses NIS+ (NIS Version 3) in conjunction with files.
#
# "hosts:" and "services:" in this file are used only if the
# /etc/netconfig file contains "switch.so" as a nametoaddr library for
# "inet" transports.

# the following two lines obviate the "+" entry in /etc/passwd and
# /etc/group.
passwd:     files nisplus
group:      files nisplus

# consult /etc "files" only if nisplus is down.
hosts:      nisplus [NOTFOUND=return] files
# Uncomment  the following  line, and  comment  out  the  above,  to  use
# both  DNS  and  NIS+
# hosts:       nisplus dns [NOTFOUND=return] files

services:   nisplus [NOTFOUND=return] files
networks:   nisplus [NOTFOUND=return] files
protocols:  nisplus [NOTFOUND=return] files
rpc:        nisplus [NOTFOUND=return] files
ethers:     nisplus [NOTFOUND=return] files
netmasks:   nisplus [NOTFOUND=return] files
bootparams: nisplus [NOTFOUND=return] files

publickey:  nisplus

netgroup:   nisplus

automount:  files nisplus
aliases:    files nisplus
```

If the file does not look like the one above, change it to the version recommended for NIS+. Complete instructions are provided in Chapter 12, "Setting Up the Name Service Switch," but here is an example.

```
client1# cp /etc/nsswitch.nisplus /etc/nsswitch.conf
```

Although the instructions in Chapter 12 tell you to kill and restart the keyserver, you don't need to add this point, since you'll do so in Step 8.

6. Clean out leftover NIS+ material and processes.

If the workstation you are working on was previously used as an NIS+ server or client, remove any files that might exist in /var/nis and kill the cache manager, if it is still running. In this example, a coldstart file and a directory cache file still exist in /var/nis:

```
client1# ls /var/nis
NIS_COLD_START      NIS_SHARED_CACHE
client1# rm -rf /var/nis/*
client1# ps -ef | grep nis_cachemgr
    root   295    260 10 15:26:58 pts/0   0:00 grep nis_cachemgr
    root   286      1 57 15:21:55 ?       0:01 /usr/sbin/nis_cachemgr
client1# kill -9 286
```

This step makes sure files left in /var/nis or directory objects stored by the cache manager are completely erased so they do not conflict with the new information generated during this setup process. If you have stored any admin scripts in /var/nis, you may want to consider storing them elsewhere temporarily, until you finish setting up the root domain.

7. Initialize the client.

You can initialize a client in three different ways: by hostname, by coldstart file, or by broadcast. Select a method and follow the instructions, which begin on the pages listed below. Then proceed with Step 8.

▼	How to Initialize an NIS+ Client by Broadcast	Page	158
▼	How to Initialize an NIS+ Client by Hostname	Page	159
▼	How to Initialize an NIS+ Client by Coldstart File	Page	160

8. **Kill and restart the keyserv daemon.**
   The following step stores the client's secret key on the keyserver. Before that can be done, you must kill and restart the keyserv daemon. This also has the side effect of updating the key server's Switch information about the client.

   First kill the keyserv daemon, then remove the `.rootkey` file from the `/etc` directory, then restart it. Here is an example:

```
client1# ps -e | grep keyserv
root   145    1  67  16:34:44   ?   keyserv
       .
       .
       .
client1# kill 145
client1# rm -f /etc/.rootkey
client1# keyserv
```

9. **Run keylogin.**
   This step stores the client's secret key with the keyserver. It also saves a copy in `/etc/.rootkey`, so that the root user on the client does not have to do a keylogin to use NIS+. Use `keylogin` with the `-r` option. When prompted for a password, enter the client's root password. It must be the same as the password supplied to create the client's DES credentials:

```
client1# keylogin -r
Password: <enter-root-password>
Wrote secret key into /etc/.rootkey
```

10. **Reboot the client.**
    This step completes this task.

▼ How to Change a Workstation's Domain Name

This task changes a workstation's domain name. Since a workstation's domain name is usually set during installation, you should check it (just enter domainname without an argument) before you decide to use this task.

A Note About Specifying a Domain Name After Installation

A workstation is usually assigned to its domain during installation. On an operating network, the installation script usually obtains the domain name automatically and simply asks the installer to confirm it. During the installation proper, the workstation's domain name is assigned to a variable called domainname, and stored in the kernel. There, it is made available to any program that needs it.

However, when a workstation is rebooted, the setting of the domainname variable is lost. As a result, unless the domain name is saved somewhere, the operating system no longer knows which domain the workstation belongs to. To solve this problem, the domain name is stored in a file called /etc/defaultdomain.

When the workstation is rebooted, the kernel automatically obtains the domain name from this file and resets the domainname variable. However, only at reboot is the variable updated automatically. If you change a workstation's domain name sometime after installation, you must also edit the /etc/defaultdomain file; if you don't, after the next reboot, the workstation will revert to its previous domain name.

Security Considerations

You must perform this task as root on the workstation whose domain name you will change.

Information You Need

- The workstation's superuser password
- The new domain name.

Instructions

1. **Log on to the workstation and become superuser.**
   The examples in this task use "rootmaster" as the workstation and "Wiz.Com." as the new domain name.

```
rootmaster% su
Password: <enter-password>
```

2. **Change the workstation's domain name.**

Enter the new name with the `domainname` command, as shown below. Do not use a trailing dot.

```
rootmaster#  domainname Wiz.Com
```

If the workstation was an NIS client, it may no longer be able to get NIS service.

3. **Verify the result.**

Use the `domainname` command again, this time without an argument, to display the server's current domain.

```
rootmaster#  domainname
Wiz.Com
```

4. **Save the new domain name.**

Redirect the output of the `domainname` command into the `/etc/defaultdomain` file.

```
rootmaster#  domainname > /etc/defaultdomain
```

5. **At a convenient time, reboot the workstation.**

Even after entering the new domain name into the `/etc/defaultdomain` file, some processes may still operate with the old domain name. To ensure that all processes are using the new domain name, reboot the workstation.

Since you may be performing this task in a sequence of many other tasks, examine the work remaining to be done on the workstation before rebooting. Otherwise, you might find yourself rebooting several times instead of just once.

This step completes this task.

To Return To . . .

Where You Left Off in:	Go To:
▼ How to Set Up the Root Domain	*Page 119*
▼ How to Set Up an NIS+ Client	*Page 152*

▼ How to Initialize an NIS+ Client by Broadcast

This method initializes an NIS+ client by sending an IP broadcast on the client's subnet.

This is the simplest way to set up a client, but also the least secure. The NIS+ server that responds to the broadcast sends the client all the information that the client needs in its coldstart file, including the server's public key. Presumably, only an NIS+ server will respond to the broadcast. However, since the client has no way of knowing whether the workstation that responded to the broadcast is indeed a trusted server, this is the least secure method of setting up a client. As a result, this method is only recommended for sites with small, secure networks.

Security Considerations

You must perform this task as root on the client.

Prerequisites

At least one NIS+ server must exist on the same subnet as the client.

Information You Need

You need the root password to the client.

Instructions

1. **Initialize the client.**

   This step initializes the client and creates a NIS_COLD_START file in its /var/nis directory. Use the nisinit command with the -c and -B options:

   ```
   Client1# nisinit -c -B
   This machine is in the Wiz.Com. NIS+ domain.
   Setting up NIS+ client ...
   All done.
   ```

   An NIS+ server on the same subnet will reply to the broadcast and add its location information into the client's coldstart file.

   This step completes this task.

To Return To . . .

Where You Left Off In:	Go To:
▼ How to Set Up an NIS+ Client	*Page 155*

▼ How to Initialize an NIS+ Client by Hostname

Initializing a client by hostname consists of explicitly identifying the IP address of its trusted server. This server's name, location information, and public keys are then placed in the client's coldstart file.

This method is more secure than the broadcast method because it actually specifies the IP address of the trusted server, rather than relying on a server to identify itself. However, if a router exists between the client and the trusted server, it could intercept messages to the "trusted" IP address and route them to an untrusted server.

Security Considerations

You must perform this operation as root on the client.

Prerequisites

* The NIS+ service must be running in the client's domain.

* The client must have an entry in its /etc/hosts file for the trusted server.

Information You Need

You need the name and IP address of the trusted server.

Instructions

1. **Check the client's** /etc/hosts **file.**
   Make sure the client has an entry for the trusted server.

2. **Initialize the client.**

This step initializes the client and creates a NIS_COLD_START file in its /var/nis directory. Use the nisinit command with the -c and -H options. This example uses rootmaster as the trusted server:

```
Client1# nisinit -c -H rootmaster
This machine is in the Wiz.Com. NIS+ domain.
Setting up NIS+ client ...
All done.
```

The nisinit utility looks for the server's address in the client's /etc/hosts file, so don't append a domain name to the server. If you do, the utility won't be able to find its address.

This step completes this task.

To Return To...

Where You Left Off In:	Go To:
▼ How to Set Up an NIS+ Client	*Page 155*

▼ How to Initialize an NIS+ Client by Coldstart File

This task initializes an NIS+ client by using the coldstart file of another NIS+ client — preferably from the same domain. This is the most secure method of setting up an NIS+ client. It ensures that the client obtains its NIS+ information from a trusted server — something that cannot be guaranteed by the hostname or broadcast method.

Security Considerations

You must perform this task as root on the client.

Prerequisites

The servers specified in the coldstart file must already be set up and running NIS+.

Information You Need

You need the name and location of the coldstart file you will copy.

Instructions

1. **Copy the other client's coldstart file.**
   Copy the other client's coldstart file into a directory in the new client. This may be easier to do while logged on as yourself rather than as root on the client. Be sure to switch back to root before initializing the client.

   Don't copy the other client's file into /var/nis, though, because during initialization that directory gets overwritten. This example copies the coldstart file of "client1" into the /tmp directory of "client2."

   ```
   client2# exit
   client2% rcp client1:/var/nis/NIS_COLD_START /tmp
   client2% su
   ```

2. **Initialize the client from the coldstart file.**
   Use the nisinit command with the -c and -C options, as shown below.

   ```
   client2# nisinit -c -C /tmp/NIS_COLD_START
   This machine is in the Wiz.Com. NIS+ domain.
   Setting up NIS+ client ...
   All done.
   ```

   This step completes this task.

   To Return To . . .

Where You Left Off In:	Go To:
▼ How to Set Up an NIS+ Client	*Page 155*

Summary

This is a summary of the steps required to set up a client. It assumes the simplest case, so be sure you are familiar with the more thorough task descriptions before you use this summary as a reference. For brevity, this summary does not show the responses to each command.

```rootmaster%```	1. Log on to domain's master.
```rootmaster% nisaddcred -p \```	2. Create DES credentials for client.
``` unix.client1.Wiz.Com -P \```	
``` client1.Wiz.Com. des```	
```client1# rlogin client1 -l root```	3. Log on, as root, to the client.
```Password: <enter-password>```	
```client1# domainname Wiz.Com```	4. Assign the client a domain name.
```client1# domainname > /etc/ \```	
``` defaultdomain```	
```client1# more /etc/nsswitch.conf```	5. Check the switch configuration file.
```client1# rm -rf /var/nis/*```	6. Clean out /var/nis.
```client1# nisinit -c -H rootmaster```	7. Initialize the client.
``client1# ps -ef	grep keyserv```	8. Kill and restart the keyserver.
```client1# kill -9 <process-id>```	
```client1# keyserv```	
```client1# keylogin -r```	9. Keylogin the client.
```Password: <enter-root-password>```	
```client1# init 6```	10. Reboot the client.

Setting Up NIS+ Servers 10 ≡

This chapter provides step-by-step procedures for three server-related tasks:

▼ How to Set Up an NIS+ Server	Page	164
▼ How to Add a Replica to an Existing Domain	Page	167
▼ How to Change a Server's Security Level	Page	168

The first task describes how to set up an NIS+ server. The second describes how to add a server to an existing domain, whether root or non-root. The third describes how to change a server's security level, whether to upgrade it for normal DES operation or to downgrade it for debugging. A summary of each task is provided at the end of the chapter.

Differences Between Standard and NIS-Compatible Server Setup Procedures

The differences between a NIS-compatible and a standard NIS+ server are the same as for the root master server. The NIS+ daemon for an NIS-compatible server must be started with the -Y option, which allows the server to answer requests from NIS clients. This is described in Step 2, in the first task below. The equivalent step for standard NIS+ servers is Step 3.

As you may recall, the instructions for setting up the root master server in NIS-compatibility mode (Chapter 7) also required a -Y flag with the `nissetup` utility, which creates the NIS+ tables with the proper permissions for a NIS-compatible domain. That step is not included in the server setup task because with every server other than the root master, the `nissetup` utility is not used until the server is associated with a domain (as described in Chapter 11, "Setting Up a Non-Root Domain.).

▼ How to Set Up an NIS+ Server

This task applies to any NIS+ server except the root master; that is, to a root replica, a non-root master, or a non-root replica, whether running in NIS-compatibility mode or not. This task only sets up the server; it does not specify which domain it supports or whether it is a master or a replica. That is done by the tasks in Chapter 11, "Setting Up a Non-Root Domain."

Here is a summary of the entire setup process:

Step	1	Log on —as root— to the client that will become the replica server.
Step	2	—NIS-Compatibility Only— Start the NIS+ daemon with -Y.
Step	3	—Standard NIS+ Only— Start the NIS+ daemon.
Step	4	Start the NIS+ Cache Manager.

Security Considerations

You must perform this operation as root on the server. The security level at which you start the server (Step 4) determines the credentials that its clients must have. For instance, if the server is set up with security level 2, the clients in the domain it supports must have DES credentials. If you have set up the client according to the instructions in this book, the client has DES credentials in the root domain, and you can start the server with security level 2.

Prerequisites

- The root domain must already be set up — see Chapter 7, "Setting Up the Root Domain."

- The server must have already been initialized as an NIS+ client — see Chapter 9, "Setting Up an NIS+ Client."

Information You Need

- The root password of the client that will become the server

- The name of the server's domain

- The IP address of the parent server.

Instructions

1. **Log on —as root— to the client that will become the replica server.**

2. **—NIS-Compatibility Only— Start the NIS+ daemon with -Y.**

   Perform this step only if you are setting up the server in NIS-compatibility mode; if setting up a standard NIS+ server, perform Step 3 instead.

   This step consists of two sub-steps, a and b. Step a starts the NIS+ daemon in NIS-compatibility mode and Step b makes sure that when the server is rebooted, the NIS+ daemon restarts in NIS-compatibility mode.

   a. Use `rpc.nisd` **with the** `-Y` **flag.**

   ```
   compatserver# rpc.nisd -Y
   ```

   The `-Y` option invokes an interface that answers NIS requests in addition to NIS+ requests.

   b. Edit the `/etc/init.d/rpc` **file.**

   Search for the string `EMULYP="Y"` in the `/etc/init.d/rpc` file and uncomment the whole line (remove the # character from the beginning of the line). Be sure to save the file.

   ```
   compatserver# vi /etc/init.d/rpc

       ---uncomment the line that contains EMULYP="Y"---
   ```

   This step creates a directory with the same name as the server and the server's `.log` file. They are placed in `/var/nis`.

   ```
   compatserver# ls -F
   NIS_COLD_START    compatserver/    compatserver.log
   ```

   The `compatserver.log` file is the transaction log (described in Chapter 2). You can examine the contents of the transaction log by using the `nislog` command, described in Chapter 16, "Administering NIS+ Directories."

3. **—Standard NIS+ Only— Start the NIS+ daemon.**
Use the `rpc.nisd -r` command without any flags.

```
server# rpc.nisd
```

To verify that the NIS+ daemon is indeed running, use the `ps` command, as shown below:

```
server# ps -ef | grep rpc.nisd
root 1081     1 61  16:43:33  ?        0:01  rpc.nisd
root 1087  1004 11  16:44:09  pts/1 0:00  grep rpc.nisd
```

This step creates a directory with the same name as the server and the server's `.log` file. They are placed in `/var/nis`.

```
compatserver# ls -F
NIS_COLD_START    compatserver/   compatserver.log
```

The `compatserver.log` file is the transaction log (described in Chapter 2). You can examine the contents of the transaction log by using the `nislog` command, described in Chapter 16, "Administering NIS+ Directories."

4. **Start the NIS+ Cache Manager.**
The NIS+ Cache Manager caches location information about the NIS+ servers that support other NIS+ domains. To start the Cache Manager, just enter the `nis_cachemgr` command, as shown below.

```
server# nis_cachemgr
```

This step completes this task. A task summary is provided at the end of the chapter.

▼ How to Add a Replica to an Existing Domain

This task describes how to add a replica server to an existing domain, whether root or non-root. Here is a list of the steps:

Step	1	Log on —as root— to the domain's master server.
Step	2	Add the replica to the domain.
Step	3	Checkpoint the domain's directory object.

Security Considerations

The NIS+ principal performing this operation must have Modify rights to the domain's directory object.

Prerequisites

• The server that will be designated a replica must have already been set up.

• The domain must have already been set up and assigned a master server.

Information You Need

• The name of the server

• The name of the domain.

Instructions

1. **Log on —as root— to the domain's master server.**

2. **Add the replica to the domain.**

Namespace   Servers

root   adds replica
directory

Use the `nismkdir` command with the `-s` option, as shown in the example below. The example adds the replica "rootreplica" to the "Wiz.Com." domain:

```
rootmaster# nismkdir -s rootreplica  Wiz.Com.
```

When you use the `nismkdir` command on a directory object that already exists, it does not recreate the directory, it simply modifies it according to the flags you provide. In this case, the `-s` flag assigns the domain an additional replica server. You can verify that the replica was added by examining the directory object's definition, using the `niscat -o` command.

3. **Checkpoint the domain's directory object.**
   If you have followed the suggestions in the Planning chapter and set up the domain's tables immediately after completing the domain setup, you can now propagate the tables down to the replica. This is accomplished by checkpointing the domain's directory object. The checkpoint makes the master ask its replicas whether they have the latest information. The new replica, of course, replies negatively, so the master downloads it a copy of its tables.

   Use the `nisping` command, with the `-C` (upper-case) option:

   ```
   rootmaster# nisping -C Wiz.Com.
   ```

   For more information about `nisping`, see Chapter 16, "Administering NIS+ Directories."

   This step completes this task. A summary is provided at the end of this chapter.

▼ How to Change a Server's Security Level

This task changes the security level of a previously set up NIS+ server. You can assign it security level 0 (lowest), 1, or 2 (highest). The default is 2.

Security Considerations

You must perform this task as root on the server. If changing to security level 1, at least one NIS+ principal must have LOCAL credentials in the Cred table of the server's home domain. Otherwise, the server will be unable to authenticate anyone and no one will be able to operate on that domain. If changing to security level 2, at least one NIS+ principal must have DES credentials in the domain's Cred table. Security level 0 requires no credentials.

Instructions

1. **Log on —as root— to the server.**

2. **Find the process ID of the NIS+ daemon.**

   Use the ps command as shown below.

   ```
   server# ps -e | grep rpc.nisd
   root 1081     1  61  16:43:33  ?       0:01  rpc.nisd
   root 1386  1004  11  16:44:09  pts/1   0:00  grep rpc.nisd
   ```

3. **Kill the NIS+ daemon.**

   Use the kill command as shown below. Note that this will interrupt NIS+ service.

   ```
   server# kill 1081
   ```

   If you reinvoke the ps command, it should no longer list the daemon process.

   ```
   server# ps -ef | grep rpc.nisd
   root  1094  1004  11  16:54:28  pts/1  0:00 grep rpc.nisd
   ```

4. **Kill the NIS+ cache manager.**

   Use the ps command to find its process id, and then kill it, as shown below.

   ```
   server# ps -e | grep nis_cachemgr
   root 1299     1  61  12:57:31  ?       0:01  nis_cachemgr
   root 1387  1004  11  16:57:34  pts/1   0:00  grep nis_cachemgr
   server# kill 1299
   server# rm /var/nis/NIS_SHARED_DIRCACHE
   ```

   Also be sure to remove /var/nis/NIS_SHARED_DIRCACHE, since it may contain old information.

5. **Restart the NIS+ daemon with the desired security level.**

   Use the rpc.nisd command as shown below.

   ```
   server# rpc.nisd -S security-level
   ```

Security-level can be 0 (lowest), 1, or 2 (highest).   Security level 2 is the default; to select it, you don't have to use the -S option.

To verify that the NIS+ daemon is indeed running, use the ps command, as shown below:

```
server# ps -ef | grep rpc.nisd
root 1081     1  61  16:43:33  ?       0:01  rpc.nisd -S 0
root 1087  1004  11  16:44:09  pts/1  0:00  grep rpc.nisd
```

6. **Restart the NIS+ Cache Manager.**
   Use the nis_cachemgr command, as shown below.

```
server# nis_cachemgr
```

This step completes this task.   A summary is provided below.

Summary

Below is a summary of the tasks described in this chapter. It assumes the simplest case, so be sure you are familiar with the more thorough task descriptions before you use this summary as a reference. Also, this summary does not show the server's responses to each command.

To Set up an NIS+ Server:

`server# `**`su`**
 	
`server#    `**`rpc.nisd -Y`**
`server#    `**`vi /etc/inet.d/rpc`**
`server# `**`rpc.nisd`**
`server# `**`nis_cachemgr`**
	1. Log on, as root, to the server.
	2. NIS-compat only:
	   a. Start daemon with -Y.
	   b. Uncomment EMULYP="Y" line.
	3. NIS+-Only: Start daemon.
	4. Start the NIS+ cache manager.

How to Add a Replica to an Existing Domain:

`rootmaster% `**`su`** `# `**`nismkdir -s rootreplica Wiz.Com.`** `# `**`nisping -C Wiz.Com.`**	1. Log on, as root, to domain's master. 2. Designate the new replica. 3. Checkpoint the domain's directory.

To Change a Server's Security Level:

`server# `**`su`** `server# `**`ps -ef	grep rpc.nisd`** `server# `**`kill`** *`<process-id>`* `server# `**`ps -ef	grep nis_cachemgr`** `server# `**`kill`** *`<process-id>`* `server# `**`rm /var/nis/NIS_CACHEDIR`** `server# `**`rpc.nisd -S`** *`<security-level>`* `server# `**`nis_cachemgr`**	1. Log on, as root, to the server. 2. Find the process id of the daemon. 3. Kill the daemon. 4. Kill the cache manager. 5. Restart the NIS+ daemon. 6. Restart the NIS+ cache manager.

Setting Up a Non-Root Domain 11 ≡

This chapter provides step-by-step instructions for setting up a non-root domain. If you follow the guidelines in the Planning chapter, you'll start setting up a non-root domain *after* you have set up its servers.

▼ How to Set Up a Non-Root Domain   Page   173

A summary of the task is provided at the end of the chapter.

Differences Between Standard and NIS-Compatible Setup Procedures

The differences between a NIS-compatible and a standard NIS+ server are the same as for the root domain. The NIS+ daemon for each server in an NIS-compatible domain should have been started with the -Y option, as instructed in Chapter 10.

An NIS compatible domain also requires its tables to provide Read rights for the Nobody category, which allows NIS clients to access the information stored in them. This is accomplished with the -Y option to the `nissetup` command, in Step 4. The standard NIS+ domain version uses the same command but without the -Y option, so it is described in the same step.

▼ How to Set Up a Non-Root Domain

This task describes how to set up a non-root domain, whether in NIS-compatibility mode or in standard NIS+ mode. Setting up a non-root domain involves the following tasks:
- Establishing security for the domain
- Creating the domain's directories
- Creating the domain's tables
- Designating the domain's servers

However, as with setting up the root domain, these tasks cannot be performed sequentially. To make the set up process easier to execute, they have been broken down into individual steps, and the steps have been arranged into the most efficient order.

Here is a summary of the entire setup process:

Step	1	Log on to the domain's master server.
Step	2	Name the domain's administrative group.
Step	3	Create the domain's directory and designate its servers.
Step	4	Create the domain's subdirectories and tables.
Step	5	Create the domain's admin group.
Step	6	Assign full group access rights to the directory object.
Step	7	Add the servers to the domain's admin group.
Step	8	Add credentials for other administrators.
Step	9	Add the administrators to the domain's admin group.

Security Considerations

In most sites, to preserve the security of the parent domain, only the parent domain's master server or an administrator who belongs to the parent domain's admin group is allowed to create a domain beneath it. Although this is a policy decision and not a requirement of NIS+, the instructions in this chapter assume that you are following that policy. Of course, the parent domain's admin group must have Create rights to the parent directory object. To verify this, use the `niscat -o` command:

```
rootmaster# niscat -o Wiz.Com.
Object Name    : Wiz
Owner          : rootmaster
Group          : admin.Wiz.Com.
Domain         : Com.
Access Rights  : r---rmcdrmcdr---
   .
   .
   .
```

If you are more concerned about convenience than security, you could simply make the new domain's master server a member of its parent domain's admin group and then perform the entire procedure from the server. Use the `nisgrpadm` command, described in Chapter 13, "Administering NIS+ Groups."

Prerequisites
- The parent domain must be set up and running.
- The server that will be designated as this domain's master must be initialized and running NIS+.
- If you will designate a replica server, it must have an entry in the master's /etc/hosts file.

Information You Need
- The name of the new domain (for Step 3)
- The name of the new domain's master and replica servers
- The name of the new domain's admin group (for Step 2)
- Userids of the administrators who will belong to the new domain's admin group (for Step 8).

Instructions

1. **Log on to the domain's master server.**
   Log on to the server that you will designate as the new domain's master. The steps in this task use the server named "salesmaster," which belongs to the Wiz.Com. domain, and will become the master server of the Sales.Wiz.Com. domain. The administrator performing this task is "topadmin.Wiz.Com.," a member of the admin.Wiz.Com. group. That group has full access rights to the Wiz.Com. directory object.

2. **Name the domain's administrative group.**
   Although you won't actually create the admin group until Step 5, you need to identify it now. This enables the nismkdir command used in the following step to create the directory object with the proper access rights for the group. It does the same for the nissetup utility used in Step 4.

   Set the value of the environment variable NIS_GROUP to the name of the domain's admin group. Here are two examples, one for csh users, and one for sh/ksh users. They both set NIS_GROUP to "admin.Sales.Wiz.Com."

```
salesmaster# setenv NIS_GROUP admin.Sales.Wiz.Com.      # for csh

salesmaster# NIS_GROUP=admin.Sales.Wiz.Com.             # for sh/ksh
salesmaster# export NIS_GROUP                           # for sh/ksh
```

3. Create the domain's directory and designate its servers.

Namespace   Servers

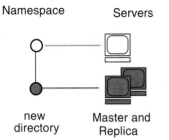

new   Master and
directory   Replica

The nismkdir command, in one step, creates the new domain's directory and designates its supporting servers. It has the following syntax:

nismkdir –m *master* –s *replica* *domain*

The –m flag designates its master server, and the –s flag designates its replica. Here is an example:

```
salesmaster# nismkdir -m salesmaster -s salesreplica Sales.Wiz.Com.
```

The directory is loaded into /var/nis, but to view it, use the niscat -o command:

```
salesmaster# niscat -o Sales.Wiz.Com.
Object Name    : Sales
Owner          : topadmin.Wiz.Com.
Group          : admin.Sales.Wiz.Com.
Domain         : Wiz.Com.
Access Rights  : ----rmcdr---r---
      .
      .
      .
```

Unlike the root directory, this directory object *does* have the proper group assignment. As a result, you won't have to use nischgrp.

4. Create the domain's subdirectories and tables.

Namespace   Servers

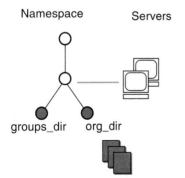

groups_dir   org_dir

This step adds the "org_dir" and "groups_dir" directories, and the NIS+ tables, beneath the new directory object. Use the nissetup utility, but be sure to add the new domain name. And, for a NIS-compatible domain, include the –Y flag. Here are examples of both versions:

```
salesmaster# /usr/lib/nis/nissetup -Y Sales.Wiz.Com.

   —OR—

salesmaster# /usr/lib/nis/nissetup  Sales.Wiz.Com.
```

Each object added by the utility is listed in the output:

```
salesmaster# /usr/lib/nis/nissetup
org_dir.Sales.Wiz.Com. created
groups_dir.Sales.Wiz.Com. created
auto_master.org_dir.Sales.Wiz.Com. created
auto_home.org_dir.Sales.Wiz.Com. created
bootparams.org_dir.Sales.Wiz.Com. created
cred.org_dir.Sales.Wiz.Com. created
ethers.org_dir.Sales.Wiz.Com. created
group.org_dir.Sales.Wiz.Com. created
hosts.org_dir.Sales.Wiz.Com. created
mail_aliases.org_dir.Sales.Wiz.Com. created
sendmailvars.org_dir.Sales.Wiz.Com. created
netmasks.org_dir.Sales.Wiz.Com. created
netgroup.org_dir.Sales.Wiz.Com. created
networks.org_dir.Sales.Wiz.Com. created
passwd.org_dir.Sales.Wiz.Com. created
protocols.org_dir.Sales.Wiz.Com. created
rpc.org_dir.Sales.Wiz.Com. created
services.org_dir.Sales.Wiz.Com. created
timezone.org_dir.Sales.Wiz.Com. created
```

The -Y option creates the same tables and subdirectories as for a standard NIS+ domain, but assigns Read rights to the Nobody category so that requests from NIS clients, which are unauthenticated, can access information in the NIS+ tables.

If you are curious, you can verify the existence of the org_dir and groups_dir directories by looking in your domain's equivalent of /var/nis/salesmaster. They are listed along with the root object and other NIS+ files. The tables are listed under the org_dir directory. You can examine the contents of any table by using the niscat command, described in Chapter 17 (although at this point the tables are empty).

5. **Create the domain's admin group.**
   This step creates the admin group named in Step 2. Use the `nisgrpadm` command with the `-c` option. The example below creates the "admin.Sales.Wiz.Com." group:

   ```
   salesmaster# nisgrpadm -c admin.Sales.Wiz.Com.
   Group "admin.Sales.Wiz.Com." created.
   ```

   This step only creates the group — it does not identify its members. That is done in the next step.

6. **Assign full group access rights to the directory object.**
   By default, the directory object only grants its group Read access, which makes the group no more useful than the World category. To make the setup of clients and subdomains easier, change the access rights that the directory object grants its group from Read to Read, Modify, Create, and Destroy. Use the `nischmod` command, as shown below:

   ```
   salesmaster# nischmod g+rmcd Sales.Wiz.Com.
   ```

   Complete instructions for using the `nischmod` command are provided in Chapter 15, "Administering NIS+ Access Rights."

7. **Add the servers to the domain's admin group.**
   At this point, the domain's group has no members. Add the master and replica servers, using the `nisgrpadm` command with the `-a` option. The first argument is the group name, the rest are the names of the new members. This example adds "salesmaster.Wiz.Com." and "salesreplica.Wiz.Com." to the "admin.Sales.Wiz.Com." group:

   ```
   salesmaster# nisgrpadm -a admin.Sales.Wiz.Com. \
                salesmaster.Wiz.Com. salesreplica.Wiz.Com.
   Added "salesmaster.Wiz.Com." to group "admin.Sales.Wiz.Com."
   Added "salesreplica.Wiz.Com." to group "admin.Sales.Wiz.Com."
   ```

To verify that the servers are indeed members of the group, use the `nisgrpadm` command with the `-l` option (see Chapter 13, "Administering NIS+ Groups"):

```
salesmaster# nisgrpadm -l admin.Sales.Wiz.Com.
Group entry for "admin.Sales.Wiz.Com." group:
    Explicit members:
        salesmaster.Wiz.Com.
        salesreplica.Wiz.Com.
    No implicit members
    No recursive members
    No explicit nonmembers
    No implicit nonmembers
    No recursive nonmembers
```

8. **Add credentials for other administrators.**

Add the credentials of the other administrators who will work in the domain. For administrators who already have DES credentials in another domain, simply add LOCAL credentials. Use the `nisaddcred` command, as shown below. For example:

```
salesmaster# nisaddcred -p 33355 local -P topadmin.Wiz.Com. local
```

For administrators that do not yet have credentials, you can proceed in two different ways. One way is to ask them to add their own credentials. However, they will have to do this as root. Here is an example in which an administrator with a UID of 22244 and a principal name of "moe.Sales.Wiz.Com."adds his own credentials to the Sales.Wiz.Com. domain.

```
salesmaster# nisaddcred -p 22244 -P moe.Sales.Wiz.Com. local
salesmaster# nisaddcred -p unix.22244@Sales.Wiz.Com \
                        -P moe.Sales.Wiz.Com. des
Adding key pair for unix.22244@Sales.Wiz.Com.
Enter login password: <enter-moe's-login-password>
```

The other way is for you to create temporary credentials for the other administrators, using dummy passwords (note that each administrator must have an entry in the NIS+ Passwd table):

```
salesmaster# /usr/lib/nis/nisaddent -a -f
              /etc/passwd.xfr   passwd
salesmaster# nisaddcred -p 22244 -P moe.Sales.Wiz.Com. local
salesmaster# nisaddcred -p unix.22244@Sales.Wiz.Com \
                        -P moe.Sales.Wiz.Com. des
Adding key pair for unix.22244@Sales.Wiz.Com.
Enter moe's login password: <enter-dummy-password>
nisaddcred: WARNING: password differs from login passwd.
Retype password: <re-enter-dummy-password>
```

Each administrator can later change his or her network password using the chkey command. Chapter 14, "Administering NIS+ Credentials," describes how to do this.

9. **Add the administrators to the domain's admin group.**
   You don't have to wait for the other administrators to change their dummy passwords to perform this step. Use the nisgrpadm command with the -a option. The first argument is the group name, the remaining arguments are the names of the administrators. This example adds the administrator "moe" to the "admin.Sales.Wiz.Com." group:

```
salesmaster# nisgrpadm -a admin.Sales.Wiz.Com. \
                        moe.Sales.Wiz.Com.
Added "moe.Sales.Wiz.Com." to group "admin.Sales.Wiz.Com.".
```

This step completes this task. A summary of this task is provided below.

Summary

This is a summary of the steps required to set up a non-root domain. It assumes the simplest case, so be sure you are familiar with the more thorough task descriptions before you use this summary as a reference. Also, this summary does not show the server's responses to each command.

How to Set Up a Non-Root Domain:

`salesmaster% su`	1. Log on, as root, to domain's master.
`# NIS_GROUP=admin.Sales.Wiz.Com.`	2. Name the domain's admin group.
`# export NIS_GROUP`	
`# nismkdir -m salesmaster -s \`	3. Create the domain's directory and
`        salesreplica Sales.Wiz.Com.`	designate its servers.
`# /usr/lib/nis/nissetup`	4. Create org_dir, groups_dir, and tables.
`        Sales.Wiz.Com.`	
`# nisgrpadm -c admin.Sales.Wiz.Com.`	5. Create the domain's admin group.
`# nischmod g+rmcd Sales.Wiz.Com.`	6. Assign full group rights to the domain's directory.
`# nisgrpadm -a admin.Sales.Wiz.Com. \`	7. Add servers to admin group.
`        salesmaster.Wiz.Com. \`	
`        salesreplica.Wiz.Com.`	8. Add credentials for other admins.
`# nisaddcred -p 33355 local`	
`# nisaddcred -p 22244`	
`        -P moe.Sales.Wiz.Com. local`	
`# nisaddcred -p \`	
`        unix.22244@Sales.Wiz.Com. \`	
`        -P moe.Sales.Wiz.Com. des`	
`# nisgrpadm -a admin.Sales.Wiz.Com. \`	9. Add admins to domain's admin group.
`        moe.Sales.Wiz.Com.`	

Setting Up the Name Service Switch

12

This section provides the following step-by-step instructions for using the Name Service Switch:

▼	How to Select an Alternate Configuration File	Page	183
▼	How to Select a Configuration for using DNS	Page	185
▼	How to Add Compatibility with +/- Syntax	Page	186

These tasks are so brief that no summary is provided at the end of the chapter.

▼ How to Select an Alternate Configuration File

This task describes how to select an alternate Switch configuration file for an NIS+ client. Make sure the sources called out in the file are properly set up. In other words, if you are going to select the NIS+ version, the client must eventually have access to NIS+ service; if you are going to select the local files version, those files must be properly set up on the client. Here is a list of the steps:

Step	1	Log on —as root— to the client.
Step	2	Copy the alternate file over the nsswitch.conf file.
Step	3	Kill and restart the key server at an appropriate time.
Step	4	Reboot the workstation at an appropriate time.

Security Considerations

You must perform this operation as root.

Instructions

1. **Log on —as root— to the client.**

2. **Copy the alternate file over the** nsswitch.conf **file.**
   The /etc/nsswitch.conf file is the "working" configuration file used by the Name
   Service Switch. Also in the /etc directory are three alternate versions of the file: one for
   NIS+, one for NIS, and one for local files. To select one, simply copy it over the working
   file. Of course, you can create additional alternates. Here are four examples:

```
client1# cd /etc
client1# cp nsswitch.nisplus nsswitch.conf     # NIS+ version
client1# cp nsswitch.nis nsswitch.conf         # NIS version
client1# cp nsswitch.files nsswitch.conf       # local files version
client1# cp nsswitch.custom  nsswitch.conf     # custom version
```

3. **Kill and restart the key server at an appropriate time.**
   The key server reads the publickey entry in the Name Service Switch configuration file
   only when the key server is started. As a result, if you change the switch configuration
   file, the key server does not become aware of changes to the publickey entry until it is
   restarted.   If you are performing this task as part of the task called "*How to Set Up an
   NIS+ Client*," in Chapter 9, you don't need to kill and restart the keyserver now, since
   you'll do that as part of the overall client setup procedure.

   If you are performing this task independently, or as part of the task called "*How to Set Up
   the Root Domain*," in Chapter 7, you can kill and restart the keyserver now.

   To kill and restart the keyserver, first identify its process id, using grep -e. Then use the
   kill command. After killing it, remove the /etc/.rootkey file. To restart it, simply
   enter the keyserv command. Here is an example:

```
client1# ps -e | grep keyserv
root   145    1  67  16:34:44   ?    keyserv
client1# kill 145
client1# rm -f /etc/.rootkey
client1# keyserv
```

4. **Reboot the workstation at an appropriate time.**
   Because some library routines do not periodically check the nsswitch.conf file to see
   whether it has been changed, you must reboot the workstation to make sure those
   routines have the latest information in the file. If selecting a different configuration file as
   part of a setup procedure, wait until an appropriate time to reboot.

This step completes this task.

To Return To . . .

Where You Left Off in:	Go To:
▼ How to Set Up an NIS+ Client	*Page 152*
▼ How to Set Up the Root Domain	*Page 120*

▼ How to Select a Configuration for using DNS

This task describes how to set up the Name Service Switch configuration file so that a `getXXbyYY()` client can also use the DNS service. Here is a list of the steps:

Step 1 Log on —as root— to an NIS+ client.

Step 2 Open the /etc/nsswitch.conf file.

Step 3 Specify DNS as a source of hosts information.

Step 4 Save the file and reboot the workstation.

Security Considerations

You must perform this operation as root.

Instructions

1. **Log on —as root— to an NIS+ client.**

2. **Open the** `/etc/nsswitch.conf` **file.**

3. **Specify DNS as a source of hosts information.**
   DNS can be the only source or an additional source for the hosts information. Locate the hosts line and use "dns" in one of the ways shown below:

```
hosts:    nisplus dns [NOTFOUND=return] files
hosts:    nis dns [NOTFOUND=return] files
hosts:    files dns
```

4. **Save the file and reboot the workstation.**
Because some library routines do not periodically check the `nsswitch.conf` file to see whether it has been changed, you must reboot the workstation to make sure those routines have the latest information in the file.

This step completes this task.

▼ How to Add Compatibility with +/- Syntax

This task describes how to add compatibility with the +/- syntax used in `/etc/passwd`, `/etc/shadow`[1], and `/etc/group` files. Here is a list of the steps:

Step	1	Log on —as root— to an NIS+ client.
Step	2	Open the /etc/nsswitch.conf file.
Step	3	Change the passwd and groups sources to compat.
Step	4	Save the file and reboot the workstation.

Security Considerations
You must perform this operation as root.

Instructions

1. **Log on —as root— to an NIS+ client.**

2. **Open the** `/etc/nsswitch.conf` **file.**

3. **Change the passwd and groups sources to** `compat`.

```
passwd:   compat
group:    compat
```

This provides the same semantics as in SunOS 4.1: it looks up an `/etc` files and NIS maps as indicated by the +/- entries in the files.

---

1. This file is consulted to verify a user's login password.

If you would like to use the +/- semantics with NIS+ instead of NIS, add the following two entries to the `nsswitch.conf` file:

```
passwd_compat:   nisplus
group_compat:    nisplus
```

4. **Save the file and reboot the workstation.**
   Because some library routines do not periodically check the `nsswitch.conf` file to see whether it has been changed, you must reboot the workstation to make sure those routines have the latest information in the file.

   This step completes this task.

Part 3 — Administering NIS+

13   *Administering NIS+ Groups*

This chapter describes how to use the `nisgrpadm` command to perform a variety of group administration tasks, from creating an NIS+ group to testing for membership in one.

14   *Administering NIS+ Credentials*

This chapter describes how to use the commands that administer NIS+ credentials, `nisaddcred` and `nispasswd`; and other commands related to credential administration, `nisupdkeys` and `keylogin`.

15   *Administering NIS+ Access Rights*

This chapter describes how to use the commands that administer access rights to NIS+ objects and entries, such as `nisaddcred`, `nischmod`, `nischown`, `nischgrp`, and the `-c` and `-a` options of `nistbladm`.

16   *Administering NIS+ Directories*

This chapter describes how to use the commands that administer NIS+ directories, `nismkdir` and `nisrmdir`; the related commands `nisls`, `nis_cachemgr`, `nisshowcache`, and `nischttl`; and the utilities `rpc.nisd` and `nisinit`.

17   *Administering NIS+ Tables*

This chapter describes how to use the commands that administer NIS+ tables and the information in them, `nistbladm`, `niscat`, `nismatch`, `nisgrep`, `nisln`, and `nisaddent`, including the `nissetup` utility.

Administering NIS+ Groups 13

This chapter describes how to use NIS+ group administration commands to perform the following tasks:

▼ How to Specify Group Members in all Commands	Page 192
`niscat -o`	Page 193
▼ How to List the Object Properties of a Group	Page 193
`nisgrpadm`	Page 194
▼ How to Create an NIS+ Group	Page 194
▼ How to Delete an NIS+ Group	Page 195
▼ How to Add Members to an NIS+ Group	Page 196
▼ How to List the Members of an NIS+ Group	Page 197
▼ How to Remove Members from an NIS+ Group	Page 198
▼ How to Test for Membership in an NIS+ Group	Page 198

Related Commands

The `nisgrpadm` command performs most group administration tasks, but several other commands affect groups as well:

Command	Description	See
nissetup	Creates, among other things, the directory in which a domain's groups are stored: groups_dir	Chapter 17
nisls	Lists the contents of the groups_dir directory; in other words, all the groups in a domain	Chapter 16
nischgrp	Assigns a group to any NIS+ object	Chapter 15
nisdefaults	Lists, among other things, the group that will be assigned to any new NIS+ object.	Chapter 15
NIS_GROUP	An environment variable that overrides the value of `nisdefaults` for the shell in which it is set.	Chapter 15

▼ How to Specify Group Members in all Commands

NIS+ groups can have three types of members: explicit, implicit, and recursive:

```
member       ::=  explicit-member
                  implicit-member
                  recursive-member

explicit-member   ::=  principal-name
implicit-member   ::=  @group-name . domain-name
recursive-member  ::=  * . domain-name
```

Explicit members are individual NIS+ principals. They are identified, in all group administration commands, by their principal name. The name does not have to be fully qualified if entered from its default domain.

Implicit members are all the NIS+ principals that are members of another NIS+ group. They are identified by their NIS+ group name, preceded by the @ symbol. The operation you select applies to all the members in the group.

Recursive members are all the NIS+ principals who belong to an NIS+ domain. They are identified by their domain name, preceded by the * symbol and a dot. The operation you select applies to all the members in the group.

Non-Members

NIS+ groups also accept non-members in all three categories, explicit, implicit, and recursive. Non-members are identified by a minus sign in front of their name:

explicit-non-member	::=	*–principal-name*
implicit-non-member	::=	*–@group-name . domain-name*
recursive-non-member	::=	*–* . domain-name*

`niscat -o`

The `niscat -o` command can be used to list the object properties of an NIS+ group. To use it, you must have Read access to the groups_dir directory in which the group is stored.

▼ How to List the Object Properties of a Group

To list the object properties of a group, use `niscat -o` and the group's fully-qualified name, which must include its "groups_dir" subdirectory:

> `niscat -o` *group-name*`.groups_dir.`*domain-name*

For example:

```
rootmaster# niscat -o misc.groups_dir.Wiz.Com.
Object Name    : misc
Owner          : rootmaster.Wiz.Com.
Group          : admin.Wiz.Com.
Domain         : groups_dir.Wiz.Com.
Access Rights  : ----rmcdr---r---
Time to Live   : 1:0:0
Object Type    : GROUP
Group Flags    :
Group Members  : rootmaster.Wiz.Com.
                 topadmin.Wiz.Com.
                 *.admin.Wiz.Com.
                 @.Eng.Wiz.Com.
```

Several of the group's properties are inherited from the NIS_DEFAULTS environment variable, unless they were overridden when the group was created. The Group Flags field is currently unused. In the list of group members, the * symbol identifies member domains and the @ symbol identifies member groups. See the syntax below for an explanation. A better arranged list of members is provided by the `nisgrpadm -l` command, on page 197.

nisgrpadm

The nisgrpadm command creates, deletes, and performs miscellaneous administration operations on NIS+ groups. To use nisgrpadm, you must have access rights appropriate for the operation:

This Operation	Requires This Access Right	To This Object
Create a Group	Create	groups_dir directory
Destroy a Group	Destroy	groups_dir directory
List the Members	Read	the group object
Add Members	Modify	the group object
Remove Members	Modify	the group object

Syntax

The nisgrpadm has two main forms, one for working with groups, one for working with group members.

—To create or delete a group, or to lists its members:

```
nisgrpadm -c group-name.domain-name
nisgrpadm -d group-name
nisgrpadm -l group-name
```

—To add or remove members, or determine if they belong to the group:

```
nisgrpadm -a group-name  member...
nisgrpadm -r group-name  member...
nisgrpadm -t group-name  member...
```

All operations except create (-c) accept a partially-qualified *group-name*. However, even for the -c option, nisgrpadm does not require the use of "groups_dir" in the *group-name* argument. In fact, it won't accept it.

▼ How to Create an NIS+ Group

To create an NIS+ group, you must have Create rights to the groups_dir directory of the group's domain. Use the -c option and a fully-qualified group name:

```
nisgrpadm -c group-name.domain-name
```

The example below creates three groups named admin. The first is in the Wiz.Com. domain, the second in Sales.Wiz.Com., and the third in Eng.Wiz.Com.. All three are created from the master server of their respective domains.

```
rootmaster# nisgrpadm -c admin.Wiz.Com.
Group "admin.Wiz.Com." created.
salesmaster# nisgrpadm -c admin.Sales.Wiz.Com.
Group "admin.Sales.Wiz.Com." created.
engmaster# nisgrpadm -c admin.Eng.Wiz.Com.
Group "admin.Eng.Wiz.Com." created.
```

The group you create will inherit all the object properties specified in the NIS_DEFAULTS variable; that is, its owner, owning group, access rights, time-to-live, and search path. You can view these defaults by using the nisdefaults command (described in Chapter 15). Used without options, it provides this output:

```
rootmaster# nisdefaults
Principal Name  : rootmaster.Wiz.Com.
Domain Name     : Wiz.Com.
Host Name       : rootmaster.WIz.Com.
Group Name      :
Access Rights   : ----rmcdr---r---
Time to live    : 12:0:0
Search Path     : Wiz.Com.
```

The owner is listed in the "Principal Name:" field. The owning group is listed only if you have set the NIS_GROUP environment variable.

Of course, you can override any of these defaults at the time you create the group by using the -D option:

```
salesmaster# nisgrpadm -D group=special.Sales.Wiz.Com. \
             -a admin.Sales.Wiz.Com.
Group "admin.Sales.Wiz.Com." created.
```

▼ How to Delete an NIS+ Group

To delete an NIS+ group, you must have Destroy rights to the groups_dir directory in the group's domain. Use the -d option:

```
nisgrpadm -d group-name
```

If the default domain is set properly, you don't have to fully-qualify the group name. However, you should check first (use `nisdefaults`), because you could unintentionally delete a group in another domain. The example below deletes the test.Sales.Wiz.Com. group.

```
salesmaster% nisgrpadm -d test.Sales.Wiz.Com.
Group "test.Sales.Wiz.Com." destroyed.
```

▼ How to Add Members to an NIS+ Group

To add members to an NIS+ group you must have modify rights to the group object. Use the -a option:

nisgrpadm -a *group-name members* . . .

As described earlier, you can add principals (explicit members), groups (implicit members), and domains (recursive members). You don't have to fully-qualify the name of the group or the name of the members who belong to the default domain. This example adds the NIS+ principals "grace" and "beth", both from the default domain, Alma.Home.Com., and the principals "nahny" and "umpa", from the Villas.Home.Com. domain, to the group "diapers.Alma.Home.Com."

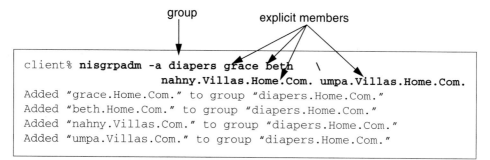

```
client% nisgrpadm -a diapers grace beth      \
                  nahny.Villas.Home.Com. umpa.Villas.Home.Com.
Added "grace.Home.Com." to group "diapers.Home.Com."
Added "beth.Home.Com." to group "diapers.Home.Com."
Added "nahny.Villas.Com." to group "diapers.Home.Com."
Added "umpa.Villas.Com." to group "diapers.Home.Com."
```

To verify the operation, use the `nisgrpadm -l` option. Look for the members under the "Explicit members" category.

This example adds the NIS+ group "admin.Wiz.Com." to the "admin.Eng.Wiz.Com." group. It is entered from a client of the "Eng.Wiz.Com." domain. Note the @ symbol in front of the group name.

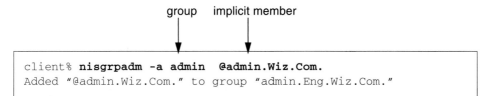

```
client% nisgrpadm -a admin  @admin.Wiz.Com.
Added "@admin.Wiz.Com." to group "admin.Eng.Wiz.Com."
```

This example adds all the NIS+ principals in the Wiz.Com. domain to the "all.Wiz.Com." group. It is entered from a client in the Wiz.Com. domain. Note the * symbol *and the dot* in front of the domain name.

```
client% nisgrpadm -a all  *.Wiz.Com.
Added "*.Wiz.Com." to group "all.Eng.Wiz.Com."
```

▼ How to List the Members of an NIS+ Group

To list the members of an NIS+ group, you must have Read rights to the group object. Use the -l option:

```
nisgrpadm -l group-name
```

This example lists the members of the "admin.Eng.Wiz.Com." group. It is entered from a client in the Eng.Wiz.Com. group:

```
client% nisgrpadm -l admin
Group entry for "admin.Eng.Wiz.Com." group:
    No explicit members
    Implicit members:
         @admin.Wiz.Com.
    No recursive members
    No explicit non-members
    No implicit non-members
    No recursive non-members
```

▼ How to Remove Members from an NIS+ Group

To remove members from an NIS+ group, you must have Modify rights to the group object. Use the -r option:

> nisgrpadm -r *group-name* *members* . . .

This example removes the NIS+ principals "grace" and "nahny.Villas.Home.Com." from the "diapers.Alma.Home.Com." group. It is entered from a client in the Alma.Home.Com. domain:

```
client% nisgrpadm -r diapers grace nahny.Villas.Home.Com.
Removed "grace.Alma.Home.Com." from group
    "diapers.Alma.Home.Com.".
```

This example removes the "admin.Wiz.Com." group from the "admin.Eng.Wiz.Com. group. It is entered from a client in the Eng.Wiz.Com. domain:

```
client% nisgrpadm -r admin @admin.Wiz.Com.
Removed "@admin.Wiz.Com." from group "admin.Eng.Wiz.Com.".
```

▼ How to Test for Membership in an NIS+ Group

To find out whether an NIS+ principal is a member of a particular NIS+ group you must have Read access to the group object. Use the -t option:

> nisgrpadm -t *group-name* *members* . . .

This example tests whether the NIS+ principal "topadmin" belongs to the "admin.Wiz.Com." group. It is entered from a client in the Wiz.Com. domain.

```
client% nisgrpadm -t topadmin  admin
"topadmin.Wiz.Com." is a member of group "admin.Wiz.Com.".
```

This example tests whether the NIS+ principal "joe," from the Sales.Wiz.Com. domain, belongs to the "admin.SalesWiz.Com." group. It is entered from a client in the Wiz.Com. domain.

```
client% nisgrpadm -t joe.Sales.Wiz.Com.  admin.Sales.Wiz.Com.
"joe.Sales.Wiz.Com." is a member of group "admin.Sales.Wiz.Com.".
```

Administering NIS+ Credentials 14 ≡

This chapter describes how to use the NIS+ credential administration commands to perform the following tasks.

nisaddcred	Page 201
▼ How to Create the Root Master's Credentials	Page 203
▼ How to Create Your Own Credentials	Page 203
▼ How to Create Credentials for Others	Page 204
▼ How to Remove Credentials	Page 208
chkey	Page 209
▼ How to Change Your DES Keys	Page 209
nispasswd	Page 210
▼ How to Display Password Information	Page 212
▼ How to Change Passwords	Page 213
nisupdkeys	Page 214
▼ How to Update All Public Keys in a Directory	Page 215
▼ How to Update the Keys of a Particular Server	Page 215
▼ How to Clear Public Keys	Page 215
▼ How to Update IP Addresses	Page 216
keylogin	Page 216
▼ How to Keylogin	Page 216

Related Commands

The commands listed above handle most credential-related administration tasks, but two other commands can provide marginally useful information about credentials:

Command	Description	See
`niscat -o`	Lists an object's properties. By looking in the Public Key field of the object's server, you can tell whether the object definition is storing the server's public key.	Chapter 16
`niscat`	Lists the contents of the Cred table. By looking through the entries, you can tell whether a principal has LOCAL and DES credentials	Chapter 17

Where Credential-Related Information is Stored

Credential-related information, such as secret keys and passwords, is stored in many locations throughout the namespace. NIS+ updates this information periodically, depending on the time-to-live values of the objects that store it, but sometimes, between updates, it gets out of sync. As a result, you may find that operations that should work, don't work. Table 14-1, below, lists all the objects, tables, and files that store credential-related information and how to reset it. Although this book does not have a troubleshooting chapter, you may find this table very helpful.

Item	Stores	To Reset or Change
Cred table	NIS+ principal's secret key and public key. These are the master copies of these keys.	First remove the credentials, then re-create a new one. Use `nisaddcred` for both operations.
Directory object	A copy of the public key of each server that supports it.	Run the `nisupdkeys` command on the directory object. It is in `/usr/lib/nis`.
Keyserver	The secret key of the NIS+ principal who is currently logged in.	Run `keylogin` for a client user or `keylogin -r` for a client workstation.
NIS+ Daemon	Copies of directory objects, which in turn contain copies of their servers' public keys.	Kill the daemon and the cache manager. Then restart both.

All About Administering NIS+

Item	Stores	To Reset or Change
Directory cache	A copy of directory objects, which in turn contain copies of their servers' public keys.	Kill the NIS+ cache manager and remove the NIS_SHARED_CACHE from /var/nis. Then restart the cache manager using the nis_cachemgr command.
Coldstart file	A copy of a directory object, which in turn contains copies of its servers' public keys.	In the root master, kill the NIS+ daemon and restart it. The daemon reloads new information into the existing NIS_COLD_START file. In a client, re-initialize the client with nisinit -c. The client's trusted server reloads new information into the client's existing coldstart file.
Passwd Table	A user's password or a workstation's root password.	Use the nispasswd command. It changes the password in the NIS+ Passwd table and updates it in the Cred table.
Passwd File	A user's password or a workstation's root password.	Use the passwd command, whether logged on as root or as yourself, whichever is appropriate.
Passwd Map	A user's password or a workstation's root password.	Use yppasswd.

nisaddcred

The nisaddcred command creates and removes LOCAL and DES credentials. You can use it to create credentials for yourself or for another NIS+ principal, whether in the local domain or in another domain. To create or remove a credential, you must have Modify rights to the domain's Cred table. In addition, the principal whose credentials you are creating must have an entry either in the NIS+ Passwd table or in the server's /etc/hosts table.

Syntax

—*To create the root master's credentials:*

```
nisaddcred des
```

—*To create your own credentials:*

```
nisaddcred local
nisaddcred des
```

—*To create credentials for another NIS+ principal:*

```
nisaddcred -p uid -P principal-name local [ domain ]
nisaddcred -p rpc-netname -P principal-name des [ domain ]
```

—*To remove credentials:*

```
nisaddcred -r principal-name
```

Secure RPC Netname vs NIS+ Principal Name

When creating credentials, you will often have to enter a principal's *rpc-netname* and *principal-name*. It is easy to confuse their syntaxes, so here is a clear explanation of each.

A secure RPC netname is a name whose syntax is enforced by the RPC protocol. Therefore, it departs slightly from NIS+ naming conventions:

> *rpc-netname*   ::= unix.*uid@domain*
>   unix.*hostname@domain*

It always begins with the unix. prefix and ends with a domain name. However, the domain name *does not* contain a trailing dot. If it identifies a user, it requires the user's UID. If it identifies a workstation, it requires the workstation's hostname. It is always preceded by the -p (lower-case) flag.

An NIS+ principal follows the normal NIS+ naming conventions, but it must always be fully-qualified:

> *principal-name*   ::= *principal.domain.*

Whether it identifies a client user or a client workstation, it begins with the principal's *name*, followed by a dot and the complete domain name, ending in a dot. When used to create credentials, it is always preceded by the -P (upper-case) flag. When used to remove credentials, it does not use the -P flag.

▼ How to Create the Root Master's Credentials

The root master can only have DES credentials. You can only create them while logged on as root and running the NIS+ daemon in security level 0. Use the command without any options:

```
nisaddcred des
```

Here is an example:

```
rootmaster# nisaddcred des
DES principal name : unix.rootmaster@Wiz.Com
Adding key pair for unix.rootmaster@Wiz.Com (rootmaster.Wiz.Com.).
Enter login password: <enter-login-password>
Wrote secret key into /etc/.rootkey
```

When prompted for a login password, enter the root master's root password. If you prefer to enter a different password, see the instructions in "*How to Set Up the Root Domain*" on page 117.

▼ How to Create Your Own Credentials

In your home domain, you must have both LOCAL and DES credentials. If you need to create them yourself, you will run into a circular problem. You cannot create credentials unless you have Modify rights to the domain's Cred table, but you cannot have such rights until you have credentials. You have to step out of the loop somehow. The most secure way is to log on as root to your domain's master server and create them from there.

You can create LOCAL credentials for yourself in any other domain, provided you have Modify rights to the domain's Cred table. After you have created your home domain credentials, you can acquire Modify rights by becoming a member of the domain's admin group —just make sure that group has Modify rights.

Also, whether in your home domain or in another, you must have an entry in the domain's Passwd table or /etc/passwd file.

To create your home domain credentials, use the nisaddcred command twice, once for each type of credential:

```
nisaddcred -p uid   -P principal-name local
nisaddcred -p rpc-netname -P principal-name des
```

Here is an example that adds both types of credentials to the root domain for an administrator named "topadmin," who has a UID of 11177. It is entered as root from the root master server.

```
rootmaster# nisaddcred -p 11177 -P topadmin.Wiz.Com. local
rootmaster# nisaddcred -p unix.11177@Wiz.Com \
                       -P topadmin.Wiz.Com. des
Adding key pair for unix.11177@Wiz.Com (topadmin.Wiz.Com.).
Enter login password: <enter-login-password>
```

When prompted, enter your login password. If you prefer to enter a different password, see the instructions in Step 18 of *"How to Set Up the Root Domain,","* in Chapter 7.

▼ How to Create Credentials for Others

This task describes how to create credentials for other NIS+ principals, whether client users or client workstations. There are several variations to this task, so they will be explained one at a time, each in its own subtask:

▼ Credentials for Client Users	Page 204
▼ Credentials for Client Workstations	Page 207
▼ Adding Client User Credentials to Other Domains	Page 208

▼ Credentials for Client Users

You can create credentials for client users in their home domain, whether or not you know their login password. However, these three conditions must be met:

- You must have Modify rights to their domain's Cred table.
- They must have an entry in their domain's Passwd table or in the master server's /etc/passwd file.
- You must know their UID.

If you know the principal's login password, the procedure is straightforward. Use nisaddcred twice, once for each type of credential, and identify the principal with the -p and -P flags:

```
nisaddcred -p uid -P principal-name local
nisaddcred -p unix.uid@domain -P principal-name des
```

If the principal's home domain is different from the default domain, append a domain name to the end of the command:

```
nisaddcred -p uid -P principal-name local domain
nisaddcred -p unix.uid@domain -P principal-name des domain
```

Here are some examples:

```
salesmaster# nisaddcred -p 22244 -P joe.Sales.Wiz.Com. local
salesmaster# nisaddcred -p unix.22244@Sales.Wiz.Com \
                        -P joe.Sales.Wiz.Com. des
Adding key pair for unix.22244@Sales.Wiz.Com
(joe.Sales.Wiz.Com.).
Enter login password: <enter-joe's-login-password>
Retype password: <re-enter-password>
```

The example above creates LOCAL and DES credentials for an administrator named "joe" whose home domain is "Sales.Wiz.Com." The default domain is also "Sales.Wiz.Com.," since the command is entered from that domain's master server. This example creates the same credentials, but is entered from the root master:

```
rootmaster# nisaddcred -p 22244 -P joe.Sales.Wiz.Com. local \
                        Sales.Wiz.Com.
rootmaster# nisaddcred -p unix.22244@Wiz.Com \
                        -P joe.Sales.Wiz.Com. des   Sales.Wiz.Com.
Adding key pair for unix.22244@Sales.Wiz.Com
(joe.Sales.Wiz.Com.).
Enter login password: <enter-joe's-login-password>
Retype password: <re-enter-password>
```

If you don't know the client user's password, you can still create his or her credentials. Just use a dummy password and have the client user change it later with the `chkey` command. Here is an example that creates dummy credentials for an administrator named "bob" in the Wiz.Com. domain:

rootmaster# **nisaddcred -p 11199** \
    -P bob.Wiz.Com. local
rootmaster# **nisaddcred** \
    -p unix.11199@Wiz.Com \
    -P bob.Wiz.Com. des
Adding key pair for unix.11199@Wiz.Com
(bob.Wiz.Com.).
Enter bob's login password:
    <enter-dummy-password>
nisaddcred: WARNING: password differs
from login passwd.
Retype password:
    <re-enter-dummy-password>
	# Create LOCAL credential for bob.
	
	# Create DES credential for bob.
	
	#
	#
	#
	
	# Enter dummy password for bob.
	
	#
	
	# Re-enter dummy password.

% **rlogin rootmaster -1 bob** Password: *<enter-login-password>* Password does not decrypt secret key for unix.11199@Wiz.Com. $ **keylogin** Password: *<enter-dummy-password>* $ **chkey** Updating nisplus publickey database Generating new key for 'unix.11199@Wiz.Com'. Enter login password: *<enter-login-password>* Retype password: *<re-enter-login-password>* Done.	# Bob logs into rootmaster. # Bob enters real login password. # Bob gets error message but is # allowed to login anyway. # Bob does keylogin. # Bob enters dummy password. # Bob does chkey. # # # Bob enters real login password. # Bob re-enters real login # password.

First, you would create the client user's credentials in the usual way, but using a dummy login password. NIS+ would warn you and ask you to re-enter it. When you did, the operation would be complete. The domain's Cred table would contain the client user's credential information based on the dummy password. The domain's Passwd table (or /etc/passwd file), however, would still have the "correct" entry.

Then, the client user would log into the domain's master server, entering his or her *correct* login password (since the login operation checks the password entry in the Passwd table or /etc/passwd file). From there, the client user would first keylogin, using the dummy password (since a keylogin checks the Cred table), and then use the chkey command to change the Cred entry to the real thing.

▼ **Credentials for Client Workstations**

You can create DES credentials for client workstations only in their home domain. The following conditions must be met:

- You must know the workstation's root password.
- You must have Modify rights to their domain's Cred table.
- They must have an entry in their domain's Passwd table or in the master server's /etc/passwd file.

Use nisaddcred with the -p and -P flags:

    nisaddcred -p unix.*hostname@domain* -P *principal-name* des

If the principal's home domain is different from the default domain, append a domain name to the end of the command:

    nisaddcred -p unix.*hostname@domain* -P *principal-name* des *domain*

Here are two examples, one entered from the client's home domain (Sales.Wiz.Com.), the other from the domain above it (Wiz.Com.):

```
salesmaster# nisaddcred -p unix.client1@Sales.Wiz.Com \
                   -P client1.Sales.Wiz.Com. des
Adding key pair for unix.client1@Sales.Wiz.Com
(client1.Sales.Wiz.Com.).
Enter client1.Sales.Wiz.Com.'s root login password: <enter-password>
Retype password: <re-enter-password>
```

```
rootmaster# nisaddcred -p unix.client1@Sales.Wiz.Com. \
                   -p client1.Sales.Wiz.Com. des  Sales.Wiz.Com.
Adding key pair for unix.client1@Sales.Wiz.Com
(client1.Sales.Wiz.Com.).
Enter client1.Sales.Wiz.Com.'s root login password: <enter-password>
Retype password: <re-enter-password>
```

▼ Adding Client User Credentials to Other Domains

To add a client user's LOCAL credentials to another domain —after they have been created in the client's home domain, you must have Modify rights to the other domain's Cred table and you must know the client user's UID and principal name.

    nisaddcred -p *uid* -P *principal-name* local [*domain*]

If you enter the command from a remote domain, be sure to append the domain name to the command. Following are two examples that add LOCAL credentials for the administrator "topadmin.Wiz.Com." to the "Sales.Wiz.Com." domain. The first one is entered from the Sales.Wiz.Com. domain's master server, the second is entered from the root master server.

```
salesmaster# nisaddcred -p 33355 local -P topadmin.Wiz.Com. local
```

```
rootmaster# nisaddcred -p 33355 local -P topadmin.Wiz.Com. \
                      local  Sales.Wiz.Com.
```

▼ How to Remove Credentials

The nisaddcred command removes a principal's credentials, but both at a time and only from the local domain. To use it, you must have Modify rights to the local domain's Cred table. Use the -r option and specify the principal with its NIS+ principal name:

    nisaddcred -r *principal-name*

The following two examples remove the LOCAL and DES credentials for the administrator "topadmin.Wiz.Com." from the root domain, and LOCAL credentials from the Sales.Wiz.Com. domain. Note that they must be entered from different servers.

```
rootmaster# nisaddcred -r topadmin.Wiz.Com.

salesmaster# nisaddcred -r topadmin.Wiz.Com.
```

To verify that the credential was indeed removed, run `nismatch` on the Cred table, as shown below. For more information about `nismatch`, see Chapter 17, "*Administering NIS+ Tables.*"

```
rootmaster# nismatch topadmin.Wiz.Com. cred.org_dir
salesmaster# nismatch topadmin.Wiz.Com. cred.org_dir
```

chkey

The `chkey` command changes an NIS+ principal's public and secret keys stored in the Cred table. It does not affect the principal's entry either in the Passwd table or in the `/etc/passwd` file. In fact, this command is often used to make a principal's entry in the Cred table correspond to its entry in the Passwd table.

The `chkey` command interacts with the keyserver, the Cred table, and the Passwd table. When you invoke it, it tries to identify you with the keyserver. Therefore, you must keylogin before using it. However, the keyserver needs the password that was used to generate your keys in the Cred table. That may be different from your normal login password, depending on how your credentials were created.

For all this to work, you must also have an entry in the Passwd table. If you don't have an entry, or if you forget to keylogin, `chkey` will give you the following error message:

```
chkey: unable to locate password record for uid uid
```

Once it identifies you, it prompts you for a new password, which it then uses to generate a new set of public and private keys. It stores those keys in the Cred table, provided you have Modify rights to it.

▼ How to Change Your DES Keys

To change your DES keys with the `chkey` command, you need:

- Modify rights to your domain's Cred table
- The password from which your entry in the Cred table was formed
- An entry in the domain's Passwd table.
- Your login password.

First, keylogin, using your current password, then use chkey. Here is an example:

```
rootmaster% keylogin
Password: < enter-current-password >
rootmaster% chkey
Updating nisplus publickey database
Generating new key for 'unix.11199@Wiz.Com'.
Enter login password: <enter-new-password>
Retype password: <re-enter-new-password>
Done.
```

If you want to use chkey again before you logout, you don't have to keylogin again.

nispasswd

The nispasswd command changes or displays information stored in the NIS+ Password table. If you use it to change a principal's actual password, it tries to update the principal's secret key in the Cred table. If you have Modify rights to the Cred table and if the principal's login and network passwords are the same, it will update the keys in the Cred table. Otherwise, it changes the password, but does not change the secret keys. This means that the secret keys in the Cred table will have been formed with a password that is now different from the one stored in the Passwd table. In that case, you'll either have to change the keys with the chkey command, or keylogin after each login.

The Name Service Switch determines which processes obtain the new password. If the source for Password information in the Switch is nisplus, all processes will use the new password. However, if the source is nis or files, processes that use the standard getpwnam and getspnam interfaces (such as rlogin and ftp), will look elsewhere for the password information, and so will not get the new password stored in the NIS+ table. For more information about the Name Service Switch, see Chapter 5, "Understanding the Name Service Switch."

If you are the owner of the Password table, provided you have the proper credentials, you can change password information at any time and without constraints. However, if you are not the owner, you must comply with aging and construction constraints.

When you attempt to change a password, if the old password has not aged sufficiently (i.e., number of days since last change is less than *min*), NIS+ will terminate and not carry out the change.

The new password must have at least six characters, but no more than eight. It must contain at least two letters and at least one number or special character. Make sure the password is not derived in any way from the user's login name. Also make sure the new password has at least three characters that are different from the old password.

To use the `nispasswd` command, you must have the access rights appropriate for the operation:

This Operation	Requires These Rights	To This Object
Displaying information	Read	The Password entry
Changing Information	Modify	The Password entry
Adding New Information	Modify	The Password Table

Related Commands

The `nispasswd` command provides capabilities that are similar to those offered by other commands. The table below summarizes their differences.

Command	Description
passwd	Changes information in the workstation's `/etc/passwd` and `/etc/shadow` file.
yppasswd	Changes information in the NIS password map. Has no effect on the NIS+ Passwd table.

Command	Description
nispasswd	Changes and displays information in the NIS+ Password table. When a principal's password is changed, nispasswd tries to update principal's secret key in the Cred table. Its options are customized for the Password tables making the command easier to use for that table than the nistbladm command. It also allows an administrator to lock and force passwords, tasks that nistbladm doesn't allow.
nistbladm	Creates, changes, and displays information about any NIS+ table, including the Password table. Although the nispasswd command is easier to use for the Password table, nistbladm allows you to: - Create new entries - Delete an existing entry - Change the UID and GID fields in the Password table - Change the LastChanged, Inactive, and Expired fields in the Shadow table - Change access rights and other security-related attributes of the Password table.
niscat	Can be used to display the contents of the Passwd table.

Syntax

—To display information from the Passwd table

```
nispasswd -a
nispasswd -d username
```

—To change a password

```
nispasswd [ username ]
```

—To operate on the Password table of another domain

```
nispasswd [options] -D domainname
```

▼ How to Display Password Information

You can use the nispasswd command to display Password information about all users in a domain or about one particular user. To display information about all users, use the -a option:

```
nispasswd -a
```

Only the entries and columns for which you have Read permission will be displayed. To display the entry for a particular user, use the -d option. Without a username, it displays your password entry:

```
nispasswd -d
nispasswd -d username
```

Entries are displayed with the following format:

```
username    status    mm/dd/yy    min    max    warn
```

Field	Description
username	The user's login name
status	The user's password status. "PS" indicates the account has a password. "LK" indicates the account is locked. "NP" indicates the account has no password.
mm/dd/yy	The date, using Greenwich Mean Time, that the user's password was last changed.
min	The minimum number of days since the last change that must pass before the password can be changed again.
max	The maximum number of days since the last change that can pass before the password must be changed.
warn	The number of days' notice that a user is given before her password expires.

To display entries from a Password table in another domain, use the -D option:

```
nispasswd -a -D domainname
nispasswd -d -D domainname
```

▼ How to Change Passwords

To change your own password, enter the nispasswd command without any arguments:

```
nispasswd
```

To change the password of another user in the local domain, add a *username*:

```
nispasswd username
```

To change the password of another user in a remote domain, also add the -D flag:

```
nispasswd username -D domainname
```

NIS+ prompts you once for the old password and twice for the new one. If you are the owner of the Passwd table, NIS+ does not prompt you for the old password. If you make a mistake and the two entries for the new password don't match, NIS+ will ask you again for the new password.

nisupdkeys

The public keys of NIS+ servers are stored in several locations throughout the namespace, as listed in Table 14-1 on page 217. When new credentials are created for the server, a new public key is generated and stored in the Cred table, encrypted with the server's new password. However, the directory object still has a copy of the old public key. The nisupdkeys command is used to update that copy.

The nisupdkeys command can update the key of one particular server, or of all the servers that support a directory. It can also update the server's IP address, if that has changed, and it can remove the server's public key from the directory object. However, it cannot update the NIS_COLDSTART files on the client workstations. To update their copy, the clients should invoke the nisinit command. Or, if the NIS+ cache manager is running and more than one server is available in the coldstart file, they can wait until the time-to-live expires on the directory object. When that happens, the cache manager automatically updates the coldstart file. The default time-to-live is 12 hours.

To use the nisupdkeys command, you must have Modify rights to the directory object.

Syntax

Note that the nisupdkeys command is located in /usr/lib/nis.

—*To update keys:*

```
/usr/lib/nis/nisupdkeys [ directory ]
/usr/lib/nis/nisupdkeys -H server-name
```

—*To update IP addresses:*

```
/usr/lib/nis/nisupdkeys -a [ directory ]
/usr/lib/nis/nisupdkeys -a -H server-name
```

—*To clear keys:*

```
/usr/lib/nis/nisupdkeys -C [ directory ]
/usr/lib/nis/nisupdkeys -C -H server-name
```

When a directory name is supplied, `nisupdkeys` updates the public keys of all the servers that support that directory. If the name of a server is supplied instead, it updates the public keys of that server only. If no directory name is supplied, it updates the public keys of the local directory.

▼ How to Update All Public Keys in a Directory

To update the public keys of all servers that support a particular directory, simply provide the directory name:

```
nisupdkeys directory
```

If you don't supply a directory name, it uses the local directory. These two examples update the public keys of the root directory and a directory beneath it. They are both entered from the root master:

```
rootmaster# /usr/lib/nis/nisupdkeys
Fetch Public key for server rootmaster.Wiz.Com.
  netname= 'unix.rootmaster@Wiz.Com.'
Updating rootmaster.Wiz.Com.'s public key.
   Public key : public-key
rootmaster# /usr/lib/nis/nisupdkeys Sales.Wiz.Com.
```

▼ How to Update the Keys of a Particular Server

To update the public keys of a particular server in all the directories that store them, use the `-H` option and provide the server name:

```
nisupdkeys -H server-name
```

▼ How to Clear Public Keys

To clear all the public keys stored by a directory, use the `-C` option and specify the directory. To clear the public keys of only one server supporting that directory, use the `-C` and `-H` options.

```
nisupdkeys -C directory
nisupdkeys -C -H server-name
```

▼ How to Update IP Addresses

To update the IP addresses of one or more servers, use the -a option.

```
nisupdkeys -a directory
nisupdkeys -a -H server-name
```

keylogin

The keylogin command helps authenticate an NIS+ principal. When a principal logs in, the login process prompts for a password, which is used to authenticate the principal. Normally, this is the only time the principal is asked to provide a password. However, if the principal's DES credentials were created with a password that is different from the login password, the login password will no longer be able to authenticate the principal.

To remedy this problem, the principal must perform a keylogin, using the keylogin command, after every login. The keylogin command prompts the principal for its network password and stores it in the key server. From there, it is used by all NIS+ processes to authenticate the principal.

Syntax

```
keylogin
keylogin -r
```

The -r flag is used to keylogin a client workstation.

▼ How to Keylogin

To keylogin, simply enter the keylogin command and, when prompted, supply your network password; i.e., the password used to create your DES credentials. Before logging out, use the keylogout command. This example shows how to keylogin for a client user and a client workstation:

```
Client1% login: <login-name>
Password: <login-password>
Client1% keylogin
Password: <network-password>
Client1% su
Password: <root-password>
Client1# keylogin -r
Password: <root-network-password>
Wrote secret key into /etc/.rootkey
```

Administering NIS+ Access Rights 15⊟

This chapter describes how to use the NIS+ access rights administration commands to perform the following tasks:

▼ How to Specify Access Rights in All Commands	Page 218
nisdefaults	Page 220
▼ How to Display Default Values	Page 221
▼ How to Display the Value of NIS_DEFAULTS	Page 222
▼ How to Reset the Value of NIS_DEFAULTS	Page 223
▼ How to Override Defaults	Page 223
nischmod	Page 224
▼ How to Add Rights to an Object	Page 225
▼ How to Remove Rights to an Object	Page 225
▼ How to Add Rights to a Table Entry	Page 225
▼ How to Remove Rights to a Table Entry	Page 226
nistbladm -c,-u	Page 226
▼ How to Set Column Rights when Creating a Table	Page 226
▼ How to Add Rights to an Existing Table Column	Page 227
▼ How to Remove Rights to a Table Column	Page 228
nischown	Page 228
▼ How to Change an Object's Owner	Page 228

▼	How to Change a Table Entry's Owner	Page 229
`nischgrp`		Page 229
▼	How to Change an Object's Group	Page 230
▼	How to Change a Table Entry's Group	Page 230

▼ How to Specify Access Rights in All Commands

This section describes how to specify access rights, as well as owner, group owner, and object, when using any of the commands described in this chapter.

Syntax for Access Rights

Access rights, whether specified in an environment variable or a command, are identified with three types of arguments: *category*, *operator*, and *right*.

```
category  ::=o | g | w | a | n
operator  ::=+ | - | =
right  ::= r | m | c | d
```

The *category* refers to the category of NIS+ principal to which the *rights* will apply. The *operator* indicates the operation that will be performed with the *rights*. The *rights* are the access rights themselves. The accepted values for each are listed below.

Category	Description
o	The owner of the object or table entry.
g	The group owner of the object or table entry.
w	World: all authenticated principals
n	Nobody: all authenticated principals and all unauthenticated clients
a	All: shorthand for Owner, Group, and World. This is the default.

Operator	Description
+	Add the access rights specified by *right*.
-	Revoke the access rights specified by *right*.
=	Explicitly set the access rights specified by *right*; that is, revoke all existing rights and replace them with the new access rights.

Right	Description
r	Read the object definition or table entry
m	Modify the object definition or table entry
c	Create a table entry or column
d	Destroy a table entry or column

This example *adds* the *Read* access right to the *Owner*.

```
o+r
```

This example *adds* the *Modify* access right to the *Owner, Group*, and *World*.

```
a+m
```

This example *sets* the rights of the *Owner, Group*, and *World* to *Read*. This means that all three categories of principal now only have Read access, regardless of what access rights they had before:

```
a=r
```

This example *adds* the *Create* and *Destroy* rights to the *Owner*.

```
o+cd
```

This example *adds* the *Read* and *Modify* rights to the *World* and *Nobody*.

```
wn+rm
```

This example *removes* all four rights from the *Group, World,* and *Nobody*.

```
gwn-rmcd
```

This example combines the first two operations.

```
o+cd,wn+rm
```

Syntax for Owner and Group

To specify an owner, use an NIS+ principal name. To specify an NIS+ group, use an NIS+ group name with the domain name appended.

owner	: : =	*principal-name* . *domain-name* .
group	: : =	*group-name* . *domain-name* .

Syntax for Objects and Entries

Objects and entries use different syntaxes. Objects use simple object names, while table entries use indexed names.

> *object*   : : =   *object-name*
> *entry*   : : =   *[column-name=value, . . .]* , *table-name*

For example:

```
hosts.org_dir.Sales.Wiz.Com.
[name=butler],hosts.org_dir.Eng.Wiz.Com.
[uid=33555],passwd.org_dir.Eng.Wiz.Com.
```

(Note that in the instance above, the brackets are part of the syntax, not just the "optional" symbol of the grammar.

Indexed names can specify more than one column-value pair. If so, the operation applies only to the entries that match *all* the column-value pairs. The more column-value pairs you provide, the more stringent the search.   This example uses two pairs to specify the entry:

```
[winner=yoyoma,year=1992],races.org_dir.Wiz.Com.
```

Columns use a special version of indexed names. Because you can only work on columns with the nistbladm command, go to that section for more information. It begins on page 252.

nisdefaults

The nisdefaults command displays the seven defaults currently active in the namespace: domain, group, host, principal, access rights, directory search path, and time-to-live. NIS+ supplies preset values for these defaults. They are listed under "*Options*," below. In addition, you can specify your own security-related defaults (owner, group, access rights, and time-to-live) with the NIS_DEFAULTS environment variable. Once you set the value of NIS_DEFAULTS, every object you create from that shell will acquire those defaults, unless you override them by using the -D option when you invoke a command. This section describes how to perform tasks related to the nisdefaults command, the NIS_DEFAULTS environment variable, and the -D option.

Syntax

—To display individual defaults:

```
nisdefaults [ -dghprst ]
nisdefaults [ -dghprst ] [ -v ]
```

—To display all defaults:

```
nisdefaults [ -a ]
```

— Options:

-d	Domain. Displays the home domain of the workstation from which the command was entered.
-g	Group. Displays the group that would be assigned to the next object created from this shell. The group is taken from the NIS_GROUP environment variable.
-h	Hostname. Displays the workstation's hostname.
-p	Principal. Displays the userid or hostname of the NIS+ principal who entered the `nisdefaults` command.
-r	Rights. Displays the access rights that will be assigned to the next object or entry created from this shell. They are:

```
----rmcdr---r---
```

-s	Search Path. Displays the syntax of the search path, which indicate the domains that NIS+ will search through when looking for information. By default the search path is $. For more information about the search path, see "NIS+ Name Expansion,"," in Chapter 2.
-t	Time to live. Displays the time to live that will be assigned to the next object created from this shell. The default is 12 hours.

▼ How to Display Default Values

You can display all default values or any subset of them. To display all values, enter the `nisdefaults` command without arguments. They are displayed in verbose format. To use terse format, add the -a option. Here is an example:

```
rootmaster% nisdefaults
Domain         : Wiz.Com.
Group:         :
Hostname       : rootmaster.Wiz.Com.
Principal      : topadmin.Wiz.Com.
Access Rights  : ----rmcdr---r---
Search Path    : $
Time to live   : 12:0:0
```

To display a subset of the values, use the appropriate options The values are displayed in terse mode. To display them in verbose mode, add the -v flag.

```
rootmaster% nisdefaults -rs
----rmcdr---r---
$
```

▼ How to Change Defaults

You can change the default access rights, owner, and group by changing the value of the NIS_DEFAULTS environment variable. Use the command that is appropriate for your shell with the access=, owner=, and group= arguments:

> access=*right* . . .
> owner=*principal-name*
> group=*group-name*

You can combine two or more arguments into one line:

> owner=*principal-name*:group=*group-name*

Here are some examples:

```
client% setenv NIS_DEFAULTS access=o+r
client% NIS_DEFAULTS=access=o+r; export NIS_DEFAULTS
client% setenv NIS_DEFAULTS owner=abe.Wiz.Com.
client% setenv NIS_DEFAULTS access=o+r:owner=abe.Wiz.Com.
```

All objects and entries created from the shell in which you changed the defaults will have the new values you specified. You cannot specify default settings for a table column; the column simply inherits the defaults of the table.

▼ How to Display the Value of NIS_DEFAULTS

You can check the setting of an environment variable by using the echo command, as shown below:

```
client% echo $NIS_DEFAULTS
owner=butler:group=gamblers:access=o+rmcd
```

▼ How to Reset the Value of NIS_DEFAULTS

You can reset the NIS_DEFAULTS variable back to its original values (listed on page 221), by entering the name of the variable without arguments, using the format appropriate to your shell:

```
client# unsetenv NIS_DEFAULTS                        # for csh

client# NIS_DEFAULTS=; export NIS_DEFAULTS           # for sh/ksh
```

▼ How to Override Defaults

You can override default access rights, owner, and group, any time that you create an NIS+ object or table entry with any of these NIS+ commands:

- nismkdir - creates NIS+ directory objects
- nisaddent - transfers entries into an NIS+ table
- nistbladm - creates entries in an NIS+ table

Insert the -D option into the syntax of those commands, as shown below:

> *command* -D access=*right* ... *command-arguments*
> *command* -D owner=*principal-name command-arguments*
> *command* -D group=*group-name command-arguments*

As when setting defaults, you can combine two or more arguments into one line:

> *command* -D owner=*principal-name*, group=*group-name* \
> *command-arguments*

Remember that a column's owner and group are always the same as its table, so you cannot override them.

The following two examples override the default access rights:

```
client% nistbladm -D access=o+d  -a  name=derby  \
                                     year=1992   \
                                     winner=yoyoma \
                                     races.org_dir.Wiz.Com.

client% nismkdir -D access=o+r  Sales.Wiz.Com.
```

These two examples override the default owner:

```
Client% nistbladm -D owner=abe.Wiz.Com.  -a  name=derby  \
                                       year=1992  \
                                       winner=yoyoma \
                                       races.org_dir.Wiz.Com.

client% nismkdir -D owner=abe.Wiz.Com.  Sales.Wiz.Com.
```

These two examples override the default group:

```
client% nisaddent -D group=admin.Wiz.Com. -a -f h-file hosts
client% nismkdir -D group=admin.Wiz.Com.  Sales.Wiz.Com.
```

This example overrides the default owner and group:

```
client% nismkdir -D owner=abe.Wiz.Com.:group=admin.Wiz.Com. \
             Sales.Wiz.Com.
```

`nischmod`

The `nischmod` command operates on the access rights of an NIS+ object or table entry. It does not operate on the access rights of a table column; for columns, use the `nistbladm` command with the `-D` option. For all `nischmod` operations, you must already have Modify rights to the object or entry.

Syntax

—To add rights for an object or entry:

```
nischmod category...+right...  object-name.
nischmod category...+right...  [ column-name=value ] , table-name
```

—To remove rights for an object or entry:

```
nischmod category...-right...  object-name.
nischmod category...-right...  [ column-name=value ] , table-name
```

▼ How to Add Rights to an Object

To add access rights to an NIS+ object, use the + operator:

    nischmod *category...+right... object-name.*

This example adds Read and Modify rights to the Group of the Sales.Wiz.Com. directory object.

```
client% nischmod  g+rm    Sales.Wiz.Com.
```

▼ How to Remove Rights to an Object

To remove access rights to an NIS+ object, use the – operator:

    nischmod *category...–right... object-name*

This example removes Create and Destroy rights from the Group of the Sales.Wiz.Com. directory object.

```
client% nischmod g-cd    Sales.Wiz.Com.
```

▼ How to Add Rights to a Table Entry

To add access rights to an entry in an NIS+ table, use the + operator and an indexed name:

    nischmod *category...+right...   [column-name=value] , table-name*

This example adds Read and Modify rights to Group for an entry in the "hosts.org_dir.Wiz.Com." table. The entry is the one whose hostname column has the value of abe:

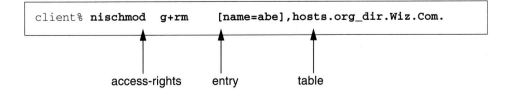

```
client% nischmod  g+rm    [name=abe],hosts.org_dir.Wiz.Com.
```

access-rights   entry   table

▼ How to Remove Rights to a Table Entry

To remove access rights to an entry in an NIS+ table, use the - operator and an indexed name:

nischmod *category*...-*right*...   [*column-name=value*] , *table-name*

This example removes Destroy rights from Group for an entry in the "hosts.org_dir.Wiz.Com." table. The entry is the one whose hostname column has the value of abe:

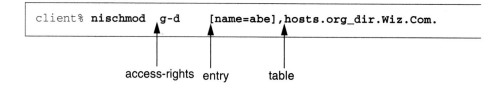

```
client% nischmod  g-d     [name=abe],hosts.org_dir.Wiz.Com.
```

access-rights entry   table

nistbladm -c,-u

The nistbladm command performs a variety of operations on NIS+ tables, as described in Chapter 17, "Administering NIS+ Tables." However, two of its options, -c and -u, enable you to perform several security-related tasks.   To use the -c option, you must have create rights to the directory under which you will create the table. To use the -u option, you must have Modify rights to the table column.

Syntax

—*To set column rights when creating a table:*

nistbladm -c *type column=access-rights*... *table-name*

—*To change rights to a particular column:*

nistbladm -u [*column=access-rights*, ...] , *table-name*

▼ How to Set Column Rights when Creating a Table

When a table is created, its columns are assigned the same rights as the table object.   To assign a column its own set of rights, append *access-rights* to each column's equal sign and separate the columns with a space:

column=access-rights   *column=access-rights*   *column=access-rights*

Here is the full syntax:

```
nistbladm  -c  type column=access-rights...      table-name
```

This example creates a table with three columns and adds Modify rights for the World to the second and third columns:

```
client% nistbladm -c races.org_dir.Wiz.Com. \
                  name= year=w+m winner=w+m races
```

For more information about the `nistbladm  -c` option, see Chapter 17, "Administering NIS+ Tables."

▼ How to Add Rights to an Existing Table Column

To add access rights to a column in an existing NIS+ table, use the u option (its full syntax is described in Chapter 17, "Administering NIS+ Tables"). Use one *column=access-rights* pair for each column whose rights you want to update. To update multiple columns, separate them with commas and enclose the entire set with square brackets:

> [*column=access-rights*]
> [*column=access-rights*, *column=access-rights*]

Here is the full syntax:

```
nistbladm  -u  [column=category...+right...], table-name
```

This example adds Read and Modify rights to Group for the "hostname" column in the "hosts.org_dir.Wiz.Com." table.

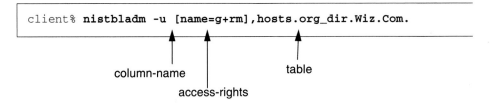

This example adds Read and Modify rights to Group for two columns in the Password table of the Wiz.Com. domain:

```
client% nistbladm -u  \
[name=g+rm,addr=g+rm],hosts.org_dir.Wiz.Com.
```

▼ How to Remove Rights to a Table Column

To remove access rights to a column in an NIS+ table, use the u option, the – operator, and an indexed name:

    nistbladm -u [*column=category...-access-rights...*],*table-name*

This example removes Group's Read and Modify rights to the "hostname" column in the "hosts.org_dir.Wiz.Com." table.

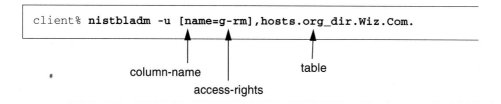

nischown

The nischown command changes the owner of one or more objects and entries. To use it, you must have Modify rights to the object or entry. The nischown command cannot change the owner of a column, since a table's columns belong the table's owner. To change a column's owner, you must change the table's owner.

Syntax

—*To change an object's owner:*

    nischown *new-owner object-name...*

—*To change an entry's owner:*

    nischown *new-owner* [*column=value,...*],*table-name...*

▼ How to Change an Object's Owner

To change an object's owner, use the following syntax:

    nischown *new-owner object-name*

All About Administering NIS+

Be sure to append the domain name to both the object name and new owner name. This example changes the owner of the Hosts table in the Wiz.Com. domain to "grant.Wiz.Com.":

```
client% nischown  grant.Wiz.Com.  hosts.org_dir.Wiz.Com.
```

▼ How to Change a Table Entry's Owner

To change a table entry's owner, use an indexed name for the entry, as shown below (this syntax is fully described on page 220):

nischown *new-owner* [*column=value*, . . .] , *table-name*

Be sure to append the domain name to both the new owner name and the table name. This example changes the owner of an entry in the Hosts table of the Wiz.Com. domain to "lee.Eng.Wiz." The entry is the one whose value in the hostname column is "virginia."

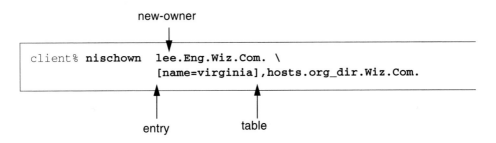

```
                   new-owner
                       |
client% nischown   lee.Eng.Wiz.Com. \
                   [name=virginia],hosts.org_dir.Wiz.Com.
                       ▲               ▲
                       |               |
                     entry           table
```

nischgrp

The nischgrp command changes the group owner of one or more objects and table entries. To use it, you must have Modify rights to the object or entry. The nischgrp command cannot change the group of a column, since the group assigned to a table's columns is the same as the group assigned to the table. To change a column's group owner, you must change the table's group owner.

Syntax

—To change an object's group:

nischgrp *new-group object-name* . . .

—*To change an entry's group:*

> nischgrp *new-group* [*column=value*, . . .] ,*table-name*. . .

▼ How to Change an Object's Group

To change an object's group, use the following syntax:

> nischgrp *new-group object-name*

Be sure to append the domain name to both the object name and new group name. This example changes the group of the Hosts table in the Wiz.Com. domain to "admins.Wiz.Com.":

---
client% **nischown admins.Wiz.Com. hosts.org_dir.Wiz.Com.**

▼ How to Change a Table Entry's Group

To change a table entry's group, use an indexed name for the entry, as shown below (this syntax is fully described on page 220):

> nischgrp *new-group* [*column=value*, . . .] ,*table-name*

Be sure to append the domain name to both the new group name and the table name. This example changes the group of an entry in the Hosts table of the Wiz.Com. domain to "admins.Eng.Wiz." The entry is the one whose value in the hostname column is "virginia."

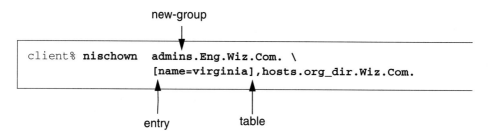

new-group

```
client% nischown   admins.Eng.Wiz.Com. \
                   [name=virginia],hosts.org_dir.Wiz.Com.
```

entry   table

Administering NIS+ Directories 16 ≡

This chapter describes how to use the NIS+ directory administration commands to perform the following tasks:

`niscat -o`	Page 232
▼ How to List the Object Properties of a Directory	Page 232
`nisls`	Page 233
▼ How to List the Contents of a Directory — Terse	Page 234
▼ How to List the Contents of a Directory — Verbose	Page 235
`nismkdir`	Page 235
▼ How to Create a Directory	Page 236
▼ How to Add a Replica to an Existing Directory	Page 237
`nisrmdir`	Page 237
▼ How to Remove a Directory	Page 237
▼ How to Disassociate a Replica from a Directory	Page 238
`nisrm`	Page 238
▼ How to Remove Non-Directory Objects	Page 238
`rpc.nisd`	Page 239
▼ How to Start the NIS+ Daemon	Page 239
▼ How to Start an NIS-Compatible NIS+ Daemon	Page 240
▼ How to Stop the NIS+ Daemon	Page 240

231

nisinit		Page 240
▼	How to Initialize a Client	Page 241
▼	How to Initialize the Root Master Server	Page 241
nis_cachemgr		Page 242
▼	How to Start the Cache Manager	Page 242
nisshowcache		Page 242
▼	How to Display the Contents of the NIS+ Cache	Page 243
nisping		Page 243
▼	How to Display the Time of the Last Update	Page 244
▼	How to Ping Replicas	Page 244
▼	How to Checkpoint a Directory	Page 245
nislog		Page 245
▼	How to Display the Contents of the Transaction Log	Page 246
nischttl		Page 248
▼	How to Change the Time-to-Live of an Object	Page 249
▼	How to Change the Time-to-Live of a Table Entry	Page 249

niscat -o

The niscat -o command can be used to list the object properties of an NIS+ directory. To use it, you must have Read access to the directory object itself.

▼ How to List the Object Properties of a Directory

To list the object properties of a directory, use niscat -o and the directory's name:

```
niscat -o directory-name
```

For example:

```
rootmaster# niscat -o Wiz.Com.
Object Name   : Wiz
Owner         : rootmaster.Wiz.Com.
Group         :
Domain        : Com.
Access Rights : r---rmcdr---r---
Time to Live  : 24:0:0
Object Type   : DIRECTORY
.
.
.
```

nisls

The `nisls` command lists the contents of an NIS+ directory. To use it, you must have Read rights to the directory object.

Syntax

—To display in terse format:

```
nisls
nisls [ -dLMR ] directory-name
```

—To display in verbose format:

```
nisls -l [ -gm ] [ -dLMR ] directory-name
```

— *Options:*

-d Directory Object. Instead of listing a directory's contents, treat it like another object.

-L Links. If the directory name is actually a link, the command follows the link and displays information about the linked directory.

-M Master. Get the information from the Master server only. Although this provides the most up to date information, it may take longer if the master server is busy.

-R Recursive. List directories recursively. That is, if a directory contains other directories, their contents are displayed as well.

-l Long. Display information in long format. Long format displays an object's type, creation time, owner, and access rights.

-g Group. When displaying information in long format, display the directory's group owner instead of its owner.

-m Modification time. When displaying information in long format, display the directory's modification time instead of its creation time.

▼ How to List the Contents of a Directory — Terse

To list the contents of a directory in the default short format, use one or more of the options listed below and a directory name. If you don't supply a directory name, NIS+ will use the default directory.

```
nisls [ -dLMR ]
nisls [ -dLMR ] directory-name
```

For example, this instance of nisls is entered from the root master server of the root domain "Wiz.Com.":

```
rootmaster% nisls
Wiz.Com.:
org_dir
groups_dir
```

Here is another example entered from the root master server:

```
rootmaster% nisls -R Sales.Wiz.Com.
Sales.Wiz.Com.:
org_dir
groups_dir

groups_dir.Sales.Wiz.Com.:
admin

org_dir.Sales.Wiz.Com.:
auto_master
auto_home
bootparams
cred
.
.
.
```

▼ How to List the Contents of a Directory — Verbose

To list the contents of a directory in the verbose format, use the -l option and one or more of the options listed below. The -g and -m options modify the attributes that are displayed. If you don't supply a directory name, NIS+ will use the default directory.

```
nisls -l [ -gm ] [ -dLMR ]
nisls -l [ -gm ] [ -dLMR ] directory-name
```

Here is an example, entered from the master server of the root domain "Wiz.Com.":

```
rootmaster% nisls -l
Wiz.Com.:
D r---rmcdr---r--- rootmaster.Wiz.Com. <date> org_dir
D r---rmcdr---r--- rootmaster.Wiz.Com. <date> groups_dir
```

nismkdir

The nismkdir command creates a non-root NIS+ directory and associates it with a master server and a root server. (To create a root directory, use the nisinit -r command, described on page 240.) The nismkdir command can also be used to add a replica to an existing directory.

There are several prerequisites to creating an NIS+ directory, as well as several related tasks. For a complete description, see Chapter 11, "Setting Up a Non-Root Domain."

Syntax

—To create a directory:

```
nismkdir -m master-server -s replica-server directory-name
```

— To add a replica to an existing directory:

```
nismkdir -s replica-server directory-name
```

▼ How to Create a Directory

To create a directory, you must have Create rights to its parent directory. Use the -m option to identify the master server and the -s option to identify the replica:

```
nismkdir -m master -s replica directory.
```

This example creates the Sales.Wiz.Com. directory and specifies its master server, "salesmaster.Wiz.Com." and its replica, "salesreplica1.Wiz.Com." It is entered from the root master server.

```
rootmaster% nismkdir -m  salesmaster.Wiz.Com. \
                    -s  salesreplica1.Wiz.Com.    Sales.Wiz.Com.
```

Although we don't advise it except for small or test-oriented namespaces, the nismkdir command does allow you to use the parent directory's servers for the new directory, instead of specifying its own. Here are two examples:

```
rootmaster% nismkdir Sales.Wiz.Com.
```

```
rootmaster% nismkdir -m salesmaster.Wiz.Com. Sales.Wiz.Com.
```

The first example creates the "Sales.Wiz.Com." directory and associates it with its parent directory's master and replica servers. The second example creates the "Sales.Wiz.Com." directory and specifies its own master server, "salesmaster.Wiz.Com." Since no replica server is specified, the new directory will have only a master server until you use `nismkdir` again to assign it a replica. If the "Sales.Wiz.Com." domain already existed, the `nismkdir` command as shown above would have made "salesmaster.Wiz.Com." its new master server and would have relegated its old master server to a replica.

▼ How to Add a Replica to an Existing Directory

To assign a new replica server to an existing directory, use the `-s` option and the name of the existing directory:

> `nismkdir` `-s` *existing-directory-name*

The `nismkdir` command realizes that the directory already exists, so it does not recreate it. It only assigns it the additional replica. Here is an example:

```
rootmaster% nismkdir -s rootreplica1.Wiz.Com. Wiz.Com.
```

nisrmdir

The `nisrmdir` command can remove a directory or simply disassociate a replica server from a directory. When it removes a directory, NIS+ first disassociates the master and replica servers from the directory, and then removes the directory.   To remove the directory, you must have Destroy rights to its parent directory. To disassociate a replica server from a directory, you must have Modify rights to the directory.

▼ How to Remove a Directory

To remove an entire directory and disassociate its master and replica servers, use the `nisrmdir` command without any options:

> `nisrmdir` *directory-name*

This example removes the "Eng.Wiz.Com." directory from beneath the Wiz.Com. directory:

```
rootmaster% nisrmdir Eng.Wiz.Com.
```

▼ How to Disassociate a Replica from a Directory

To disassociate a replica server from a directory, use the `nisrmdir` command with the `-s` option:

>   nisrmdir -s *server-name directory*

This example disassociates the "engreplica1" server from the "Eng.Wiz.Com." directory:

```
rootmaster% nisrmdir -s engreplica1 Eng.Wiz.Com.
```

`nisrm`

The `nisrm` command is similar to the standard `rm` system command. It removes any NIS+ object from the namespace, except directories and non-empty tables. To use the `nisrm` command, you must have Destroy rights to the object. However, if you don't, you can use the `-f` option, which tries to force the operation in spite of permissions.

You can remove group objects with the `nisgrpadm -d` command (see page 195), and you can empty tables with `nistbladm -r` or `nistbladm -R` (see page 254).

Syntax

— *To remove a non-directory object:*

>   nisrmdir [-if] *object-name*

— *Options:*

-i	Inquire. Asks for confirmation prior to removing an object. If the *object-name* you provide is not fully qualified, this option is used automatically.
-f	Force. Attempts to force a removal even if you don't have the proper permissions. It attempts to change the permission by using the `nischmod` command, and then tries to remove the object again.

▼ How to Remove Non-Directory Objects

To remove non-directory objects, use the `nisrm` command and provide the object names:

>   nisrm *object-name*...

This example removes a group and a table from the namespace:

```
rootmaster% nisrm -i admins.Wiz.Com. groups.org_dir.Wiz.Com.
Remove admins.Wiz.Com.? y
Remove groups.org_dir.Wiz.Com.? y
```

rpc.nisd

The rpc.nisd command starts the NIS+ daemon, which is used by an NIS+ server to answer requests from NIS+ clients. The daemon can run in NIS-compatibility mode, which enables it to answer requests from NIS clients as well. You don't need any access rights to start the NIS+ daemon, but you should be aware of all its prerequisites and related tasks. They are described in Chapter 7, "Setting Up the Root Domain," and Chapter 10, "Setting Up NIS+ Servers."

By default, the NIS+ daemon starts with security level 2.

Syntax

— *To start the daemon:*

```
rpc.nisd
rpc.nisd -r
```

— *To start the daemon in NIS-compatibility mode:*

```
rpc.nisd [ -r ] -Y
```

— *Options:*

-S *security-level*   Specifies a security level.

-f   Forces a checkpoint of the directory served by the daemon. This has the side effect of emptying the directory's transaction log and freeing disk space.

▼ How to Start the NIS+ Daemon

To start the NIS+ daemon on any server except the root master, use the command without options:

```
rpc.nisd
```

The daemon starts with security level 2, which is the default. To start the daemon on the root master server, use the -r option:

```
rpc.nisd -r
```

To start the daemon with security level 0 or 1, use the -S flag:

```
rpc.nisd -S level
rpc.nisd -r -S level
```

▼ How to Start an NIS-Compatible NIS+ Daemon

You can start the NIS+ daemon in NIS-compatibility mode in any server, including the root master. Use the -Y (upper-case) option:

```
rpc.nisd -Y
rpc.nisd -r -Y
```

If the server is rebooted, the daemon will not restart in NIS-compatibility mode unless you also uncomment the line that contains 'EMULYP="Y"' in the server's /etc/init.d/rpc file.

To start the daemon with a security level 0 or 1, use the -S flag:

```
rpc.nisd -Y -S level
rpc.nisd -r -Y -S level
```

▼ How to Stop the NIS+ Daemon

To stop the NIS+ daemon, whether it is running in normal or NIS-compatibility mode, kill it like you would any other daemon. First find its process ID, then kill it. It is also a good idea to kill the cache manager along with it. Here is an example:

```
rootmaster# ps -e | grep rpc.nisd
root 1081     1 61  16:43:33  ?      0:01  rpc.nisd -r -S 0
root 1087  1004 11  16:44:09  pts/1  0:00  grep rpc.nisd
rootmaster# kill 1081
```

nisinit

The nisinit command initializes a workstation to be an NIS+ client. As with the rpc.nisd command, you don't need any access rights to use the nisinit command, but you should be aware of its prerequisites and related tasks. They are described in Chapter 7, "Setting Up the Root Domain," and Chapter 9, "Setting Up an NIS+ Client."

Syntax

—To initialize a client:

```
nisinit -c -B
nisinit -c -H hostname
nisinit -c -C filename
```

—To initialize a root master server:

```
nisinit -r
```

 How to Initialize a Client

You can initialize a client in three different ways:

- By hostname
- By broadcast
- By coldstart file

Each way has different prerequisites and associated tasks. For instance, before you can initialize a client by hostname, the client's /etc/hosts file must list the hostname you will use. Complete instructions for each method, including prerequisites and associated tasks, are provided in Chapter 9, "Setting Up an NIS+ Client." Following is a summary of the steps that use the nisinit command.

To initialize a client by hostname, use the -c and -H options, and include the name the server from which the client will obtain its coldstart file:

```
nisinit -c -H hostname
```

To initialize a client by coldstart file, use the -c and -C options, and provide the name of the coldstart file:

```
nisinit -c -C filename
```

To initialize a client by broadcast, use the -c and -B options:

```
nisinit -c -B
```

 How to Initialize the Root Master Server

To initialize the root master server use the nisinit -r command:

```
nisinit -r
```

`nis_cachemgr`

The `nis_cachemgr` command starts the NIS+ cache manager program, which should run on all NIS+ clients. The cache manager maintains a cache of location information about the NIS+ servers that support the most frequently used directories in the namespace, including transport addresses, authentication information, and a time-to-live value.

When started, the cache manager obtains its initial information from the client's coldstart file, and downloads it into the `/var/nis/NIS_SHARED_DIRCACHE` file.

The cache manager makes requests as a client workstation. Make sure the client workstation has the proper credentials, or instead of improving performance, the cache manager will degrade it.

▼ How to Start the Cache Manager

To start the cache manager, simply enter the `nis_cachemgr` command:

```
client% nis_cachemgr
```

To stop the cache manager, kill it as you would any other process.

`nisshowcache`

The `nisshowcache` command displays the contents of a client's directory cache.

▼ How to Display the Contents of the NIS+ Cache

The `nisshowcache` command is located in `/usr/lib/nis`. It displays only the cache header and the directory names. Here is an example entered from the root master server:

```
rootmaster# /usr/lib/nis/nisshowcache

Cold Start directory:
Name : 'Wiz.Com.'
Type : NIS
Master Server :
        Name         : rootmaster.Wiz.Com.
        Public Key : Diffie-Hellman (196 bits)
        Universal addresses (6)

            .

            .

            .

Replicate:
        Name         : rootreplica1.Wiz.Com.
        Public Key : Diffie-Hellman (196 bits)
        Universal addresses (6)

            .

            .

            .

Time to live : 0:0:0
Default Access Rights :
```

nisping

The `nisping` command sends a "ping" to replica servers, telling them to ask the master server for updates immediately[1]. Before "pinging," the command checks the time of the last update received by each replica. If it is the same as the last update sent by the master, it does not send the ping to the replica.

The `nisping` command can also checkpoint a directory. This consists of telling each server in the directory, including the master, to update its information on disk from the domain's transaction log.

---

1. Actually, the replicas wait a couple of minutes.

Syntax

To display the time of the last update:

```
/usr/lib/nis/nisping  -u  [  domain  ]
```

To ping replicas:

```
/usr/lib/nis/nisping  [  domain ]
/usr/lib/nis/nisping  -H  hostname  [  domain ]
```

To checkpoint a directory:

```
/usr/lib/nis/nisping  -C  hostname  [  domain ]
```

▼ How to Display the Time of the Last Update

Use the -u option. If displays the update times for the master and replicas of the local domain, unless you specify a different domain name.

```
/usr/lib/nis/nisping  -u  [  domain  ]
```

Here is an example:

```
rootmaster# /usr/lib/nisping -u
Last updates for directory Wiz.Com.:
Master server is rootmaster.Wiz.Com.
        Last update occurred at Wed Nov 25 10:53:37 1992

Replica server is rootreplica1.Wiz.Com.
        Last update seen was Wed Nov 18 11:24:32 1992
```

▼ How to Ping Replicas

You can ping all the replicas in a domain, or one in particular. To ping all the replicas, use the command without options:

```
/usr/lib/nis/nisping
```

To ping all the replicas in a domain other than the local domain, append a domain name. To ping a particular replica, use the -H option:

```
/usr/lib/nis/nisping  -H  hostname
```

Here is an example that pings all the replicas of the local domain, Wiz.Com.:

```
rootmaster# /usr/lib/nis/nisping
Pinging replicas servering directory Wiz.Com. :
Master server is rootmaster.Wiz.Com.
        Last update occurred at Wed Nov 25 10:53:37 1992

Replica server is rootreplica1.Wiz.Com.
        Last update seen was Wed Nov 18 11:24:32 1992

        Pinging ... rootreplica1.Wiz.Com.
```

Since the update times were different, it proceeds with the ping. If the times had been identical, it would not have sent a ping.

▼ How to Checkpoint a Directory

To checkpoint a directory, use the -C option:

> /usr/lib/nis/nisping -C *directory-name*

All the servers that support a domain, including the master, transfer their information from their .log files to disk. This erases the log files and frees more disk space. While a server is checkpointing, it will still answer requests for service, but it is unavailable for updates. Here is an example of the output:

```
rootmaster# /usr/lib/nis/nisping -C
Checkpointing replicas serving directory Wiz.Com. :
Master server is rootmaster.Wiz.Com.
        Last update occurred at Wed Nov 25 10:53:37 1992

Master server is rootmaster.Wiz.Com.
checkpoint succeeded.
Replica server is rootreplica1.Wiz.Com.
        Last update seen was Wed Nov 18 11:24:32 1992

Replica server is rootreplica1.Wiz.Com.
checkpoint succeeded.
```

nislog

The nislog command displays the contents of the transaction log.

Syntax

```
/usr/sbin/nislog
/usr/sbin/nislog -h [ number ]
/usr/sbin/nislog -t [ number ]
```

▼ How to Display the Contents of the Transaction Log

To display the entire contents of the transaction log, use the nislog command without options:

```
/usr/sbin/nislog
```

To display the first (head) or last (tail) entry in the log, use the -h or -t options:

```
/usr/sbin/nislog -h
/usr/sbin/nislog -t
```

To display the first or last *n* entries, use the -h and -t options, but specify a *number*:

```
/usr/sbin/nislog -h number
/usr/sbin/nislog -t number
```

Each transaction consists of two parts: the particulars of the transaction and a copy of an object definition. Here is an example that shows the transaction log entry that was made when the Wiz.Com. directory was first created. "XID" refers to the transaction ID.

```
rootmaster# /usr/sbin/nislog -h 2
NIS Log printing facility.
NIS Log dump:
        Log state : STABLE
Number of updates    : 48
Current XID          : 39
Size of log in bytes : 18432
***UPDATES***
@@@@@@@@@@@@@@TRANSACTION@@@@@@@@@@@@@@
#00000, XID : 1
Time         : Wed Nov 25 10:50:59 1992

Directory    : Wiz.Com.
Entry type   : ADD Name
Entry timestamp : Wed Nov 25 10:50:59 1992
Principal       : rootmaster.Wiz.Com.
Object name     : org_dir.Wiz.Com.
....................Object....................
Object Name   : org_dir
Owner         : rootmaster.Wiz.Com.
Group         : admin.Wiz.Com.
Domain        : Wiz.Com.
Access Rights : r---rmcdr---r---
Time to Live  : 24:0:0
Object Type   : DIRECTORY
Name : 'org_dir.Wiz.Com.'
Type: NIS
Master Server : rootmaster.Wiz.Com.
  .
  .
  .
.............................................
@@@@@@@@@@@@@@TRANSACTION@@@@@@@@@@@@@@
#00000, XID : 2
  .
  .
  .
```

`nischttl`

The `nischttl` command changes the time-to-live value of objects and entries in the namespace. This time-to-live value is used by the Cache Manager (described in Chapter 2, "Understanding the NIS+ Namespace") to determine when to expire a cache entry. You can specify the time-to-live in total number of seconds, or in a combination of days, hours, minutes, and seconds.

The time-to-live values you assign objects or entries should depend on the stability of the object. If an object is prone to frequent change, give it a low time-to-live value. If it is steady, give it a high one. A high time-to-live is a week. A low one is less than a minute. Password entries should have time-to-live values of about 12 hours to accommodate one password change per day. Entries in tables that don't change much, such as those in the RPC table, can have values of several weeks.

To change the time-to-live of an object, you must have modify rights to that object. To change the time-to-live of a table entry, you must have modify rights to the table; failing that, to the entry; failing that, to the columns you wish to modify.

To display the current time-to-live value of an object or table entry, use the `nisdefaults -t` command, described in Chapter 15, "Administering NIS+ Access Rights."

Syntax

— *To change the time-to-live value of objects:*

```
nischttl  time-to-live object-name
nischttl [ -L ]  time-to-live object-name
```

— *To change the time-to-live value of entries:*

```
nischttl  time-to-live [column=value, ...] , table-name
nischttl [ -ALP ]  time-to-live [column=value, ...] , table-name
```

> *time-to-live* ::= *seconds* | *days* d *hours* h *minutes* m *seconds* s

— *Options:*

    -A   All. Apply the change to all the entries that match the [*column=value*] specifications that you supply.

    -L   Links. Follow links and apply the change to the linked object or entry rather than the link itself.

    -P   Path. Follow the path until there is one entry that satisfies the condition.

▼ How to Change the Time-to-Live of an Object

To change the time-to-live of an object, enter the `nischttl` command with the *time-to-live* value and the *object-name*. You can add the `-L` command to extend the change to linked objects.

```
nischttl -L time-to-live object-name
```

You can specify the *time-to-live* in seconds or a combination of days, hours, minutes, and seconds. For the former, just enter the number of seconds. For the latter, add the suffixes "`d`, `h`, `m`, and `s`" to the number of days, hours, minutes, and seconds. Here are two pairs of examples that accomplish the same thing:

```
client% nischttl 86400 Sales.Wiz.Com.
client% nischttl 24h Sales.Wiz.Com.

client% nischttl 176461 hosts.org_dir.Sales.Wiz.Com.
client% nischttl 2d1h1m1s hosts.org_dir.Sales.Wiz.Com.
```

The first pair changes the time-to-live of the Sales.Wiz.Com. directory to 91,400 seconds, or 24 hours. The second pair changes the time-to-live of all the entries in a Hosts table to 186,461 seconds, or 2 days, 1 hour, 1 minute, and 1 second.

▼ How to Change the Time-to-Live of a Table Entry

To change the time-to-live of entries, use the indexed entry format. You can use any of the options, `-A`, `-L`, or `-P`.

```
nischttl -ALP time-to-live [column=value,...],table-name
```

These examples are similar to those above, but they change the value of table entries instead of objects:

```
client% nischttl 86400 [uid=99],passwd.org_dir.Wiz.Com.
client% nischttl 24h [uid=99],passwd.org_dir.Wiz.Com.

client% nischttl 176461 [name=fred],hosts.org_dir.Wiz.Com.
client% nischttl 2d1h1m1s [name=fred],hosts.org_dir.Wiz.Com.
```

Administering NIS+ Tables 17

This chapter describes how to use the NIS+ table administration commands to perform the following tasks:

`nistbladm`		Page 252
▼	How to Create a Table	Page 253
▼	How to Delete a Table	Page 254
▼	How to Add an Entry to a Table	Page 255
▼	How to Modify a Table Entry	Page 256
▼	How to Remove a Single Entry from a Table	Page 257
▼	How to Remove Multiple Entries from a Table	Page 258
`niscat`		Page 259
▼	How to Display the Contents of a Table	Page 259
▼	How to List the Object Properties of a Table	Page 260
`nismatch, nisgrep`		Page 262
▼	How to Search Through the First Column	Page 264
▼	How to Search Through a Particular Column	Page 264
▼	How to Search Through Multiple Columns	Page 265
`nisln`		Page 265
▼	How to Create a Link	Page 266

nissetup	Page 266
▼ How to Expand a Directory into an NIS+ Domain	Page 267
▼ How to Expand it into an NIS-Compatible Domain	Page 267
nisaddent	Page 268
▼ How to Load Information From a File	Page 269
▼ How to Load Data from an NIS Map	Page 271
▼ How to Dump the Contents of an NIS+ Table to a File	Page 273

nistbladm

The nistbladm command is the primary NIS+ table administration command. With it, you can create, modify, and delete NIS+ tables and entries. To create a table, its directory must already exist. To add entries to the table, the table and columns must already be defined.

To create a table, you must have Create rights to the directory under which you will create it. To delete a table, you must have Destroy rights to the directory. To modify the contents of a table, whether to add, change, or delete entries, you must have Modify rights to the table or the entries.

Syntax

— *To create or delete a table:*

```
nistbladm -c  table-type column-spec... table-name
nistbladm -d  table-name
```

        column-spec ::=   *column*=[CSI, rights]

— *To add, modify, or remove entries:*

```
nistbladm -a
nistbladm -A  entry
nistbladm -m  new-entry old-entry
nistbladm -r
nistblamd -R  entry
```

   entry ::= *column=value* ... *table-name* |
            [*column=value*, ...], *table-name*

The *column-spec* syntax is explained under the task "*How to Create a Table*" on page 253. The *entry* syntax is explained under the task "*How to Add an Entry to a Table*" on page 255. There is an additional option, -u, for updating a table's defaults. That option is described in Chapter 15, "Administering NIS+ Access Rights."

▼ How to Create a Table

An NIS+ table must have at least one column and at least one of its columns must be searchable.   To create an NIS+ table, use the nistbladm command with the -c option:

    nistbladm -c *table-type column-spec... table-name*

The *table-type* is simply a string that identifies the table as belonging to a class of tables. It can be any string you choose.

The *column-spec* argument describes how to specify the characteristics of each column. To use the default column characteristics, simply provide the column names followed by equal signs, and separate the columns with spaces:

    column= column=

To assign the column some non-default characteristics, such as access rights that are different from those of the table as a whole, append each column's characteristics to the equal sign:

    column=[CSI,*rights*]   *column=*[CSI,*rights*]

A column can have any of the following characteristics:

S	Searchable. The nismatch command can search through the column.
I	Case-insensitive. When nismatch searches through the column, it will ignore case.
C	Encrypted.
rights	Access Rights. These access rights are over and above those granted to the table as a whole or to specific entries.

If you specify only access rights, you don't need to use a comma. If you include one or more of the S, I, or C flags, add a comma before the access rights. The syntax for access rights is described in Chapter 15, "Administering NIS+ Access Rights."

This example creates a table named "Races" in the Wiz.Com. directory (the "org_dir" directory is reserved for system tables). The table has three searchable columns, Name, Year, and Winner. (Within any table there should be no two entries with the same values for all searchable columns.)

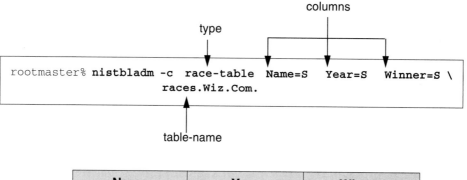

Name	**Year**	**Winner**

This is the same example as the above, but access rights are added to each column:

```
rootmaster% nistbladm -c  race-table  Name=S,w+m  Year=S,w+m \
                          Winner=S,w+m   races.Wiz.Com.
```

For more information about specifying column access rights when creating a table, see "*How to Set Column Rights when Creating a Table*" on page 226.

▼ How to Delete a Table

To delete a table, simply use the -d option and enter the table name:

```
nistbladm -d table-name
```

The table must be empty before you can delete it (see "*How to Remove a Single Entry from a Table*" on page 257). This example deletes the Races table from the "Wiz.Com." directory:

```
rootmaster% nistbladm -d  races.Wiz.Com.
```

▼ How to Add an Entry to a Table

To add an entry to a table, use the -a option (to force overwrites of existing entries, use the -A option instead) and specify a value for every column in the table:

```
nistbladm -a entry
```

To find the name of a particular column, use the niscat -o command. You can use two different syntaxes to specify an entry:

```
entry  ::= column=value  ...  table-name  |
           [column=value, ...] , table-name
```

The first consists of one or more *column=value* pairs, separated by spaces and followed by the table name. The second consists of one or more *column=value* pairs, separated by commas and enclosed in square brackets, followed by a comma and the table name. The second syntax is referred to as an *indexed-name*.

These two examples add the same entry to the races table, but they each use a different form:

```
rootmaster% nistbladm -a Name=derby  Year=1992  Winner=yoyoma \
                    races.Wiz.Com.
rootmaster% nistbladm -a [Name=derby,Year=1992,Winner=yoyoma],\
                    races.Wiz.Com.
```

Name	Year	Winner
derby	1992	yoyoma

This example adds the same entry, but uses the -A option to overwrite the existing "1992 derby" entry:

```
rootmaster% nistbladm -A Name=derby  Year=1992 \
                  Winner=chilipepper races.Wiz.Com.
```

Name	Year	Winner
derby	1992	chilipepper

You can only add one entry with each instance of the `nistbladm` command. This example adds three more entries to the `races` table:

```
rootmaster% nistbladm -a [Name=derby,Year=1991,\
                         Winner=elvis],  races.Wiz.Com.
rootmaster% nistbladm -a [Name=derby,Year=1990,\
                         Winner=LittleFeat], races.Wiz.Com.
rootmaster% nistbladm -a [Name=derby,Year=1989, \
                         Winner=bocefus], races.Wiz.Com.
```

Name	Year	Winner
derby	1992	chilipepper
derby	1991	elvis
derby	1990	LittleFeat
derby	1989	bocefus

▼ How to Modify a Table Entry

To modify a table entry, use the `-m` option:

```
nistbladm -m new-entry old-entry
```

Specify the *new-entry* with a set of *column=value* pairs. Use an indexed name to specify the *old-entry* and the table name. This example modifies an entry in the `races` table:

new entry

```
% nistbladm -m Name=derby Year=1992 Winner=LittleFeat \
  [Name=derby,Year=1992,Winner=chilipepper], races.Wiz.Com.
```

old-entry, table-name

Name	Year	Winner
derby	1992	LittleFeat
derby	1991	elvis
derby	1990	LittleFeat
derby	1989	bocefus

▼ How to Remove a Single Entry from a Table

To remove a single entry from a table, use the `-r` option:

```
nistbladm -r indexed-name
```

You can specify as few column values as you wish. If NIS+ finds duplicates, it does not remove any entry and returns an error message instead. This example removes the 1990 entry from the `races` table:

```
rootmaster% nistbladm -r [Name=derby,Year=1990, \
                    Winner=LittleFeat], races.Wiz.Com.
```

You could have removed the same entry by specifying only the Year column value, as in this example:

```
rootmaster% nistbladm -r [Year=1990],races.Wiz.Com.
```

However, you could *not* have removed the 1990 entry by specifying only the Winner column value (LittleFeat), because two entries have that same value (1992 and 1990):

Name	Year	Winner
derby	1992	LittleFeat
derby	1991	elvis
derby	1990	LittleFeat
derby	1989	bocefus

▼ How to Remove Multiple Entries from a Table

To remove multiple entries from a table, use the -R option:

```
nistbladm -R indexed-name name
```

As with the -r option, you can specify as few column values as you wish. Unlike the -r option, however, if NIS+ finds duplicates, it removes all of them. You can find the name of a table's column by using the niscat -o command. This example removes all entries in which the Winner is LittleFeat:

```
rootmaster% nistbladm -R [Winner=littlefeat],races.Wiz.Com.
```

Name	Year	Winner
derby	1992	LittleFeat
derby	1991	elvis
derby	1990	LittleFeat
derby	1989	bocefus

You can use the -R option to remove all the entries from a table. Simply do not specify any column values, as in this example:

```
rootmaster% nistbladm -R [],races.Wiz.Com.
```

niscat

The `niscat` command displays the contents of an NIS+ table. However, you can also use it to display the object properties of the table. You must have Read rights to the table, entries, or columns that you wish to display.

Syntax

— *To display the contents of a table:*

    niscat [-hM] *table-name*

— *To display the object properties of a table:*

    niscat -o *table-name*

— *Options:*

-h	Header. Displays a header line above the table entries, listing the name of each column.
-M	Master. Displays only the entries of the table stored on the Master server. This ensures you get the most up-to-date information & should be used only for debugging.
-o	Object. Displays object information about the table, such as column names, properties, and servers.

▼ How to Display the Contents of a Table

To display the contents of a table, use `niscat` with a *table-name*:

    niscat *table-name*

This example displays the contents of the table named `races`.

```
rootmaster% niscat -h races.Wiz.Com.
#name:Year:Winner
Derby:1992:LittleFeat
Derby:1991:Elvis
Derby:1990:LittleFeat
Stakes:1992:DaBulls
Stakes:1991:DaBulls
Stakes:1990:LittleFeat
AlmadenOpen:1992:LittleFeat
AlmadenOpen:1991:Buckaroo
AlmadenOpen:1990:Trigger
```

▼ How to List the Object Properties of a Table

To list the object properties of a table, use `niscat -o` and the table's name:

```
niscat -o table-name.org_dir
```

This is the best option for finding the names of a table's columns. For example:

```
rootmaster# niscat -o hosts.org_dir.Wiz.Com.
Object Name    : hosts
Owner          : rootmaster.Wiz.Com.
Group          : admin.Wiz.Com.
Domain         : org_dir.Wiz.Com.
Access Rights  : ----rmcdr---r---
Time to Live   : 12:0:0
Object Type    : TABLE
Table Type       : hosts_tbl
Number of Columns   : 4
Character Separator :
Search Path        :
Columns            :
      [0]      Name           : cname
               Attributes   : (SEARCHABLE, TEXTUAL DATA, CASE INS
                  Access Rights: ---------------
      [1]      Name           : name
               Attributes   : (SEARCHABLE, TEXTUAL DATA, CASE INS
                  Access Rights: ---------------
      [2]      Name           : addr
               Attributes   : (SEARCHABLE, TEXTUAL DATA, CASE INS
                  Access Rights: ---------------
      [3]      Name           : comment
               Attributes   : (TEXTUAL DATA)
                  Access Rights: ---------------
```

nismatch, nisgrep

The nismatch and nisgrep commands search through NIS+ tables for entries that match a particular string or regular expression, respectively. They display either the entries themselves or a count of how many entries matched. The differences between the nismatch and nisgrep commands are highlighted in the table below.

Characteristics	nismatch	nisgrep
Search Criteria	Accepts text only	Accepts regular expressions
Speed	Faster	Slower
Searches Through	Searchable columns only	All columns, whether searchable or not
Syntax of Search Criteria	*column=string* ... *tablename* [*column=string,* ...] *, tablename*	*column=exp* ... *table-name*

The tasks and examples in this section describe the syntax for both commands. To use either command, you must have Read access to the table you are searching through. The examples in this section are based on the values in the following table, named races.Wiz.Com. Only the first two columns are searchable.

Name (S)	Year (S)	Winner
Derby	1992	LittleFeat
Derby	1991	Elvis
Derby	1990	LittleFeat
Stakes	1992	Dabulls
Stakes	1991	Dabulls
Stakes	1990	LittleFeat
AlmadenOpen	1992	LittleFeat
AlmadenOpen	1991	Buckaroo
AlmadenOpen	1990	Trigger

About Regular Expressions

Regular expressions are combinations of text and symbols that you can use to search for special configurations of column values. For example, the regular expression ^Hello searches for a value that begins with Hello. When using a regular expression in the command line, be sure to enclose it in quotes, since many of the regular expression symbols have special meaning to the Bourne and C shells. For example:

```
rootmaster% nisgrep -h greeting="^Hello" phrases.Wiz.Com.
```

The regular expression symbols are summarized in Table 17-1, below.

Table 17-1Regular Expression Symbols

Symbol	Description
^*string*	Find a value that begins with *string*.
string$	Find a value that ends with *string*.
.	Find a value that has a number characters equal to the number of periods
[*chars*]	Find a value that contains any of the characters in the brackets
*expr	Find a value that has zero or more matches of the *expr*
+	Find something that appears one or more times
?	Find any value
\ '*s-char*'	Find a special character, such as ? or $.
x	y	Find a character that is either x or y

Syntax

— *To search through the first column:*

```
nismatch  string table-name
nisgrep  reg-exp table-name
```

— *To search through a particular column:*

```
nismatch  column=string  table-name
nisgrep  column=reg-exp  table-name
```

— *To search through multiple columns:*

```
nismatch  column=string  ...  table-name
nismatch  [column=string, ...] , table-name
nisgrep  column=reg-exp  ...  table-name
```

— *Options:*

-c   Count. Instead of the entries themselves, displays a count of the entries that matched the search criteria.

-h   Header. Displays a header line above the entries, listing the name of each column.

-M   Master. Displays only the entries of the table stored on the Master server. This ensures you get the most up-to-date information & should be used only for debugging.

▼ How to Search Through the First Column

To search for a particular value in the first column of a table, simply enter the first column value and a *table-name*. In `nismatch`, the value must be a string. In `nisgrep`, the value must be a regular expression.

```
nismatch -h string table-name
nisgrep   -h reg-expression table-name
```

This example searches through the "races" table for all the entries whose first column has a value of "derby":

```
rootmaster% nismatch  -h  derby  races.Wiz.Com.

rootmaster% nisgrep  -h  derby  races.Wiz.Com.
name**Year**Winner
Derby**1992**LittleFeat
Derby**1991**Elvis
Derby**1990**LittleFeat
```

▼ How to Search Through a Particular Column

To search through a particular column other than the first, use the following syntax:

```
nismatch column=string  table-name
nisgrep   column=reg-expression  table-name
```

This example searches through the `races` table for all the entries whose third column has a value of "Little Feat":

```
rootmaster% nismatch -h  Winner=LittleFeat  races.Wiz.Com.

rootmaster% nisgrep  -h  Winner=LittleFeat  races.org_dir.Wiz
Name**Year**Winner
Derby**1990**LittleFeat
Derby**1992**LittleFeat
Stakes**1990**LittleFeat
AlmadenOpen**1992**LittleFeat
```

▼ How to Search Through Multiple Columns

To search for entries with matches in two or more columns, use the following syntax:

```
nismatch  -h  column=string  ...  table-name  |
nismatch  -h  [column=string,...],table-name

nisgrep   -h  column=reg-exp  ...  table-name
```

This example searches for entries whose second column has a value of "1992" and whose first column has a value of "LittleFeat":

```
rootmaster% nismatch -h [Year=1992,Winner=LittleFeat], \
            races.Wiz.Com.

rootmaster% nisgrep -h Year=1992 Winner=LittleFeat \
            races.Wiz.Com.
Name**Year**Winner
Derby**1992**LittleFeat
AlmadenOpen**1992**LittleFeat
```

`nisln`

The `nisln` command creates symbolic links between NIS+ objects and table entries. You can use it to link objects to objects, entries to entries, or objects and entries to each other. All NIS+ administration commands accept the `-L` flag, which directs them to follow links between NIS+ objects.

To add a link to another object or entry, you must have modify rights to the source object or entry; that is, the one that will point to the other object or entry.

Syntax

— *To create a link:*

```
nisln  source target
```

— *Options:*

-L   Follow Links. If the *source* is itself a link, the new link will not be linked to it, but to that link's original source.

-D   Defaults. Specify a different set of defaults for the linked object. Defaults are described in "*How to Override Defaults*" on page 223.

▼ How to Create a Link

To add a link between one object and another, simply specify both object names, first the *source*, then the *target*. To add links between objects and entries, or between entries, use indexed names.

```
nisln  source-object  target-object
nisln  source-object  [column=value,...],table-name
nisln  [column=value,...],table-name  target-object
nisln  [column=value,...],table-name  [column=value,...],table-name
```

nissetup

The nissetup command expands an existing NIS+ directory object into a domain by creating the org_dir and groups_dir directories, and a full set of NIS+ tables. It does not, however, populate the tables with data. For that, you'll need the nisaddent command, described on page 268. Expanding a directory into a domain is part of the process of setting up a domain. For a complete description of the prerequisites and required operations, see Part II.

The nissetup command can expand a directory into a domain that supports NIS clients as well.

To use nissetup, you must have Modify rights to the directory under which you'll store the tables.

Syntax

— *To expand a directory into an NIS+ domain:*

```
/usr/lib/nis/nissetup
/usr/lib/nis/nissetup  directory-name
```

— To expand a directory into an NIS-compatible NIS+ domain::

```
/usr/lib/nis/nissetup -Y
/usr/lib/nis/nissetup -Y directory-name
```

▼ How to Expand a Directory into an NIS+ Domain

You can use the `nissetup` command with or without a directory name. If you don't supply the directory name, it uses the default directory. Each object that is added is listed in the output.

```
rootmaster# /usr/lib/nis/nissetup Wiz.Com.
rootmaster# /usr/lib/nis/nissetup
org_dir.Wiz.Com. created
groups_dir.Wiz.Com. created
auto_master.org_dir.Wiz.Com. created
auto_home.org_dir.Wiz.Com. created
bootparams.org_dir.Wiz.Com. created
cred.org_dir.Wiz.Com. created
ethers.org_dir.Wiz.Com. created
group.org_dir.Wiz.Com. created
hosts.org_dir.Wiz.Com. created
mail_aliases.org_dir.Wiz.Com. created
sendmailvars.org_dir.Wiz.Com. created
netmasks.org_dir.Wiz.Com. created
netgroup.org_dir.Wiz.Com. created
networks.org_dir.Wiz.Com. created
passwd.org_dir.Wiz.Com. created
protocols.org_dir.Wiz.Com. created
rpc.org_dir.Wiz.Com. created
services.org_dir.Wiz.Com. created
timezone.org_dir.Wiz.Com. created
```

▼ How to Expand it into an NIS-Compatible Domain

To expand a directory into a domain that supports NIS+ and NIS client requests, use the -Y flag. The tables are created with Read rights for the Nobody category so that NIS clients requests can access them.

```
rootmaster# /usr/lib/nis/nissetup -Y Test.Wiz.Com.
```

`nisaddent`

The `nisaddent` command loads information from text files and NIS maps into NIS+ tables. It can also dump the contents of NIS tables back into text files. If you are populating NIS+ tables for the first time, see the instructions in Chapter 8, "Setting Up NIS+ Tables." It describes all the prerequisites and related tasks.

You can use `nisaddent` to transfer information from one NIS+ table to another (for example, to the same type of table in another domain), but not directly. First you need to dump the contents of the table into a file, then load the file into the other table. Be sure, though, that the information in the file is formatted properly. Chapter 3, "Understanding NIS+ Tables and Information," describes the format required for each table.

When you load information into a table, you can use any of three options: replace, append, or merge. The append option simply adds the source entries to the NIS+ table. With the replace option, NIS+ first deletes all existing entries in the table and then adds the entries from the source. In a large table, this adds a large set of entries into the table's `.log` file (one set for removing the existing entries, another for adding the new ones), taking up space in `/var/nis` and making propagation to replicas time-consuming.

The merge option produces the same result as the replace option, but uses a different process, one that can greatly reduce the number of operations that must be sent to the replicas. With the merge option, NIS+ handles three types of entries differently:

* Entries that exist only in the source are added to the table.
* Entries that exist in both the source and the table are updated in the table.
* Entries that exist only in the NIS+ table are deleted from the table.

When updating a large table with a file or map whose contents are not vastly different from those of the table, the merge option can spare the server a great many operations. Because it only deletes the entries that are not duplicated in the source (the replace option deletes *all* entries, indiscriminately), it saves one delete and one add operation for every duplicate entry.

If you are loading information into the tables for the first time, you must have Create rights to the table object. If you are overwriting existing information in the tables, you must have Modify rights to the tables.

Syntax

— *To load information from text files:*

```
/usr/lib/nis/nisaddent -f filename table-type [ domain ]
/usr/lib/nis/nisaddent -f filename -t table-name table-type [ domain ]
```

All About Administering NIS+

— *To load information from NIS maps:*

```
/usr/lib/nis/nisaddent  -y  NISdomain  table-type  [  domain  ]
/usr/lib/nis/nisaddent  -y  NISdomain  -t  table-name  table-type  [  domain  ]
/usr/lib/nis/nisaddent  -Y  map  table-type  [  domain  ]
/usr/lib/nis/nisaddent  -Y  map  -t  table-name  table-type  [  domain  ]
```

— *To dump information from an NIS+ table to a file:*

```
/usr/lib/nis/nisaddent  -d  -t  table-name  >  filename
```

— *Options:*

-a   Append. Contents of the source are appended to contents of the table.

-r   Replace. Contents of the source replace contents of the table.

-m   Merge. Contents of the source are merged with contents of the table.

-d   Dump. Contents of the NIS+ table are dumped to `stdout`.

-v   Verbose. The command prints verbose status messages.

-P   Follow path. If the command was unable to find a table, follow the
            search paths specified in the environment variable `NIS_PATH`.

-A   All data. Apply the operation to all the tables in the search path.

-M   Master server. Use the tables only in the Master server of the domain.

-D   Override defaults. For the new data being loaded into the tables,
            override existing defaults. For syntax, see "*How to Override Defaults*" on
            page 223.

▼ How to Load Information From a File

You can transfer the contents of a file into an NIS table in several different ways. One
way is to use the `-f` option:

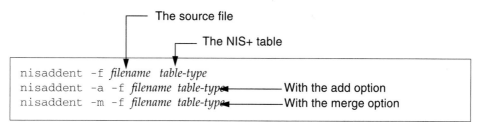

```
                The source file
                      The NIS+ table

nisaddent  -f  filename  table-type
nisaddent  -a  -f  filename  table-type ────── With the add option
nisaddent  -m  -f  filename  table-type ────── With the merge option
```

By default, -f *replaces* the contents of *table-type* in the local domain with the contents of *filename*. With the -a option added, it adds the contents of *filename* to *table-type*. With the -m option, it merges the contents of *filename* into the contents of *table-type*. These two examples load the contents of a text file named \etc\passwd.xfr into the NIS Passwd table. The first is into a table in the local domain, the second into a table in another domain:

```
rootmaster# /usr/lib/nis/nisaddent -f /etc/passwd.xfr passwd

rootmaster# usr/lib/nis/nisaddent -f /etc/passwd.xfr passwd \
            Sales.Wiz.Com.
```

Another way is to use stdin as the source. However, you cannot use the -m option with stdin. Here is an example:

```
cat filename > nisaddent   table-type
cat filename > nisaddent  -a table-type
cat filename > nisaddent  -a table-type NIS+domain
```

Here is the output of cat being piped into nisaddent:

```
cat filename | nisaddent   table-type
cat filename | nisaddent  -a table-type
```

If the NIS+ table is one of the automounter tables or a non-standard table, add the -t option and the complete name of the NIS+ table. To make it easier to find, it is highlighted in this example:

```
rootmaster# /usr/lib/nis/nisaddent -f /etc/auto_home.xfr \
            -t auto_home.org_dir.Wiz.Com. key-value

rootmaster# /usr/lib/nis/nisaddent -f /etc/auto_home.xfr \
            -t auto_home.org_dir.Sales.Wiz.Com. \
            key-value Sales.Wiz.Com.
```

▼ How to Load Data from an NIS Map

You can transfer information from an NIS map in two different ways, either by specifying the NIS domain, or by specifying the actual NIS map. If you specify the domain, NIS+ will figure out which dbm file in /var/yp/*nisdomain*[1] to use as the source, based on the *table-type*:

NIS+ Table Type	NIS Map Name
Hosts	hosts.byaddr
Password	passwd.byname
Shadow	shadow.byname
Group	ethers.byaddr
Ethers	group.byname
Netmasks	netmasks.byaddr
Networks	networks.byname
Protocols	protocols.byname
RPC	rpc.bynumber
Services	services.byname

To transfer by specifying the NIS domain, use the -y (lower-case) option and provide the NIS domain in addition to the NIS+ table type.

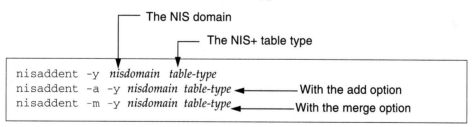

```
                            ┌── The NIS domain
                            │      ┌── The NIS+ table type
                            │      │
    nisaddent -y  nisdomain  table-type
    nisaddent -a -y  nisdomain table-type ◄──────── With the add option
    nisaddent -m -y  nisdomain table-type ◄──────── With the merge option
```

---

1. /var/yp/*nisdomain* must be local files.

By default, nisaddent replaces the contents of the NIS+ table with the contents of the NIS map. Use the -a and -m options to add or merge. Here is an example that loads the NIS Passwd table from its corresponding NIS map (passwd.byname) in the OldWiz. domain:

```
rootmaster# /usr/lib/nis/nisaddent -y OldWiz passwd

rootmaster# /usr/lib/nis/nisaddent -y OldWiz passwd \
            Sales.Wiz.Com.
```

The second example does the same thing, but for the "Sales.Wiz.Com." domain instead of the local domain, "Wiz.Com."

If the NIS+ table is one of the automounter tables or a non-standard table, add the -t option and the complete name of the NIS table, just as you would if the source were a file. To make the option easier to find, it is highlighted in these examples:

```
rootmaster# /usr/lib/nis/nisaddent -y OldWiz. \
            -t auto_home.org_dir.Wiz.Com. key-value

rootmaster# /usr/lib/nis/nisaddent -y OldWiz. \
            -t auto_home.org_dir.Wiz.Com. key-value  Sales.Wiz.Com.
```

If instead of using the dbm files for a domain, you prefer to specify a particular NIS map, use the -Y (upper-case) option and specify the map name. To make the option easier to find, it is highlighted in these examples:

```
rootmaster# /usr/lib/nis/nisaddent -Y hosts.byname hosts

rootmaster# /usr/lib/nis/nisaddent -Y hosts.byname hosts \
            Sales.Wiz.Com.
```

If the NIS map is one of the automounter maps or a non-standard map, combine the -Y option with the -t option:

```
rootmaster# /usr/lib/nis/nisaddent -Y auto_home \
            -t auto_home.org_dir.Wiz.Com. key-value

rootmaster# /usr/lib/nis/nisaddent -Y auto_home \
            -t auto_home.org_dir.Wiz.Com. key-value Sales.Wiz.Com.
```

▼ How to Dump the Contents of an NIS+ Table to a File

To dump the contents of an NIS+ table into a file, use the $-d$ and -t options. The $-d$ options tells the command to dump, and the $-t$ option specifies the NIS+ table:

```
\usr\lib\nis\nisaddent -d -t table-name > filename
```

Pre-SetupWorksheets

Use the worksheets on the following pages to record planning information priorto setup.
Chapter 6, *"Planning for Setup,"* provides a sample copy.

Domain:

Servers	Type	Name	Specifications
	Master		
	First Replica		
	Second Replica		

Credentials	Type of Principal	Type of Credential
	Servers	
	Clients	
	Administrators	
	Users	

Rights	Types of Objects	Category & Rights				
	Directories	**N**	**O**	**G**	**W**	**Use Defaults?**
	Groups	**N**	**O**	**G**	**W**	**Description**

Domain: [   ] (*Continued*)

Rights *Cont*	Types of Objects	Category & Rights				
	Tables	**N**	**O**	**G**	**W**	**Notes**
	hosts					
	bootparams					
	passwd					
	cred					
	group					
	netgroup					
	aliases					
	timezone					
	networks					
	netmasks					
	ethers					
	services					
	protocols					
	rpc					
	auto_home					
	auto_master					

Domain:

Servers	Type	Name	Specifications
	Master		
	First Replica		
	Second Replica		

Credentials	Type of Principal	Type of Credential
	Servers	
	Clients	
	Administrators	
	Users	

Rights	Types of Objects	Category & Rights				
	Directories	**N**	**O**	**G**	**W**	**Use Defaults?**
	Groups	**N**	**O**	**G**	**W**	**Description**

Domain: [   ] (*Continued*)

Rights *Cont*	Types of Objects	Category & Rights				
	Tables	**N**	**O**	**G**	**W**	**Notes**
	hosts					
	bootparams					
	passwd					
	cred					
	group					
	netgroup					
	aliases					
	timezone					
	networks					
	netmasks					
	ethers					
	services					
	protocols					
	rpc					
	auto_home					
	auto_master					

Domain:

Servers	Type	Name		Specifications
	Master			
	First Replica			
	Second Replica			

Credentials	Type of Principal	Type of Credential
	Servers	
	Clients	
	Administrators	
	Users	

Rights	Types of Objects	Category & Rights				
	Directories	**N**	**O**	**G**	**W**	**Use Defaults?**
	Groups	**N**	**O**	**G**	**W**	**Description**

Domain: |_____| (*Continued*)

Rights *Cont*	Types of Objects	Category & Rights				
	Tables	**N**	**O**	**G**	**W**	**Notes**
	hosts					
	bootparams					
	passwd					
	cred					
	group					
	netgroup					
	aliases					
	timezone					
	networks					
	netmasks					
	ethers					
	services					
	protocols					
	rpc					
	auto_home					
	auto_master					

Domain: [   ]

Servers	Type	Name	Specifications
	Master		
	First Replica		
	Second Replica		

Credentials	Type of Principal	Type of Credential
	Servers	
	Clients	
	Administrators	
	Users	

Rights	Types of Objects	Category & Rights				
	Directories	N	O	G	W	Use Defaults?
	Groups	N	O	G	W	Description

Domain: [   ] (*Continued*)

Rights *Cont*	Types of Objects	Category & Rights				
	Tables	**N**	**O**	**G**	**W**	**Notes**
	hosts					
	bootparams					
	passwd					
	cred					
	group					
	netgroup					
	aliases					
	timezone					
	networks					
	netmasks					
	ethers					
	services					
	protocols					
	rpc					
	auto_home					
	auto_master					

Index

A

access rights
    adding, 225
    adding to an entry, 225
    adding to column, 227
    how granted by server, 83
    how they are assigned, 81
    removing, 225
    removing to a column, 228
    removing to an entry, 226
    setting column rights, 226
    syntax for all commands, 218
    types of, 78
    where stored, 80
administering
    directories, 231
    NIS+ groups, 191
    tables, 251
alternate configuration files, 93
authenticated, 66
authentication name, 72
authentication type, 72
authorization categories, 78
auto_home table, 53
auto_master table, 53

B

bootparams table, 54

C

cache manager, starting, 242
changing a workstation's domain name, 156
changing passwords, 213

child directory, 25
clearing public keys, 215
client
    checking configuration file, 152
    creating DES credentials for, 151
    difference from a server, 28
    how to initialize by broadcast, 158
    how to initialize by coldstart file, 160
    how to initialize by hostname, 159
    initializing, 154, 241
    setting up, 149
client-server computing, 6
commands, list of NIS+, 20
compat keyword, 186
compatibility with +/- syntax, 186
compatibility with Solaris 1.0, overview, 19
continue, 92
Create rights, 78
creating DES credentials for root master, 127
creating input files, 52
creating root domain's admin group, 129, 178
Cred table, 72
credentials
    creating DES for client, 151
    creating DES for root master, 127
    creating for yourself, 203
    creating LOCAL for others, 204
    how they are created, 73
    removing, 208
    types of, 70

D

default search criteria, 92

defaults
    how to display, 221
    how to override, 223
    how to specify, 221
Destroy rights, 78
directory
    administering, 231
    assigning replica to, 237
    child, 25
    creating for non-root domain, 176
    creating with own servers, 236
    groups_dir, 78
    how to disassociate replica from, 238
    how to remove, 237
    listing the contents of, 234
    overview, 25
    parent, 25
    root, overview, 25
    to expand into a domain, 267
    to expand into a NIS-compatible domain, 267
displaying password information, 212
DNS, overview of, 10
DNS source, 91
domain
    adding a replica, 167
    creating directory, 176
    /etc/defaultdomain file, 156
    how to change a workstation's
        domain name, 156
    overview, 26
    purpose of, 26
    setting up non-root, 173
    specifying administrative group, 175
domainname, 119, 157
dump partition, 54

E

EMULYP="Y" string, 124, 165
entries
    how principals are allowed to create them, 87
entry
    adding access rights to, 225
    name conventions, 41
    removing access rights to, 226

ethernet address, 55
ethers table, 55
expansion, name, 42
expire, 61

G

GCOS, 60
getxxbyyy() routines, 89
GID, 60
grammar for names, 42
group
    administering, 191
    changing entry's group, 230
    changing object's group, 230
    name conventions, 41
    netgroup vs NIS+ group, 56
    owner, 78
    specifying for domain, 175
    table, 56
    workstation user group, 56
groups_dir subdirectory, 78

H

hierarchy
    differences from UNIX filesystem, 24
    of objects, 24
    tree-like structure of directories, 25
home directory, 60
hostname, 54, 55, 57
hosts, 57

I

inactive, 61
indexed name, 41
information in NIS+ tables, 51
initializing a client, 154, 241
    how to by broadcast, 158
    how to by coldstart file, 160
    how to by hostname, 159
initializing the root master server, 241
input files, creating, 52

Internet domains, 11
IP adress, 57

K

key server
    killing , 184
    killing and restarting, 155, 184
keylogin, 74, 155, 216
keyserv, 155

L

lastchg, 61
link, how to create, 266
login password, 76
login shell, 60

M

mail aliases, 58
map name, 53
master server, 29
master, root server, 29
max, 61
min, 61
Modify rights, 78
mount point, 53

N

name
    grammar, 42
    group conventions, 41
    indexed, 41
    name expansion, 42
    services, 6
    table conventions, 41
    table entry conventions, 41
Name Service Switch, 183
    how to add compatibility with +/- syntax, 185
    how to select a configuration for DNS, 185
name service switch — see "Switch", 89
namespace
    overview, 23

netgroup, 56
netmasks, 59
network name, 60
network number, 59, 60
network password, 76
networks, 60
NIS
    information storage, 15
    maps, 16
    overview of, 14
NIS+ cache,
    displaying contents of, 243
nis_cachemgr, 166, 170, 242
NIS_DEFAULTS
    how to display value of, 222
    how to reset, 223
NIS_GROUP environment variable, 81
NIS_PATH environment variable, 42
nisaddcred, 201
nisaddcred de, 203
nisaddcred des, 127, 203
nisaddcred local, 132, 152, 204
nisaddent, 137, 268
nisaddent -f, 138, 142
nisaddent -y, 142
niscat, 259
nischgrp, 229
nischmod, 224
nischown, 228
nischttl, 248
NIS-compatibility,
    transfering information from NIS+, 145
nisdefaults, 220
nisgrep, 262
nisgrpadm -a, 130, 178
nisgrpadm -c, 129, 178
nisinit, 240
nisinit -c -B, 158, 160
nisinit -c -C, 161
nisinit -r, 123
nisln, 265
nisls, 233

nismatch, 262
nismkdir, 235
nismkdir -m, 176
nispasswd, 210
nisping -C, 140, 144
nisrm, 238
nisrmdir, 237
nissetup, 266
nissetup utility, 127, 177, 267
nisshowcache, 242
nistbladm, 252
nistbladm -c, -u, 226
nisupdkeys, 131, 214
nobody, category of NIS+ principal, 79
NOTFOUND, 92
nsswitch.conf File, 90
nsswitch.conf file, default, 93
nsswitch.files file, 96
nsswitch.nis file, 95
nsswitch.nisplus file, 93

O

object
    adding access rights to, 225
    changing group, 230
    changing owner, 228
    changing time-to-live, 249
    definition, 80
    removing access rights, 225
    removing non-directory objects, 238
objects
    directory, 25
    hierarchy of, 24
    owner, 78
org_dir ways to create, 49
overriding defaults, 223
owner
    changing entry owner, 229
    changing object's owner, 228
owner, object, 78
owning group, 78

P

parent directory, 25
passwd, 211
password, 60, 61
    changing and displaying, 210
    if login is different from network, 76
planning guidelines, 101
populating tables from files, 136
port/protocol, 63
principal
    authorization categories, 78
    how access is granted to, 65
    how they are allowed to create entries, 87
principal name, 72
private data, 72
protocol name, 61
protocol number, 61
protocols, 61
public data, 72
publick key
    updating root domain's, 130
publickey file, transfering to NIS+ tables, 139
publickey map, transfering to NIS+ table, 143
purpose of network information services, 3

R

Read rights, 78
regular expressions, 263
replica server, 29
return, 92
root directory, 25
root domain
    creating the admin group, 129, 178
    updating the public key, 130
root master
    creating DES credentials, 127
root master server, 29
root partition, 54
root replica, setting up, 163
RPC, 62
RPC program name, 62

RPC program number, 62
rpc.nisd - S, 169
rpc.nisd -r -S 0, 124, 125, 165, 166

S

search criteria for switch, 92
search paths for tables, 47
searching through a table, 264
security
    access rights, 78
    authorization categories, 78
    how specified by objects, 67
    how to remove credentials, 208
    keylogin, 74
    levels of in tables, 82
    network password, 76
    nobody category, 79
    object owner, 78
    object's group owner, 78
    world category, 79
security, overview, 19
selecting an alternate Switch configuration file, 183
selecting an alternate configuration file, 183
server
    adding a replica to an existing domain, 167
    assigning replica to an existing directory, 237
    connection to directory, 28
    difference from a client, 28
    home domain vs supported domain, 36
    how grants access rights, 83
    how they enforce security, 66
    master, 29
    overview, 28
    root master, 29
    replica, 29
    setting up root replica, 163
    supporting multiple domains, 28
service name, 63
services, 63
setenv, 123, 175, 223
setting up a non-root domain, 173
setting up root replica servers, 163
setting up tables, 135

setting up the name service switch, 183
setup
    typical setup procedure, 99
shadow, 61
shell commands, list of, 20
sketching a domain hierarchy, 101
sources, 89
status=action, 93
subnet mask, 59
SUCCESS, 92
swap partition, 54
switch
    alternate configuration files, 93
    checking configuration file, 120, 152
    default search criteria, 92
    search criteria, 92
    setting up, 183
    sources, 89

T

table
    adding an entry, 255
    adding rights to column, 227
    administering, 251
    auto_home, 53
    auto_master, 53
    bootparams, 54
    changing entry owner, 229
    changing entry's group, 230
    changing time-to-live of an entry, 249
    creating, 253
    deleting, 254
    displaying its contents, 259
    entry name conventions, 41
    ethers, 55
    group, 56
    hosts, 57
    information in, 51
    levels of security, 82
    loading data from a file, 269
    loading data from a map, 271
    mail aliases, 58
    modifying an entry, 256
    name conventions, 41

netmasks, 59
networks, 60
password, 60
populating from files, 136
populating from NIS maps, 140
protocols, 61
removing an entry, 257
removing rights to a column, 228
removing several entries, 258
RPC, 62
search paths, 47
searching through a particular column, 264
searching through first column, 264
searching through multiple columns, 265
services, 63
setting column access rights, 226
setting up, 135
shadow, 61
timezone, 63
time-to-live, changing, 249
timezone, 63
transfering information from NIS+ to NIS, 145
TRYAGAIN, 92
typical setup procedure, 99

U

UID, 60
unauthenticated, 66
UNAVAIL, 92
updating
all public keys in a directory, 215
IP addresses, 215
public keys of a server, 215
user name, 60, 61

W

warn, 61
world, category of NIS+ principal, 79

Y

yppasswd, 211
ypupdate, 20
ypxfr, 20